Aviation Communication

Do you ever wonder why an airline's communication strategy can crash and burn in a crisis? A lack of understanding an acceptable aviation communication strategy can, in this fast world of social media, ruin a company's credibility in the aviation industry.

Aviation Communication: Strategy and Messages for Ensuring Success and Preventing Failures is the first go-to book to reveal to everyone in the aviation industry how to stop an organization's communication strategy from becoming the tragedy-after-the-tragedy that we've seen so often. In such instances, after the media go home, the economic, political, regulatory, and legal effects can linger for years. The strategies and messages in this book show how to prevent this along with the ultimate safety net used by those who have been successful. Readers will learn to prevent catastrophic communication mistakes with strategic templates for a wide array of scenarios, as well as 25 specific techniques that give the actual words to use to deliver the book's messages.

This book is a must-have for the international aviation business community as a tri-functional induction, training, and reference tool.

Linda J. Tavlin is the president of an international aviation communication consultancy with over 30 years' experience training organizations on how to deal with controversial audiences. Linda teaches aviation communication in the accident investigation and safety programs at Cranfield University, UK.

Aviation Communication
Strategy and Messages for Ensuring
Success and Preventing Failures

Linda J. Tavlin

LONDON AND NEW YORK

First published 2019
by Routledge
2 Park Square, Milton Park, Abingdon, Oxon OX14 4RN

and by Routledge
52 Vanderbilt Avenue, New York, NY 10017

Routledge is an imprint of the Taylor & Francis Group, an informa business

© 2019 Linda J. Tavlin

The right of Linda J. Tavlin to be identified as author of this work has been asserted by her in accordance with sections 77 and 78 of the Copyright, Designs and Patents Act 1988.

All rights reserved. No part of this book may be reprinted or reproduced or utilised in any form or by any electronic, mechanical, or other means, now known or hereafter invented, including photocopying and recording, or in any information storage or retrieval system, without permission in writing from the publishers.

Trademark notice: Product or corporate names may be trademarks or registered trademarks, and are used only for identification and explanation without intent to infringe.

British Library Cataloguing-in-Publication Data
A catalogue record for this book is available from the British Library

Library of Congress Cataloging-in-Publication Data
Names: Tavlin, Linda, author.
Title: Aviation communication : strategy and messages for ensuring success and preventing failures / Linda Tavlin.
Description: Abingdon, Oxon ; New York, NY : Routledge, 2019. | Includes bibliographical references and index.
Identifiers: LCCN 2018057104 | ISBN 9781138624801 (hbk) | ISBN 9781138624825 (pbk) | ISBN 9780429460425 (ebk)
Subjects: LCSH: Aeronautics—Information services. | Communication in organizations. | Miscommunication—Prevention. | Aeronautics—Safety measures. | Aeronautics, Commercial—Customer services.
Classification: LCC TL564 .T38 2019 | DDC 387.7068/4—dc23
LC record available at https://lccn.loc.gov/2018057104

ISBN: 978-1-138-62480-1 (hbk)
ISBN: 978-1-138-62482-5 (pbk)
ISBN: 978-0-429-46042-5 (ebk)

Typeset in Bembo
by Apex CoVantage, LLC

Printed and bound by CPI Group (UK) Ltd, Croydon, CR0 4YY

To my friend and mentor, David F. Thomas, whose support, encouragement, positive reinforcement, and most of all, friendship, have never wavered in over 30 years; I aspire to his professionalism and kindness

Contents

List of illustrations   xi
Foreword by Professor Graham Braithwaite   xii
Acknowledgments   xv

Introduction   1

1 Introduction to aviation communication – it's more than you think!   4
Three points to communication 5
Potential parties to an event 9
Audience analysis 12
Empowerment statement 17
Cultural differences in communication 18
Chapter summary 22

2 Aviation terminology and communication techniques: the basic building blocks and connective tissue   23
Terminology and lingo 23
Techniques 30
Source of support points – development of a technical data sheet 42
Chapter summary 45

3 The 4-point formula – your absolute safety net   48
Background 48
The 4-point formula 52
Rationale for the 4-point formula 53
Case studies – uses of the 4-point formula 54
Why reinvent the wheel? 63
Dealing with various audiences 67
Conclusion 68
Chapter summary 69

4 The accident investigation process and associated scenarios: who is *really* in charge? 71
Background 71
Contracting states 72
Standards and Recommended Practices 74
Investigation board formats 75
Rationale for communication 78
Levels of communication 78
Variables for reality 85
Three common threads 86
The CEO and their communication styles 89
Case study 90
Chapter summary 92

5 Strategy and messages: establishing the foundation for success or failure – the meat and the bones 93
Strategy for who speaks 93
An organization's objective for who communicates in an accident or incident 94
Reality decides who communicates 95
Messages for potential audiences in an accident or incident 96
Messages by subject 99
Chapter summary 115

6 Controversial questions and answers – situational awareness – *do*s and *don't*s: help to back out of that corner! 116
Leaving a situation 116
Don't know the answer 117
Don't know the answer but would like to respond 117
Know the answer, but don't want to respond 117
Realize you are in trouble and want to get out of it 118
Sometimes there is no winning – realize it! 118
Law enforcement vs aviation 119
Personnel event 119
Ethics situation 120
Insurance question 120
Humanizing vs apologizing 120
The causes 121
Confidentiality 122
Questions in an accident 123
Potential controversial questions 125

Dos *and* don'ts *131*
English as a second language 132
Chapter summary 133

7 **Communication response worksheets – learning to plan it all *before* something happens**   134
Communication response worksheet template – how to fill it out 134
Template 1 – accident with deaths and/or injuries 135
Template 2 – incident, part 1 139
Template 3 – safety 145
Template 4 – ethics, part 1 147
Template 5 – commercial, part 1 150
Template 6 – finance 153
Template 7 – workplace 154
Template 8 – technical 156
Chapter summary 157

8 **Sample press statements: the accident and beyond with the how *and* the why**   158
Statement/release #1 – event with deaths/injuries external 158
Statement/release #2 – event with deaths/injuries internal 160
Statement/release #3 – incident with no deaths or injuries 161
Statement/release #4 – security scrutiny 162
Statement/release #5 – regulatory event 162
Statement/release #6 – regulatory fine 163
Statement/release #7 – security/terrorism concern 164
Statement/release #8 – safety issue 165
Statement/release #9 – workplace event 166
Statement/release #10 – loss of aircraft component 166
Statement/release #11 – inaccurate or speculative statement/political posturing by outside party ("Witness has said" or "Sources have told us") 167
Statement/release #12 – environmental event (non-living) 168
Statement/release #13 – environmental event (living) 168
Statement/release #14 – something happened, and it was your fault 169
Statement/release #15 – ethics scenario 170
Statement/release #16 – whistle-blower 171
Statement/release #17 – financial troubles 172
Statement/release #18 – defense of a regulator (if a regulator is in a Category 2 status) 172

x   Contents

> Statement/release #19 – misperception that our industry is "third world" 173
> How to educate 174
> Conclusion 175
> Chapter summary 175

9 **Social media and aviation communication: when and when not?**   176
> Forms of social media 176
> Case studies 183
> Conclusion 191
> Chapter summary 191

10 **Case study – Allegiant Air, the FAA, and *60 Minutes***   194
> Allegiant Air 194
> The 60 Minutes interview and the FAA 201
> Potential impact on Allegiant Air 208
> Chapter summary 210

11 **Summary of mistakes and countermeasures**   211
> Chapter 1: Introduction to aviation communication – it's more than you think! 211
> Chapter 3: The 4-point formula and extra – your absolute safety net 214
> Chapter 4: The accident investigation process and associated scenarios: who is *really* in charge? 216
> Chapter 7: Communication response worksheets – learning to plan it all *before* something happens 217
> Chapter 9: Social media and aviation communication: when and when not? 217
> Chapter 10: Case study – Allegiant Air, the FAA, and 60 Minutes 218

Index   219

Illustrations

Charts

1.1	Potential parties to an event	8
1.2	Potential parties to this event	14
3.1	Potential parties to this event	60
9.1	Parties to this event	186
9.2	Parties to the United Airlines event	188
10.1	Parties to the *60 Minutes* story on Allegiant Air with FAA, April 2018	207

Figures

1.1	Media misperception	7
4.1	Communication safety net for MH370	73
4.2	International investigation participants	74
4.3	Strategy for reality	88
7.1	Communication strategy difference for an accident vs an incident	141
7.2	Right and wrong communication strategy for an incident	142

Tables

3.1	In summary: the 4-point formula	69
4.1	Levels of communication – who will be asked?	79
4.2	Levels of communication – what is the reality?	79
4.3	Three common threads – getting it right	86
4.4	Three common threads – getting it wrong	87
9.1	Compare what they said	189
10.1	Potential FAA messages to *60 Minutes*' criticism with techniques	203
10.2	*60 Minutes*' criticism of Allegiant Air with potential messages	206

Foreword

Ask most employees, customers, or managers what they would like to see improved in a business and the chances are that the word "communication" will appear near the top of the list. It doesn't matter what type of organization and it isn't limited to communication when things are going wrong – people have a desire and a need to understand things and that is the role of good communication.

In the 1980s, Commercial Union Insurance company used the marketing phrase, "We won't turn a crisis into a drama." Bad communication – whether it be the wrong message, the wrong timing, or the wrong audience – can turn minor events into major disasters. News of bad experiences travels swiftly, especially in an era when social media connectivity is ubiquitous. This is just part of the reason why this book is both relevant and timely.

I was delighted when Linda asked me to write the foreword to her book. Over the years, I have enjoyed many conversations with her regarding the performance of various organizations in responding to a major event. She has a clear passion for the importance of communication and delivering the right message. She is not a "media skills" trainer; that massively underrepresents what she is trying to do. Communication is about so much more than the words said – it is about the right people delivering the right message at the right time to the right audiences. It is also about knowing who can and cannot share information, especially in the highly charged atmosphere that follows a major event such as an aircraft accident, and when the appropriate party to communicate certain information is not necessarily the operator.

In my work at the Safety and Accident Investigation Centre at Cranfield University, I am privileged to mix with industry professionals from across aviation, railways, marine, and health care. All are safety-critical industries covered by complex regulatory requirements which attract a high degree of public interest when things go wrong. While it is major disasters that attract the greatest media, public, and political interest, those with an operational role will know that every day brings the potential for a crisis. Whether that potential translates into a full-blown crisis may well depend on how an individual or an organization responds.

Anyone working in a safety-critical industry has something to learn from the experience that Linda Tavlin has collected over many years, but so too do people in other roles where communication is paramount. Many of our students have benefited from her classes and workshops over the years, and so too have countless government agencies and operators. When I see a group working with her, it is clear that some of them "get it" instantly – they recognize the need for technical experts and managers to communicate effectively with a wide range of different stakeholders and cultures. Others, who perhaps come from a more technical engineering background, can find it harder to understand the importance of the topic – until they see the many examples and case studies that Linda has collected over the years. In some cases, the culture or organization that they come from adds particular traps or constraints.

I would urge the reader to take time to reflect on how the various examples included in the book might apply to their own circumstances, both now and in the future. Good fortune has hidden some of the examples of poor communication because other events prove themselves to be more newsworthy. Having "got away with it" once is not a great strategy for future success and attempts to bury bad news by releasing it just ahead of a public holiday weekend are becoming less effective!

Major events may range from fatal accidents to business disruptions. All have the capacity to be business harming and reputation damaging if handled poorly. In the case of transport accidents, which have the potential to cause many deaths, good communication is essential to providing timely support for family members and friends who may be anxious about their loved ones. It is also critical to reassuring passengers and investors that the companies and government agencies that are involved are taking things seriously and responding appropriately. A loss of confidence in a brand, product, or sector can have long-lasting business implications.

While those responding to safety events are the obvious beneficiaries of reading this book, there are also plenty of lessons for managers across industry and government about communicating under pressure. In an increasingly connected world where the threat of service disruption can come from many sources – safety, security, extreme weather, natural disasters, power or communications outages, and so on – the demand for effective and timely communication is growing. Naturally, the customer wants to know what is going on and what the company is doing about it; but so do the other stakeholders.

Not everyone wants to use that information positively either. The news media has a voracious appetite and, it seems, social media an even greater one. Potential litigators and those with regulatory or law enforcement responsibilities will be listening carefully, too. These are not reasons to avoid communication, not least because any void will be filled and if not by the professionals, then by the so-called experts and commentators. Their messages can be even more damaging than how customers interpret silence or "No comment" from the responsible organization.

Linda's 4-point formula is a valuable tool for anyone who may have a message to deliver. The examples she provides help to bring it to life and will provide inspiration for developing an organization's plans for communication. While none of us know precisely what potential crises may develop, the formula provides an essential framework for preparation.

Professor Graham Braithwaite
Cranfield University, UK

Acknowledgments

Although I am the sole author of this book, I could not have done it without the help and support of the following people:

I will be forever thankful to the publisher, Taylor & Francis, without whom I would not have had this wonderful opportunity, and to their support team: my editor, Guy Loft, who put me at ease, and his assistant, Matthew Ranscombe, who answered all questions and made it sound a lot simpler than it really was; and lastly my copy-editor, Gareth Vaughan, whom I thank for his patience and professionalism doing what I could never do and seeing things I could not see.

There are several people I would like to thank for the professional help and support they gave me, all in their own way; no matter how large or small, it was all of great value.

First, Tony Fernandes, who allowed me to use his name in my intro, although it was he who deserves all the accolades for the awesome job he did in his communication handling in the aftermath of the AirAsia Flight 8501 tragedy.

To Professor Graham Braithwaite, who runs the best Aviation Accident Investigation program on earth – even HM Queen Elizabeth II thought so – and I'm honored to have him write my foreword.

To Chuck Sambulchino, the best "book doctor" around.

To Bo Lingam, the "inside man" and my go-to guy who will always tell me when I get it wrong.

To all those who gave their aviation advice: The Honorable John Goglia, Carol Giles, Fred Leonelli, Captain Barry Wiscznowski, Captain David Evans, Captain David Eisner, Javier Venegas, Takis Adimidis, Bas Gerressen, David Barry, and Sue Warner-Bean.

To all those who gave their professional advice: Scott Alevy, Cary Spencer, James T. Dilday, Dr Carol Kyros Walker, and Matthew Tavlin.

Of equal importance to thank were those who inspired and supported me personally: Cynthia Wulfsberg, David Freedland, Dennis Wachs, Gary Hastings, Donna Starr, Abby Z. Funk, and Nancy J. Anderson, who once sat through my class and said, "This class should be a book." And now it is!

Introduction

When the template for the "disaster after the disaster" is out there, do you ever wonder why companies – and I mean big companies that should know better – keep following it? We know the results. Stock prices drop. There is loss of business. Regulatory fines are issued. Political repercussions abound. And that's just a few of the consequences. Let's blame the media! Let's blame the unions! Everyone but us – where the blame really lies.

I became tired of seeing the disaster after the disaster due to a bad communication strategy or bad messages, so I wrote a book with the solutions – *Aviation Communication: Ensuring Success and Preventing Failure* – to take the lessons I have learned, and that have worked throughout the world, and bring them to everyone.

The cause of these communication disasters is the wrong strategy, a bad strategy, or better yet, no strategy. All too often the blame is laid at the door of the media, the unions, or some other group; an organization's own strategy for communication and messages should be blamed instead. The problem is that communication is not a public relations or media issue but an issue that requires skills for every employee who deals with any audience, from the internal mundane workplace issue to the large-scale international crisis.

The strategy and messages in this book have worked for those who've used them in the past. Beginning on the foundation laid down in Chapter 1 and followed by the basic building blocks (techniques) in Chapter 2, readers will be provided with the same strategy that made the difference between success and failure in past communication challenges. The message will follow the strategy consistently throughout the book for reinforcement.

In my 30 years in this business and over 20 years of teaching aviation professionals at universities, I have never come across anyone who received this information during their initial aviation training. I certainly have never come across anyone on the commercial side of the industry who has ever been instructed on technical aviation issues and aviation is their product.

Investigators and regulators all over the world have used these messages and strategy. And if they have no problem with them, industry shouldn't either. Sometimes industry forget they would not be selling tickets if the regulators had not given them the authority to do so.

Aviation Communication not only gives employees the strategy and techniques but tells them the messages for each subject and how to deliver them, from the technical to the commercial to what may seem like the mundane workplace event. Never before has a book been written for the aviation industry with these three purposes, and which can be used as an induction tool, a reference book, and a training manual. Many advisors tell industry what to do but not how to say it. Chapters 5 and 6 will finally give readers the exact words they need to take all that advice they have so often heard.

Let's take the media out of the equation for a moment. Employees need to communicate with various audiences on a daily basis, including customers, passengers, regulators, travel industry professionals, local community groups, and many others. They all need to have the messages and strategies that are contained in this book to deal effectively with these groups. After all, an organization is only going to do as well as the ability of these groups to deal with these audiences.

In the subsequent chapters there will be controversial questions with drafted responses, and a chapter with hypothetical press releases that will not make recent, familiar mistakes, showing the technique used from Chapter 2 and the philosophy behind it. The book will prove that a crash is an investigation first and not a media event. That is the key to getting it right.

In many of my classes, when I ask, "Who do you think in recent times has done a good job in communicating after a worst-case scenario?" The answer is invariably, "Tony Fernandes of AirAsia."[1] In the aftermath of the Indonesia AirAsia 8501 tragedy of December 2014, Tony Fernandes, the CEO of not one but nine airlines at that time, addressed the investigators of the world and told them exactly what he did in preparation for what no airline executive or airline employee around the world hopes will ever happen.[2] Readers of this book can learn the same formula that he used in Chapter 3, the 4-point formula. It is also the same thing Air France used in the aftermath of the Concorde tragedy.

Fortunately, the worst-case scenario is now a rare event in aviation. However, a crisis can be defined in many ways. It can be a workplace event, an environmental event, or something that may seem as mundane as a lost bag. However, to the person who lost the bag, it is a crisis. There needs to be communication for all these situations. This book is applicable daily and therefore addresses the reality that communication is not just about dealing with the media and families – and that is what makes this different from the ordinary PR book. This book is for everyday use. So why wait?

Communication is not an after-the-fact activity. You need to know what you are going to say *before* an event occurs. So many times, clients say, "How do I know what I'm going to say until something happens?" Why wait? After reading this book, they no longer have to wait until something happens. We've seen too many times that this strategy does not work.

Aviation Communication will take you through the techniques in Chapter 2, the strategy for the worst-case scenario in Chapter 3, to the messages for all subjects in Chapter 4, the controversial questions and answers in Chapter 5, how to put it all together with templates in Chapter 6, and a lot more. You will want to read this now and keep it on your shelf as your go-to aviation communication advisor.

Notes

1 Teo Cheng Wee (2014) "AirAsia Flight QZ8501: Boss Tony Fernandes Draws Positive Feedback with Personal Touch," The Straits Times, December 31, https://www.straitstimes.com/asia/se-asia/airasia-flight-qz8501.
2 Tony Fernandes (2016) "A Family Affair: AirAsia Group in Light of Indonesia AirAsia Flight QZ8501," *Forum Magazine*, ISASI, Spring, p. 16.

1 Introduction to aviation communication – it's more than you think!

According to the Air Transportation Action Group (ATAG), there are 9.9 million people directly employed worldwide in the aviation industry. All of them need to communicate with one audience or another daily while doing their jobs, whether they are on the technical, commercial, or regulatory side of the industry. The problem with the subject of communication is that it is intangible and subjective, so if there are 50 people with whom you are speaking, there are likely to be 50 different definitions or interpretations of what your communication means. It cannot be controlled by one organization or department. That is just the way it is, whether the corporate powers that be like it or not.

Communication is defined throughout this book as the ability to convey a fact, policy, or thought to any audience, and in the aviation industry that is a lot of people. For the purpose of this discussion, communication is what any employee or affiliated employee may be faced with in their position or work with an organization dealing with the aviation industry, whether it be a regulator, operator, manufacturer, defense contracting professional, investigator, union, media outlet, customer, passenger, employee and beyond. It applies to anyone in any department who may have to communicate with an audience because of the nature of the work they do or in response to a situation that occurs and could include but is not limited to: accidents/incidents; workplace events; regulatory events; affiliate issues; customer issues; personnel events; environmental events; etc.

If I must cite one example that proves the fundamental nature of communication, it would be the events surrounding the tragic disappearance of Malaysia Airlines Flight MH370 in March 2014. To date, no actual plane has been found. There is no known nor confirmed crash (except for several aircraft parts), no regulatory actions, or anything else. Yet here is a company and a country that were discredited in the eyes of the world.[1] What did they do that was so wrong? It was their communication that proved to be fundamental. Communication is not the icing on the cake. It *is* the cake.

Three points to communication

Have a message

> **Mistake #1** – Having a strategy that says, "How do we know what our message is until something happens?"

This is not true. There are messages about the job a person does that can be carried around at all times. There are messages about an organization that can be carried around at all times as well, and there are general messages about the aviation industry that can be carried around at all times.

Examples of a message about the job you do would be:

- My job is to take this aircraft from point A to point B.
- My job is to see that the monthly payroll is carried out on time.
- My job is to ensure that our customers receive the service to which they are entitled.

Examples of a message about my/"our organization" would be:

- "Our organization's" job is to ensure compliance with the Federal Aviation Regulations.
- "Our organization's" job is to safely facilitate 5,000 daily operations through this airport.

When an employee from any department in the aviation industry is asked, "What is the safest aircraft," is that an aviation question or a question specific to an organization? The response would be the same no matter what country, organization, or person is responding, thus making it an aviation question. It does not matter what the situation is. The answer to that question should be known based on any scenario in which it may be asked. There is no reason why anyone in aviation should not know the answer to that question.

Another example of a general aviation message that is applicable to all of the industry would be: "Before any aircraft takes off it must be certified airworthy."

> **Countermeasure to mistake #1** – An understanding of aviation messages should be learned as a tool during initial aviation training for new employees. After all, aviation is your business. No tickets can be sold without an air operator's certificate.

Practice your message

> **Mistake #2** – Practicing for all situations with the same strategy using a briefing book with questions and answers is acceptable.

Your message is your ammunition but all the ammunition in the world will not help you if you cannot aim and shoot. Everyone has a different level of communication skill strength, so it is a good idea to practice the delivery of your message. Some people are good at dealing with technical audiences but terrible with emotional audiences and some people are better at dealing with political or regulatory audiences.

One of the many comments I receive is that people in various workforces think that because they deal at high levels on a daily basis, they do not need to practice their messages, skills, or anything else. This is due to arrogance and the often false assumption that others are as familiar or well versed in operational facets as those who work within the structure every day. The world has seen the results of unpracticed messages too often.

> **Countermeasure to mistake #2** – Do not practice for all situations with the same strategy. Determine if you are going to educate, clear up a misunderstanding, or fit into a situation whose theme has already been determined.

It's a thought process

> **Mistake #3** – Preparing for all situations with the same strategy.

Communication is a thought process. If a question is asked, the answer may be one of several options. For example, one may be asked, "How are you going to apologize for this terrible mistake?" One response could be, "I'm sorry. I'll never do it again." Another response could be, "We have nothing to apologize for." A third response could be, "We are always sorry when a tragedy like this occurs." One audience could be your director/CEO/commander. Another audience could be a union. A third audience could be family members/emotional audiences. Each one of those responses might be apapropriate with one of those audiences but you certainly would not go to a family member and say, "We have nothing to apologize for." You need to think on your feet and develop your response strategy. Communication with regulators needs a different strategy altogether, and far more factual understanding than communication with customers. In all cases, communication must be forthright and factual.

> **Countermeasure to mistake #3** – The lead for these strategies should be the safety/operations departments to ensure they do not conflict with their ability to deal effectively with their target audience.

Figure 1.1 shows an archaic perception of communication. It implies that the media is the center of everything and all the other potential parties to an event should defer to the media. Clients many times say to me, "If we don't do this, the media will crucify us, or worse." This philosophy leads them to develop a reactionary strategy and will lead to failure.

This may have been the way things were before the introduction of the 24-hour news cycle back in 1980, but that 24-hour reporting life inspired competition between news services. Then, with the introduction of cell phones, everyone could be a photo journalist, and anyone might end up on the evening news or on a news blog through no fault (or with no control) of their own. That was followed by the advent and proliferation of social media. Now events are photographed, recorded, and published digitally almost as they happen. Media itself is no longer at levels of old: in today's environment, more people get their news digitally than from print or by watching television newscasts.

To say that this is just a new phenomenon since the onset of social media is a fallacy. Within one hour of Swissair Flight 111 crashing, I heard someone on

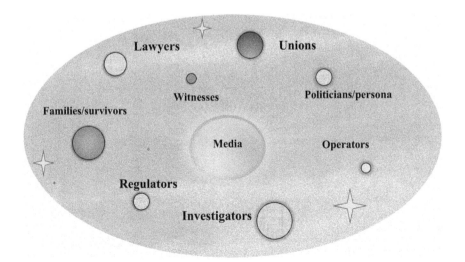

Figure 1.1 Media misperception

8 Introduction to aviation communication

CNN comparing it to the ValuJet crash of 1996 because there had been smoke reported in the cockpit. The Swissair tragedy took place on September 2, 1998, before the onset of social media. Granted, the time element was much quicker but the concept is the same – information coming out, whether right or wrong, in the immediate aftermath of an event. And the immediate perceptions are often lasting facts.

Figure 1.1 focuses on the media as though they are the epicenter of everything. It portrays them as though they are the sun and all the other potential parties to an event are planets orbiting the sun. If an organization has a strategy which incorporates the above older philosophy, then it is a strategy that gives social and traditional media the power to control how the event is reported and perceived. It means you will not be proactively in control of your message and you will be left with a strategy that limits you to reactively answer questions. If that happens, no matter who the audience is, you will be in a position where the party asking the questions is able to control where they take the discussion because you will merely be following and reacting. The reality is reflected in Chart 1.1.

Chart 1.1 shows the potential parties to an event. Each of these potential parties has their own style of communicating. Failing to take into consideration their styles of communicating when developing a communication strategy will leave you with a strategy that does not meet today's communications reality.

Let's examine one by one the various styles of communicating and what each brings to an event.

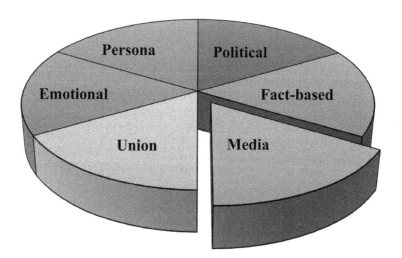

Chart 1.1 Potential parties to an event

Potential parties to an event

Fact-based communication

The fact-based style of communicating is what all people in the aviation industry should practice, unless they are representing a union perspective. The good thing about the aviation industry is its interlocking system of checks, balances, and oversight. Nothing that is done in the aviation industry is arbitrary. There is data, proof of what has happened or what an organization has done, examples of audits, safety, and proactivity.

When you represent the fact-based perspective, you are there because you represent "our organization" and the process. If you make the mistake of representing yourself, giving your opinion or something similar, you lose the ability to represent the fact-based perspective.

Political-style communication

The next style of communicating is the political style. This does not necessarily refer to an elected official. It is a style of communicating for someone who comes forward, states what they want (generally self-serving), and a year later when a report comes out, or a lawsuit is completed, the statement may or may not be proven to be true or factual – and a fact-based party to the event must then counteract the political statement. An example of political-style communication is someone who appears on television within an hour of something happening as the proclaimed industry expert without having any hands-on working relationship with the event at hand, nor verified factual knowledge of the situation. Another example that fits into this category would be the "witnesses have said" or "sources have told us."

Persona communication

A persona is an individual with stature or star power. People seek him/her out for attention or he/she may seek out attention. He/she attracts attention to an event as well as to themselves. You never know if you will have a persona as a party to an event. An example of this would be a corporate CEO with star power such as a Sir Richard Branson. If something happened with Virgin Atlantic, people would expect to hear from him. If it were another airline, the world would not necessarily be familiar with who was the head of the organization. In addition, you never know who might be on an aircraft.

Emotional-style communication

The emotional audience is anyone (individual or collective) who identifies with something that happened. They want two things from an organization. First, they want you to be sympathetic. Second, they want you to be accessible.

This means that you must come forward and face them. If you do not do these two things, you run the risk of fueling the adversarial nature of this audience. If that happens, you will never be done nor successful. The emotional audience triggers the political audience.

One example of when the emotional audience triggered the political audience was the aftermath of the forcible removal of a passenger from a United Airlines flight at O'Hare International Airport in April 2017. The CEO's initial statement was met with much criticism and fuelled the adversarial emotional audience.[2] In this case, the emotional audience was anyone who identified with the "victim," a passenger. Every member of the traveling public is a potential passenger, and nearly all are in a position to dictate public opinion. That outcry triggered a public reaction from politicians as to whether there should be industry-wide legislation as a remedy for the actions that led to the chain reaction.

Union-style communication

> **Mistake #4** – "We don't have a union, so we don't need a strategy for dealing with a union."

The aviation industry is fraught with and influenced by organized labour unions, from those who maintain the aircraft (such as the International Association of Machinists and Aerospace Workers – IAM) to the those who manufacture aircraft and equipment to the personnel who operate the aircraft in the air (such as the Air Line Pilots Association, International – ALPA) to the industry on the ground and in the air. The number one objective of unions is to defend their members. Organizations who also fall into this category include those who pay to have organizational membership. Unions can insert themselves into dialogue or issues by posturing or using an event to focus on an issue, even if they have no immediate stake in that particular issue or event. An example of posturing would be to say, "We know this issue is going to be a problem so if it happens, don't blame us." This is how they absolve themselves in the future. This is exactly what they are structured to do, but organizations that do not incorporate this power into their strategy do not have a strategy that deals with reality.

I may ask an organization, "What is your strategy to deal with a union?" The response might be, "We do not have a union, so we do not need a union strategy." My next question is, "Do you ever fly into a city/country where their air traffic controllers are unionized or have outsourced union maintenance?" Most do and therefore if they have an event that has external involvement, they must have a strategy that considers input from unions, even if they do not have a union. The danger in doing this is if you have party status, there is the possibility of being removed from the investigation. Another example of union input would be when the union may not have a specific role in an event but rather a specific interest in those involved in that event.

> **Countermeasure to mistake #4** – Incorporate into your communication strategy the idea that your organization may need to deal with a union, whether or not your organization has one.

Media-style communication

As you can see from Chart 1.1, the media segment is just one party to an event and not the center of the event. Print media is a business. Electronic media is entertainment and journalism is a class people take in college: true, journalism is swiftly disappearing as reporters have given way to commentators with an agenda. If an organization understands and accepts that, they need to have a strategy that takes it into account. If their messages are not substantive and are nothing more than public relations clichés, then those clichés are going to be picked up as sound bites and there will be nothing substantive to offset the other side nor make a meaningful contribution to the discussion.

Many nationalities and cultures feel that their media is more oppressive than other media. Clients from various countries frequently say to me that "people do not understand how our media is. Our media is more aggressive than other media." Then I hear the same experiences related over and over. If it isn't something you experience daily, when it does happen it can be overwhelming, but it is that way for everyone within the sphere of that media environment. With major events being universal and aviation being a multinational industry, the media that shows up is generally an international unit.

> **Mistake #5** – Organizations strategize to talk to the media.

So many times, clients say, "It isn't fair" or "I was taken out of context." Let's examine these two statements separately.

First, when one says, "it isn't fair," it may not seem fair on the surface because a different party to an event may have a different objective to yours. Your strategy must take into consideration an understanding of the objectives of the other parties to the event prior to the development of your strategy. People like to blame the media for everything. It is generally not the media that are the problem. It is the people who use the media to assert their position or agenda. The media are a tool and if you are not looking at them as a tool, then you do not have a strategy that meets reality. When you go to speak to the media, you are not simply talking to the media. It is important to remember that you are talking through the media to the audience(s) listening to the media. The media are just a tool for your end game – to use it to reach those audiences you want to receive your message. Ask yourself when developing a strategy, "Who do I want to hear this message?" and not just what that message is.

Second, the statement that one is being taken out of context is an excuse. Clarity is your responsibility. When a party feels they have been taken out of context, it generally means that they had the wrong strategy for the situation in which they find themselves. Here is a common example of what I hear. What they may tell me is, "I met with the media for 45 minutes and all they showed on the evening news was 30 seconds and therefore it was taken out of context." I explain that no one gets more than 30 seconds (if that) (see Chapter 2) on the evening news. Therefore, so the fact that they spent 45 minutes with them was their first mistake.

When I ask if they were the one who generated the story, most of the people I work with tell me no. This is their second mistake. The problem here is not the media. The problem is the way the client prepared for meeting with the media. The media went through the 45 minutes and took what fit into their story since it was not the client who generated the story. The client went to answer questions. The media asked questions until they got the 30-second sound bite or answer that fit into their perceived story. That's it! The client was not "taken out of context." Often, the reporters have already determined the thrust of their story and are simply searching for answers that support that story line. Again – journalism has changed. Reporters will lead the interview to statements that support their pre-conceived premise *if* they are allowed to do so. This happens when the interviewee goes with a strategy to just answer questions and has no messages of their own. Is that the fault of the interviewer? No.

> **Countermeasure to mistake #5** – Have a strategy that considers your audience beyond the media.

Mistake #6 – "It's the media's fault!"

> **Countermeasure to mistake #6** – Understand it is not the media's fault. It's the people who use the media.

Audience analysis

Prior to getting into a situation where you need to communicate, you need to ask yourself, "Why am I going? Am I going to educate? Am I going to clear up a misunderstanding? Or, has the theme of what I am doing already been determined?" If the latter is true, then there is no amount of facts that will change the situation and you need to figure out how to fit into the situation. Each one of these situations requires a different strategy and possibly a different communicator with a different communication style and skills.

Going to educate

If you are going to educate, your strategy needs to be one where the person doing the communicating has both good communication skills and good technical expertise. There is a longer back and forth exchange and the person who does the communicating needs to have messages, know the technical background, and provide proof for those messages. They also need to know how to facilitate their way in and out of their messages using techniques of communication without being manipulated into "opening doors."

Example

An example of how to educate is a straight question and answer session between two people:

Question: Is this operation safe?
Answer: If you look at the fact that we have been in business for 20 years, we have 1,000 operations annually, and are certified by our regulators and the regulators of all ten countries where we do business, you would know we are safe.
Question: I have been told that there is a cover-up of information regarding this event.
Answer: We've been in the business for 20 years and one of the good things about the industry is its interlocking system of checks, balances, and oversight; so it would be very difficult for anyone to cover anything up. And that is not our practice.

Clearing up a misunderstanding

An example of this might be when a disgruntled employee becomes a whistle-blower and claims that a particular technology being used compromises safety. The technology, being based on principles of engineering, would have been certified. Therefore, it is key to send a good technical communicator who is able to provide facts in a credible manner to support the positive and proven elements of the technology. However, it is not going to be a situation where you can educate with a series of challenges and rebuttals that can be supported by messages and then backed up by support points in an exchange between two people. This is a situation where there are numerous parties to the event, each providing different perspectives. Because you represent the fact-based perspective, you might be able to clear up the misunderstanding with the message and the facts, but you must also take into consideration the other parties' agendas. The person doing the communicating must also be a good overall communicator and not just a good technical communicator.

14 Introduction to aviation communication

Example

An air traffic controller was reprimanded for counter-manning Traffic Collision Avoidance System (TCAS – aviation terminology, see Chapter 2). He is disgruntled and goes to the media (using it as a tool) to say that the technology is an "accident waiting to happen." The controller's union supports him and goes on to say that technology takes precedence and further postures by saying, "if it causes a crash, don't come to us." The pilots' union representative says, "I'd be more concerned if TCAS wasn't there." The media gets input from a British expert who is a persona. Because TCAS is technology, the media then goes to the regulator who certified the technology. The regulator should be able to use facts, figures, and data to defend the technology. The pilots are represented by their union and their message to defend the technology is to make themselves part of the process (see Chapter 2, technique #24) by saying, "They would be more concerned if TCAS were not on the plane." They used a very simple message and technique to defend technology. This indicates how each of the parties to the above scenario relate to it and how complicated the scenario of clearing up a misunderstanding can be. If an organization prepares by simply reviewing a briefing book and planning on answering questions, then their strategy is doomed to fail. Chart 1.2 illustrates the potential parties to an event like this and how they should interact.

The theme has already been determined

If this is a situation in which the theme or thrust of the argument has already been determined, then the communicator needs to figure out how best to fit

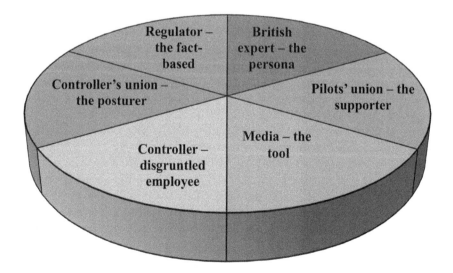

Chart 1.2 Potential parties to this event

into that situation, because there are no amount of facts that will change the theme of the situation. This is an example I heard at a congressional hearing: A politician said to a manufacturer, "My brother is afraid to fly. How am I going to convince him aviation is safe?" This is really a non-question, but the manufacturer was based in this congressman's district, so he did not want to be controversial.

Another question that was asked of a regulator by a congressman during those hearings was, "What did your metallurgist say about this?" "We don't have a metallurgist on our staff," was the response. The next question was, "Don't you think you should have a metallurgist on staff?" This was because this congressman happened to have a metallurgist on staff he wanted the regulator to hire. Therefore, there were no amount of facts that were going change the line of questions.

Mistake #7 – Organizations compartmentalize communication. "We have people to do that!"

Many organizations hear the word communication and they believe they can defer to their internal offices of corporate communication. This has nothing to do with reality in today's world, as every employee's responsibilities includes communication. It is simply not a strategy that works. All employees in aviation and aviation-related jobs are required to communicate with one audience or another on a daily basis. Can you imagine a travel agent who believes they do not need to communicate? Travel agents may need to communicate the safety of an airline or an aircraft in the same way an operator or a regulator must. It's about establishing a level of trust in any service or product you offer.

Countermeasure to mistake #7 – There needs to be an established and vetted policy statement and corporate/organizational definition for communication with accountability (making it every employee's responsibility) and the policy should be harmonized throughout the organization.

Mistake #8 – "We have executives who communicate for us, so we do not have to worry."

Many organizations or employees of organizations believe that they have superiors, executives, commanding officers, or others who will do the communicating for them, so they do not have to worry. This is another strategy that will not work because it does not meet the reality in today's world of multinational organizations and social media.

> **Countermeasure to mistake #8** – Make sure that all employees understand it is their responsibility to communicate and that clear and transparent communication is the foundation of a business, as opposed to meaningless public relations clichés. It does not belong solely to a "department" or a "person."

Mistake #9 – "We are protected because we have a 'policy.'"

> **Countermeasure to mistake #9** – Have a communication policy that meets reality with an empowerment statement that is non-punitive.

Most organizations I work with have policies in place that outline who can speak to whom, and when. This strategy will not work because it is not an inanimate organization that decides who speaks. It is the person who "asks" the question and to whom they direct their inquiries. If I walk up to an employee and ask, "What happened?" I have chosen that person to be the spokesperson. I do not care what some organizational policy says or allows that person to say. Whatever words come out of his or her mouth are what I am going to use as the response.

Mistake #10 – Spokespeople are those who speak to the media.

> **Countermeasure to Mistake #10** – Define a spokesperson as any employee who has to speak to any audience on behalf of the company.

Corporate assignments do not always determine who will be thrust into the role of spokesperson. A person is made a spokesperson by those walking up and asking an employee the question, "What happened?" To those asking the questions, it does not matter what some organizational policy says or allows their employees to say. The words that come out of an employee's mouth are what are going to be used as the attributed response. If a representative of an organization goes before a political body, board, or commission to testify, he or she must answer truthfully whatever question is asked. The organization is going to fare only as well as the ability of their representative to communicate, in a given situation, whether it be to congress/parliament or some other political body, regulatory agency, public forum, family, customer, investigator, media outlet, or another aviation-related audience.

Empowerment statement

Organizations often have a ridiculous philosophy when providing a rationale for a strategy. I hear this all the time: "We do not want to authorize anyone to talk because then we will have a lot of employees going around trying to be media stars." In my more than three decades in business, working all over the world, I have yet to meet the employee who has said, "Yes, I am dying to be a media star, work with the media, run up to them and tell them everything in the face of a tragedy when 200 people have just died in a tragic plane crash." What I have encountered are a lot of airline and airline-related professionals who sincerely want to do a good job and who are more afraid of what will happen to them in their own organization if they, through no fault of their own, end up on the evening news because someone recorded them on a cell phone and put it on YouTube while they were just trying to do their job.

Generally, I have found punitive measures are politically motivated and turf-oriented. They are destructive to a strategy on many levels. First, they are intimidating to a workforce. Second, they put people in charge of developing strategies without the expertise to do so, like ships without rudders. If we are talking about upset recovery training, falsification of maintenance records, or aircraft certification, then public relations people are not qualified to be the lead strategists on those issues because they are not versed on the issues. The issues are already beyond the expertise of corporate communication employees before something happens. Third, they create internal ill will. It is a sad commentary when employees are more afraid of what will happen to them in their own employment ranks than of talking to the media.

It is much better to empower people to say what needs to be said to protect an organization and be able to say something but give away nothing. If you say nothing, then you leave the conclusions open and generally appear evasive and with something to hide. In most organizations, employees will not say anything unless they see a policy in writing allowing them to do so without fear of punitive action. An empowerment statement could alleviate all of this and provide consistency.

First, consider the rationale for an empowerment statement. The following example might explain to employees the thought process behind a sample empowerment statement:

> Because management has the highest confidence in the employees of "our organization," this policy is intended to provide the tools and messages needed for our employees to communicate in the most difficult of situations. These tools and messages, along with our employees' capabilities and ability to exercise good judgment, give management the confidence in our

employees to do what is necessary in a given situation without overextending their expertise. The guidance and communication that are authorized can be found in Chapter 3 (the 4-point formula).

Second, it is vital to make clear the rationale and policy for the empowerment statement. This gives employees the authority to speak:

"Our organization" does not encourage employees or affiliates to seek out attention from the media or other organizations. However, we recognize that there are times when our employees and affiliates may be in a situation in which they are confronted by various audiences, due to the nature of the industry and the inevitable focus resulting from the event. When this occurs, it may be necessary for our employees and our affiliates to communicate as the exception, not the rule. *This policy authorizes communication when necessary within the parameters outlined below.*

Third, consider the authority. This sample empowerment statement is an example of something that gives employees the authority they need to communicate in a worst-case scenario.

"Our organization's" management recognizes that our employees may often find themselves in this situation, especially in the worst-case scenario. If any employee does find himself/herself in this situation with no time or option to strategize on a response, this is *authorization to communicate* according to the *4-point formula* with guidance given *without fear of punitive action*. (Note: The 4-point formula is covered in Chapter 3.)

Cultural differences in communication

Understanding intercultural communication is very important for anyone working across countries or continents, including those working for multinational companies either in their home country or abroad. In aviation, most organizations deal with this reality.

> **Mistake #9** – Not taking into consideration other countries' cultural styles of communication and working them into your strategies.

Having different parties to an event or situation is one thing with which to deal, but the issues of differences in cultural styles of communication and process objectives from country to country also play a role. Some countries are passive communicators, while others are more aggressive without necessarily being aggressive. This is not meant to be a book about the psychological styles of communication; we are just talking about generalities here for the sake of wide classification.

Let me clarify for the sake of this discussion: Passive would mean being more diplomatic and not being comfortable questioning authority; not taking the lead, and politely answering questions. More aggressive styles would be more politically charged and driven, less intimidated by authority. Here are some general examples to be considered when developing strategies.

For example, we all know that one of the most important objectives in Asian cultures is not losing face. Here is an example of how that can affect communication in a non-crash-related situation:

A regulator went to an Asian country to conduct an assessment of a 145 Repair Station Certificate (aviation terminology, Chapter 2). They asked the customer a question, but the customer did not exactly understand what was being asked. Because the regulator was considered the authority in the eyes of the customer, and in this Asian culture it was considered rude to question authority, they did not tell the regulator that they did not understand the issue itself. They ended up giving the regulator the wrong information. The regulator thought the organization did not know what they were talking about and recommended them for a recertification. This was all because of a difference in cultural styles of communication.

In a more serious example, if something happens to a company from Asia and the event takes place in the United States – as with Asiana Airlines Flight 214 which crashed in San Francisco on July 6, 2013 – the company needs a strategy for a crash that happens in San Francisco and that is handled appropriately given that it is an event in the United States, not South Korea. Asiana Airlines did not communicate as a corporation for many hours.[3] In a discussion about this in one of my classes, a student said, "I think they were waiting for the CEO to return to Seoul." But the crash did not take place in Seoul!

In the Middle East, one of the main characteristics of the cultural style of communication or process is to be accommodating. They are very polite and diplomatic, and they do not want to deliver bad news or to say that they don't know something, so they may end up saying what they think someone wants to hear. For example, a hypothetical question could be, "How many people were there?" They may not be sure how many people were there, but do not want to say they don't know. They may therefore respond with something like, "I think there were 14." The words "I think" suggest that they are not sure, as opposed to the fact-based response, "There were 14 people there." They don't want to say they don't know so they are being accommodating by modifying their response with the qualifier "I think."

Generally speaking, in Europe the focus is on the *process* in their communication process. They rarely go from point A to point D without going through points B and C. Many times, you will hear Europeans in presentations and meetings say, "and the next point is x, and the next point is y."

In the United States people often have great difficulty with the communication process. For one thing, the communication process in the United States is politically and liability driven. Second, there are many people behind the scenes who will try to tweak the process to change its outcome – because it is politically and liability driven. Therefore, in a case such as this, the media is not the problem. It is the people who use the media who are the problem. No one knows who does something and it does not matter who does it. What matters is that the process allows for it to happen and no one has control over it. If a more passive culture is not accustomed to this, it is very difficult to deal with the process, which could make for very damaging cultural perceptions.

Because the process is politically and liability driven in the United States, the objective many times is simply to win. Therefore, behind the scenes you will often see people throw out a conclusion to try to change the direction or actual conclusion. The objective is to try and help make groups receive the facts to *support* a specific conclusion before getting the full set of facts to *determine* the conclusion. This is what makes the US process one of the most difficult to navigate.

In Latin American countries, the cultural style of communication is characterised by diplomacy and protocol. Sometimes it is mistakenly thought that things can be resolved through diplomatic channels, and these channels might override the regulatory channels.

The Latin communication style is very complimentary and courteous, sometimes masking what Latin people feel might be offensive or embarrassing. One thing that is difficult to talk about is accomplishments, because they are generally humble and modest communicators, and to use facts to support accomplishments could be perceived as boastful. Unfortunately, this tends to weaken a fact-based case.

> **Countermeasure to mistake #9** – Have a plan to consider the cultural style of communication for every area in which you do business and ensure that your representatives in those countries are equipped and empowered to act on your behalf.

Mistake #10 – Not taking into consideration other countries' cultural styles of communication and working them into your strategies.

Australia has a very strong and aggressive cultural style of communication. Their aviation industry can be very political. They have never had a major event (i.e. a large-scale crash by international standards), but any regional event they can bring major political attention and reaction to. When you communicate in Australia it is very straightforward and direct, but you had better back it up with facts and support points (techniques, Chapter 2). They want data, examples, and proof and they want it fast. If you are representing a culture that is more passive or modest in terms of espousing your accomplishments, you may not be as prepared as you need to be to communicate in this environment. That is one reason why it is a difficult culture in which to communicate. I received my "highest" compliment from an Australian man, an airline safety director. He said, "You're such a great Sheila you're almost a bloke." That pretty much says it all.

> **Countermeasure to mistake #10** – Have a plan to consider the cultural style of communication for every area in which you do business and ensure that your representatives in those countries are equipped and empowered to act on your behalf based on the way the process works in that country, not yours.

Cultural communication stereotypes

Cultural stereotypes are obstacles that do get in the way of international communication. Here is another example of what I mean: The French are frequently stereotyped as being arrogant. In this case, I was going to work with a French client and my brother asked me if I would ask him why the French hate Americans. I inquired as to why he would say that. He replied, "The French all know how to speak English and refuse to do so," to which I asked, "Where do you get that?" He said, "He had friends who went to Paris and that was their experience." He went on to say, "Well, they are that way in Paris but if you get into the countryside they are nice." (This is a frequent American perceived stereotype regarding the French.) I asked him, "How many French people do you know?" He replied, "None, but I've heard." That is the problem. It is part of lore –a perception handed down from person to person based on one person's experience. A misperception left unchecked becomes entrenched, and then becomes a *perceived* fact (techniques, Chapter 2). This does not mean it is true.

I have worked with French people for many years and this experience shows that perception to not be true. The French cultural style of communication is very formal, conservative, and polite. It is misunderstood, and therefore formality has been stereotyped as "arrogance" because of other cultures' inability to understand them. The American cultural style of communication is more informal and liberal. For example, it is a much more common practice to say something like, "Let's do lunch," which may be taken as a meaningless gesture of comradery. When you ask a French person if they speak English, they may say "*non*." To someone of another culture, the French may, in fact, speak a little English. But, to a French person, if they do not speak *perfect* English (i.e. they haven't yet mastered it), they believe that they do not speak English at all, and therefore they say "*non*."

Chapter summary

1. Three points of communication
   - Have a message
   - Practice your message
   - It's a thought process
2. Potential parties to the event
   - Fact-based
   - Political
   - Persona
   - Emotional
   - Union
   - Media
3. Audience analysis
   - Going to educate
   - Going to clear up a misunderstanding
   - Fitting into someone else's story
4. Empowerment statement
5. Cultural differences in communication
   - Cultural communication stereotypes

Notes

1 Jonathan Tilley (2014) "Analysis: Malaysia Airlines' Mishandled Response to MH370 Crisis," *PRWeek*, March 21
2 Erin McCann (2017) "United's Apologies: A Timeline," *The New York Times*, April 14.
3 Susan Carey, Rachel Feintzeig, and Kanga Kong (2013) "Asiana's Response to Plane Crash Draws Notice," *Wall Street Journal*, July 9.

2 Aviation terminology and communication techniques

The basic building blocks and connective tissue

The terminology in this chapter requires more explanation than a glossary could provide. It is the basic terminology applicable for not just technical people but also commercial professionals, travel professionals, airport operators, and others. This terminology is the basic language used – though not necessarily in day-to-day operations. However, if issues arise, it is good to be aware of what is meant, even if one does not have to communicate about these issues directly. Additionally, workplace and commercial terminology are also applicable to the technical workforce.

The fact that some of the terminology is technical but crosses over to the commercial audience, and vice versa, necessitates that it be more than just a glossary. In many cases in aviation it is the commercial audience who will be the first people to respond on a technical issue. If customers want to know whether a particular aircraft type or airline is safe, they are not going to call the safety department of Boeing, Airbus, or British Airways. They are going to ask their travel agent, a sales representative, or airport personnel.

Terminology and lingo

60 Minutes – An American newsmagazine television program that initially employed the investigative journalism known as "gotcha journalism" – surprise visits, hidden cameras, and ambush techniques. Similar programs are popular in other countries such as Canada and Australia. It debuted in 1968 and has won many awards through the years. Today the persona of *60 Minutes* has changed considerably since the beginning to that of a sophisticated newsmagazine program that enjoys great respect.

AAIB – The Air Accident Investigation Branch is an independent unit within the United Kingdom's Ministry of Transport. They are responsible for the investigation of aircraft accidents and serious incidents within the United Kingdom, its overseas territories, and crown dependencies. Being one of the world's leading accident investigation organizations, they are frequently called upon to provide assistance and expertise to international air accident investigations and organizations due to their resources – both technical and human. They follow the ICAO Annex 13 and UK statutory obligations for accident investigation.

AC – Advisory Circular is a document published by the FAA giving guidance on aviation issues.

ADFAA – The Aviation Disaster Family Assistance Act, enacted in 1996, is designed to provide support for the families of victims of commercial airline crashes occurring in the United States. The National Transportation Safety Board (NTSB), the government agency charged with investigating all domestic civil aviation crashes, is responsible for executing the ADFAA, in response to which it issued detailed guidelines applicable to airlines and federal agencies. The ADFAA was enacted to resolve persistent problems in the treatment of grieving families in the aftermath of commercial airline crashes. Some of these problems included:

- Harassment of families by lawyers.
- Procedures for notification of families.
- Family assistance.
- Government stonewalling.
- Family communication.

Airworthiness Directive – A directive issued by the FAA to correct an unsafe condition.

Airworthy – Deemed acceptable for flight by a regulator.

ALPA – The Air Line Pilots' Association is the largest pilot union in the world. It represents more than 60,000 pilots from 34 US and Canadian airlines. It was founded in 1931 and is a member of the AFL–CIO.

AOC – The Air Operators Certificate is the approval granted by a national aviation authority to an aircraft operator to allow it to use aircraft for commercial purposes.

ATSB – The Australian Transportation Safety Board is the agency charged with investigating civil aviation accidents in Australia. They are many times called upon to assist other countries in accident investigation.

BEA – The Bureau d'Enquêtes et d'Anaylses (Investigation and Analysis Bureau for Civil Aviation Safety) is an agency of the French government responsible for investigating aviation accidents and incidents. The BEA makes safety recommendations based on what is learned from their investigations. It is under the authority of the Ministry of Ecology, Sustainable Development, Transport and Housing. They are responsible for investigating all aircraft accidents occurring in French territory or airspace, as well as accidents involving French aircraft occurring in international airspace or in other countries if the local authorities do not open a technical enquiry. They may also assist foreign investigation authorities upon request. It is respected as one of the top investigative organizations in the world and many times its assistance is sought from other countries due to its resources – both technical and human.

CFIT – Controlled flight into terrain is an accident in which an airworthy aircraft, under pilot control, is unintentionally flown into the ground, a mountain, a body of water, or an obstacle. In a typical CFIT scenario, the crew is unaware of the impending disaster until it is too late.

Codeshare – An aviation business agreement where two airlines share in the same flight. Each airline publishes and markets the flight under its own airline designator and flight number as part of its published timetable or schedule, and this helps the airlines to expand their markets.

Corrective action – Action to eliminate or mitigate the cause or reduce the effects of the nonconformity, noncompliance, or other undesirable situation.

Criminality – The concept that exists in various countries that an accident or incident is a criminal event while also a technical investigation. This can complicate a technical investigation as there are conflicting objectives. The outcome can generate a manslaughter case for those organizations/individuals found to have contributed to the event.

EASA – The European Aviation Safety Administration is the umbrella civil aviation regulatory agency of Europe. Their mission is to promote the highest common standards of safety and environmental protection in civil aviation.

ECAC – The European Civil Aviation Conference is an intergovernmental organization which was established by the International Civil Aviation Organization (ICAO) and the Council of Europe. The ECAC promotes the continued development of a safe, efficient, and sustainable European air transport system. In doing so, it seeks to harmonize civil aviation policies and practices amongst its member states and promote understanding on policy matters between its member states and other parts of the world. Its strategic priorities are safety, security, and the environment.

EEO – Equal employment opportunity attempts to ensure that there is equal opportunity for employment throughout a workplace.

EIR – Enforcement investigation reports may be opened by the FAA for various reasons. Some of these reasons could be routine surveillance by the FAA, whistle-blower or employee complaint, or a problem could be initiated from a customer or outside source.

ETOPS – Extended-range Twin-engine Operational Performance Standards are rules which permit twin-engine aircraft to fly routes which, at some point, are more than 60 minutes flying time away from the nearest airport suitable for emergency landing.

FAA – Federal Aviation Administration is the US government agency regulating all aspects of the aviation industry.

Federal Family Assistance Plan for Aviation Disaster – The 2008 revision of the Aviation Disaster Family Assistance Acts of 1996 and 1997 (see **VST** below).

Flight Safety Foundation – A nonprofit, international organization that does research on behalf of aviation safety through task forces, education, and seminars. They conduct annual seminars attended by hundreds of aviation safety professionals from both government and industry.

FOIA – The Freedom of Information Act is a federal freedom of information law that allows for the full or partial disclosure of previously unreleased information and documents controlled by the United States government and other governments, although it may have another name in other governments. The Act defines agency records that are subject to disclosure and outlines the mandatory disclosure procedures. Over 100 countries around the world have some form of freedom of information legislation.

FOQA – Flight Operations Quality Assurance or Flight Data Management (FDM) is the process of collecting and analyzing data from flights to improve safety and efficiency of flight operations, air traffic control procedures, and aircraft.

GASP – The Global Air Safety Plan is a plan under ICAO that prioritizes and supports the continuous improvement of global civil aviation safety.

Ground handling agents – Airlines with less-frequent services or fewer resources at a given location sometimes subcontract ground handling or on-call aircraft maintenance to another airline, as it is a cheaper alternative to setting up their own ground handling or maintenance capabilities.

Harmonization – This is an effort by regulators to try and make the regulatory and certification processes consistent from country to country.

IAM – The International Association of Machinists and Aerospace Workers is the largest labour union in North America, representing over 700,000 members of a diverse current and retired workforce.

IASA – Under the International Aviation Safety Assessment Program, the FAA determines whether another country's oversight of its air carriers that operate, or seek to operate, in the United States, or codeshare with a US air carrier, complies with safety standards established by the International Civil Aviation Organization (ICAO). If the FAA determines that it does not comply, they may downgrade that country's regulator to a Category 2 (CAT 2) status. (The indented term below is FAA-related.)

    Category 2 (CAT 2) – If a country is downgraded to a Category 2 status, it means the air carriers from the downgraded state cannot initiate new service and are restricted to current levels of any existing service to the United States while corrective actions are underway. They may not add any new routes or change anything about their operations specifications while in a CAT 2 status. During this time, the FAA does not support reciprocal codeshare arrangements between air carriers for the assessed state and US carriers. Also, during this time, the foreign air carrier serving the United States is subject to additional inspections at US airports. Although the issue is with the government and not an operator, the action could have great commercial impact on an operator.

IATA – The International Air Transport Association is the major international trade association representing the world's airlines. It has approximately 278 members and represents approximately 117 countries. It is not a regulatory authority. (The indented term below is IATA-related.)

    IOSA – The IATA Operational Safety Audit is an internationally accepted evaluation system designed to assess the operational management and control systems of an airline. All members of IATA must undergo an assessment every two years.

ICAO – International Civil Aviation Organization. (The terms indented below are ICAO-related).

Annex 13 – These are provisions laid down by the International Civil Aviation Convention as to how states shall investigate or delegate the investigation of accidents which have occurred in their territory. Serious incidents should be investigated by states or by other organizations, such as dedicated accident/incident investigation bodies or aviation service provider organizations. When an accident happens involving an international civil aviation flight, Annex 13 sets out the rules on the notification, investigation and reporting of the accident. It sets out the rights on who should conduct the investigation, which parties can be involved, what rights each party has, how the investigation should be conducted, and how the results should be reported. Annex 13 also states that the sole objective of the investigation of an accident or incident is to prevent accidents and incidents and that the investigation is not to apportion blame or liability.

Annex 19 – A new annex dedicated to states' safety management responsibilities and processes framed under the State Safety Programme (SSP). This was developed to address the potential risks of future growth of international aviation and deal with them in a proactive manner. It was the first new ICAO annex developed in over 30 years.

Accident – An occurrence associated with the operation of an aircraft which takes place between the time any person boards the aircraft with the intention of flight until all such persons have disembarked, in which:

a) a person is fatally or seriously injured as a result of:

- being in the aircraft, or
- direct contact with any part of the aircraft, including parts which have become detached from the aircraft, or
- direct exposure to jet blast, except when the injuries are from natural causes, self-inflicted or inflicted by other persons, or when the injuries are to stowaways hiding outside the areas normally available to the passengers and crew; or

b) the aircraft sustains damage or structural failure which:
- adversely affects the structural strength, performance or flight characteristics of the aircraft, and
- would normally require major repair or replacement of the affected component, *except* for engine failure or damage, when the damage is limited to the engine, its cowlings or accessories; or for damage limited to propellers, wing tips, antennas, tires, brakes, fairings, small dents or puncture holes in the aircraft skin; or

c) the aircraft is missing or is completely inaccessible.[1]

Incident – An occurrence, other than an accident, associated with the operation of an aircraft which affects or could affect the safety of operation.[2]

Accredited representative – A person designated by a state, based on his or her qualifications, to participate in an investigation conducted by another state.[3] The accredited representative is the team leader of the state's investigation team. It is a common mistake for members of industry to misunderstand who is the team leader of the investigation team.

Party system – An investigation system in which the organization conducting the investigation invites parties with specialized technical knowledge and expertise to participate in the process on groups such as airframe, operations, or air traffic. Those without appropriate technical expertise, such as insurance companies or lawyers, are excluded from this process.

ISASI – The International Society of Air Safety Investigators was formed to promote air safety through the exchange of ideas, experiences, and information about aircraft accident investigations, and to aid in the advancement of flight safety. There are regional subchapters of ISASI.

JAA – The Joint Airworthiness Authority was an associated body of the ECAC representing the civil aviation regulatory authorities of a number of European states who had agreed to co-operate in developing and implementing common safety regulatory standards and procedures. It was not a regulatory body, as regulations were achieved through the member authorities. It preceded the EASA.

Just culture – The effort not to lay blame in the aftermath of an aviation accident or incident and not consider them criminal events. Just culture does not lay blame or assign fault, but rather looks for cause in the name of safety and prevention. Some countries consider an accident a criminal event from the start while companies have a philosophy to practice just culture by not implementing punitive measures for inadvertent errors. Other companies take punitive measures against their workforce which does nothing for learning from past mistakes in the name of prevention. Below is a hypothetical example of a corporate philosophy that does not practice just culture, have a safety philosophy, or a safety management system.

On a particular date, the pilot of our Flight 123 with flight crew A, B, and C did not strictly follow our standard operating procedure (SOP) and the first officer did not speak verbatim to our required standard resulting in a go-around. Oversight managers have direct management responsibility. In order to make an example of everyone concerned, we are going to take the following actions:

1. We will notify everyone and punish financially the supervisory managers of these pilots to show that management is responsible for the actions of the crew.
2. We will punish pilot A by publicly notifying everyone of his infraction, fine him a dollar amount, and downgrade his professional status.
3. We will punish pilot B by publicly notifying everyone of his infraction, fine him a dollar amount, and downgrade his professional status.
4. We will punish pilot C by publicly notifying everyone of his infraction, fine him a dollar amount, and downgrade his professional status.

We hope everyone will learn this lesson in the name of safety.

LCC – A low-cost carrier is an airline without most of the traditional services provided in the fare, resulting in lower fares and fewer comforts. It is sometimes known as a no-frills, discount, or budget carrier. They cover a wide range of business models, ranging from what customers might refer to as "cattle cars" to offering services almost on par with a mainline operator.

Letter of investigation – A document that serves the dual purpose of notifying someone that they are under investigation for a possible violation and providing an opportunity for the alleged violator to explain their version of the events.

Lip service – To give an insincere commitment by just saying you are going to do something to appease the other person, but have no intention of going through with it.

LOC – A letter of correction follows an initial warning notice given by the FAA and confirms an FAA decision in an administrative action. It states the necessary corrective action the alleged violator has taken or agrees to take. If the agreed corrective action is not fully completed, legal enforcement action may be taken.

LOFT – Line-oriented flight training is training in a simulator with a complete crew using representative flight segments that contain normal, abnormal, and emergency procedures that may be expected in line operations.

MAU – Monthly active users is a key performance indicator associated with social networking.

MRO – Maintenance repair and overhaul is an essential requirement to ensure that aircraft are maintained in predetermined conditions of airworthiness to safely transport passengers and cargo.

145 Repair Station Certificate – Federal Aviation Regulation 145 or FAR 145 describes how to obtain a repair station certificate from the FAA. It also contains the rules a certificated repair station must follow in the performance of maintenance or alterations of an aircraft, airframe, aircraft engine, propeller, appliance, or component part.

NPCA – A Notice of Proposed Certificate Action is a demand by the FAA to a certificate holder informing the alleged violator to either respond or suffer certificate amendment, revocation, or suspension. An NPCA can be issued on a regular or emergency basis.

NPCP – The Notice of Proposed Civil Penalty is a monetary penalty levied by the FAA against a certificate holder for regulatory violations.

NTSB – The National Transportation Safety Board is an independent multimodal agency that advances transportation safety by investigating occurrences in the marine, pipeline, rail, and air modes of transportation, which is much like the Transportation Safety Board of Canada.

Pencil-whipping – This is a term that refers to the practice of signing off on work that was never really done or to approve a document without reviewing it.

SARPs – The Standard and Recommended Practices, as defined by ICAO.

SAT – The Special Assistance Team is the name given by some organizations to those designated to interface with family and loved ones of aviation disaster victims.

SDR – The Service Difficulty Report is a report submitted to the FAA by certificate holders and repair stations that provide the airworthiness statistical data necessary for planning, directing, controlling, and evaluating certain assigned safety-related programs. The purpose of this system is to document, receipt, and rapidly publicize reports of conditions adversely affecting the airworthiness of aeronautical products.

SMS – The Safety Management System is a systemic approach to managing safety that service providers are responsible for establishing and is overseen by states according to ICAO requirements. It encompasses necessary organizational structures, accountabilities, and procedures. Although it has the word "safety" in it, it is meant to be an organization-wide approach to doing business and not a manual on a shelf, although some organizations do see it that way.

SOPs – Standard operating procedures.

TCAS – The Traffic Collision Avoidance System or Traffic Alert and Collision Avoidance System is designed to reduce the incidence of mid-air collisions between aircraft. It was developed by the industry in response to a number of accidents that could have been prevented.

TSB – The Transportation Safety Board of Canada is an independent multimodal agency that advances transportation safety by investigating occurrences in the marine, pipeline, rail, and air modes of transportation, which is much like the National Transportation Safety Board of the United States. The TSB's expertise and assistance is often sought in international accident investigation.

VST – The Victim Support Team within the AFDAA has seven tasks required of operators that mandate how they provide response requirements to family members.

Whistle-blower – A person or a group of people who are informants against an organization, company, or person on issues they believe are not appropriate. They may or may not be identified. This could come in the form of an employee who was fired by an organization. What they say may or may not be accurate.

Techniques

The techniques below are useful for any industry with any audience and are appropriate for any employee to use within the workplace. They are not meant to be used with just the media.

Technique #1: Have a message

It is necessary to have a message for each situation you face – even if that message is "I do not know." You do not have to wait for something to happen to determine what the message is. There are aviation messages that belong to the industry and it is important to formulate and practice them prior to anything happening. There are messages you can carry around with you at all times. There are messages about the job you do, your organization, and the industry itself.

It is your message that will carry you through language and cultural differences. You must have a message in order to accomplish the following:

1. *Control the outcome.* To be able to do this, you must have a message. You cannot do this without a message.
2. *Educate or inform.* To be able to accomplish this, you must have a message. If you just go prepared to answer questions, you are going with a strategy to react. Even though you may have prepared by going through possible question and answer practice sessions, you must have something basic that you want to convey.
3. *Correct a misunderstanding.* You cannot do this without a message that offers an alternative to show why those with whom you are communicating do not fully understand. If you are the subject matter expert, you should always know more about your subject than the person asking the questions.
4. *Change the subject.* You cannot change a subject unless you have something to change it to.

Close the door on a subject. If you do not want to talk on a subject, it is appropriate to close the door on that discussion, but if you are not armed with a message, you will just sit there with nothing to say once you close the door.

Examples

Messages about your job:

- My job is airport operations and from that I can tell you …
- My job is aircraft maintenance and that is a question about flight operations …

Messages about your organization:

- I'm a tour operator and that is an issue for the airport.
- I work for the airport and that is something to ask the operator.

Messages about the industry:

- We are always looking to improve on our past performance.
- This industry is based on a complex system of checks and balances.
- Nothing in industry is arbitrary.
- The system is safe.

Technique #2: Develop support points

A message by itself is not enough. It only means something to you. For you to make a point with your audiences, you must back up your messages with support points. You do not have to use in-depth statistics, just a couple of facts. They do not have to be numbers. To say that "the system is safe" is not enough. When you have a message and back it up with support points, this is how you cut off someone's line of questioning.

Examples

Message: The system is safe. For example:

- *Support point 1:* We have implemented a new system of checks and balances and …
- *Support point 2:* We have recently updated all our training.

Message: We do a good job. It's based on more than one criterion. For example:

- *Support point 1:* We have been ranked by our peers five years in a row as the top in customer service.
- *Support point 2:* Our profit margin is up by 13 percent over last year.

Technique #3: Low level of expertise/defer to the experts

You are not expected to discuss subjects that are out of your area of expertise. While you are not expected to discuss subjects in which you are not involved, there may be general things you know about the subject that you want to discuss. For example, if you are a commercial person, you may be asked a question about a maintenance issue. Although you do not work in the area of maintenance, you may want to say something. If you choose to do that, you first want to establish a low level of expertise.

Establishing a low level of expertise is the equivalent of laying out a safety net. For example, if you first establish a low level of expertise and then answer the question, but you are then asked a follow-up question that you do not want to answer, or that is out of your area of expertise, you can refer back to your low level of expertise. This is a legitimate way of keeping control by closing a door and not allowing yourself to be manipulated into opening a door you do not want to open. For example:

> Bad example: I think that happened because … (This will eventually get to a question you will not be able to answer, and you will lose credibility.) This response would be, "Oh really? Please tell me how." Then you are stuck.
>
> Good example: That is a question about maintenance and as I said, I am in the finance department, but generally speaking I can tell you that …

Eventually you are going to come to a question to which you do not want to respond. You then use your low level of expertise to cut off someone's line of questioning:

> As I said before, my area of expertise is maintenance.
> Or
> We are just one small part of a larger investigation team (because no one but the investigators are going to answer – see Chapter 4).
> Or
> That's a law enforcement issue, not a commercial issue, and my area of expertise is commercial.

Technique #4: Establish credibility

The opposite technique from a low level of expertise is to establish credibility whenever possible. This not only establishes you as the expert but gives credibility to the response. It's important to do this because if you are representing the fact-based perspective, you want to be seen as the subject expert.
Good examples:

- I've been in this industry *for 15 years* and from that I can tell you …
- I *worked hands-on* with this issue and this is not accurate …
- *You may not be aware* of what we have done …

The little phrase of "You may not be aware" is very powerful because it elevates you as one with expertise over those to whom you are speaking.

Technique #5: Give them credibility

The opposite of technique #4, which is establishing your credibility, is to establish the other party's credibility. This shows them that you know they probably already have the answer or know the reasons why you cannot say more than you are saying. (Note: This is a polite way of saying, "Don't ask me any more stupid questions.")

A good example would be: "As *I know you are aware*, as an operator we are just one small part of a larger team."

Technique #6: Use of statistics/facts

There are three ways to use statistics. You must always try and use facts whenever possible because you work in a fact-based industry with much oversight. The three ways to use statistics are:

1. To put things in perspective.
2. Trends vs. numbers.
3. Percentages.

Consider these examples:

- *Put into perspective:* This is used to quantify something in order to put it into perspective. You would do this by saying "This is one person out of a workforce of 3,000." The time to use this is in the ethics scenario.
- *Trends:* The number may be high, but the trend may be a reduction of 25 percent.

     o Question: The number of mid-air collisions over Dublin is double anywhere else in Europe.
     o Answer: Yes, the number is high, but that reflects a trend of a 25 percent reduction from the past year.

The time to use this would be when you are talking about the trends in accident rates decreasing over the years.

- *Percentages:* The number one may seem low, but it may be one out of only three, which is still 33 percent. An example of this would be if you had been trying to show that you were proactive in your efforts to move women through the ranks of management but had small numbers.

Technique #7: Take the high road

You may be asked negative questions. Deal with negative questions by rising above the negativity of the question. If you fight back, it will only stand to devalue your point. It is called taking the high road. Consider these examples:

Question: Do you have people who work for "your organization" whose better days are behind them?
Bad example: Every workplace has people who work past their usefulness.
Good example: If you mean people who are close to retirement, we certainly value their expertise and experience in "our organization."
Question: Who has been the worst CEO of your company in recent times?
Bad example: The one who just left the company.
Good example: They have all made a contribution.

Technique #8: Humanize

If an event is a tragedy or emotional issue, it is necessary to communicate in a humanistic manner. An emotional issue can also be any workplace or personnel situation. Consider the following examples:

Good example: First of all, let me extend my deepest sympathies to the families and friends …

Good example: I am sorry to see any of my co-workers feel this way.
Good example: We are all members of this community and therefore have sentiments about what has happened.

A tragedy does not have to be the worst-case scenario of an accident. Consider the following scenario and examples:

Scenario: An animal (pet) was killed while coming onto airport property.
Bad example: The owner should have kept a better eye on their pet.
Good example: We feel very bad for the people who lost their beloved pet. We know how pets can be like family.

Technique #9: Turn a negative into a positive

This is a very difficult technique. It is usually the opposite of what you would expect. If all you do is prepare to respond to questions, you could be manipulated into discussing something that is not the point. Consider the following example:

Question: Are you 100 percent safe?
Bad example: No organization can be 100 percent safe.

The problem with the response is that you have quantified what you are not, so the follow-up question would be to ask, "Okay, then what percentage of safety are you at?" Then you realize you have gone down the wrong path with your response. Consider an alternative response:

Good example: We will never consider ourselves 100 percent safe because we do not want to become complacent. We are always looking to improve on our past performance because to us safety is a marathon with no finish line; however, we are 100 percent safety-conscious.
Follow-up question: What do you mean by safety-conscious?
Response: It means at "our organization" we take every opportunity to learn from where others made mistakes and put procedures in place to prevent ourselves from making the same mistakes. We also have processes within our company to identify and correct errors, possible errors, or better ways to do something.

Another area where you can use the negative to positive technique is on-the-job training. Consider this scenario:

Scenario: Are you telling me your employees are only half trained?
Response: The training of aviation professionals is *never* finished. We are always looking to update our skills to keep up with technology.

Technique #10: Bridging/closing the door

This is a technique that helps you take control of the subject. When you close the door on a subject, you use the technique of bridging to change the subject into what you want to speak about. However, if you have a strategy to just go and answer questions, you will not be able to do this. This is the technique you use if you find you have gone off track into an area you didn't want to go. Consider the following examples:

Question: What happened?
Bad example: I don't know. (Lets them keep control.)
Good example: We are just one small part of a larger team so for the sake of accuracy you are going to want to speak to the team leaders. But, in the meantime, what I can tell you is this … (the bridge).

Let's say there is a question you do not want to respond to. (You feel trapped.) Close the door and use the technique of bridging to change the subject into what you want to discuss:

Good example: That's an important question but what is more important to realize is …
Note: You can use this with a number of audiences, including a political audience, media, internal to an organization in meetings, fielding questions at a conference, etc.

Technique #11: Defuse negative words or inaccurate statements

It is critical to defuse negative words or inaccurate statements as soon as you hear them because a misperception left unchecked becomes a perception. It is then the misperception with which you will have to contend, and the misperception becomes a reality in the minds of the audience. Consider these examples:

Question: Why did you cover up this report?"
Bad example: Who said we covered up this report? (It keeps the idea of cover-up going.)
Good example: First, we did not cover up anything. With all the systems of checks and balances in this industry, it is impossible to cover up anything.
Question: Why did you allow this to occur?
Bad example: People were on vacation, we were short-staffed, and it happened. (This implies that it was allowed to happen.)
Good example: First of all, we did not allow this to occur. …

Technique #12: It is all right to disagree

You are the expert on all issues pertaining to your organization. If you hear someone saying something you disagree with, you must disagree immediately. In order to make it a fact-based response, first establish authority/expertise (see technical data sheet, section 2.3), use facts and statistics, and then disagree. Consider these examples:

Question: Anyone saying that to fly today is safe is either blind, dumb, or crazy, and that would not bother me so much, but it came from a pilot with whom I was having a cup of coffee!
Bad example: I don't know why he would say that (adversarial).
Good example: Let me provide you with a few more facts that will help paint an accurate picture and show you why I disagree (refer to technical data sheet):

- We have x number of operations daily.
- We safely transport x number of people through the system every year.
- We fly to x number of locations around the world and we're certificated by those countries to do so.

Technique #13: Do not get into arguments with unnamed sources

Do not get into arguments with unnamed sources following questions beginning with "Witnesses have said …" or "Sources have told us …" Additionally, if a politician makes a claim that you know is not fact-based, you do not want to make an adversary of someone who communicates in a political style. Do not be placed in a position where you have to contradict someone when in the end the facts will deliver the conclusion.

Question sources, but do not ask who they are. It does not matter who they are. Asking who they are just invites someone to give credibility to what they say and then you could be compromising yourself politically. Consider the following examples:

Bad example: Where did you hear that?
Response: The minister of transport. (The problem with this is that now you are placed in the position of disagreeing with a minister to defend your organization, so you know that you have given the wrong response.)
Good example: I do not know where you get your information, but what I can tell you from working hands-on with this issue is that this is not true.
Good example: I do not know where you get your information, but I was in that meeting and that did not happen.

Technique #14: Determine the right message for the right time

Do not go to an emotional audience without a humanistic message. To do so would fuel the opposition of several different audiences. A standard question is, "How are you going to apologize for this terrible mistake?"

The issue is to humanize without accepting responsibility. Many times, if you say, "We're sorry," it implies acceptance of responsibility. However, if you do not extend sympathies, it can fuel the adversary of any emotional audience. Remember that any audience – whether it is media, political, or union – can also be the emotional audience. Consider these examples:

Bad example: We have nothing to apologize for.
Good example: We are always sorry when a tragedy/event/situation like this occurs.
Bad example: This was an event that never should have occurred. (But it did! So, you have just announced you had a system failure, failed to follow procedures, etc.)
Good example: Whenever a tragedy of this magnitude occurs we do know that there is always more than one contributing factor, but there are many people working together to get to the bottom of this terrible tragedy as quickly as possible to prevent it from ever occurring again.

Technique #15: Set the tone

If someone sets an unreasonably negative tone, you can reset the tone to where you would like it to be. Consider these examples:

Bad example (low tone): Thank you for coming here today to tell us why you made this mistake.
Good example (resetting the tone): I am happy to be here today to clear up this misunderstanding.

Technique #16: Do not get angry or emotional when the issue is emotional

Never get angry or emotional when the issue is emotional because you will lose all opportunity to make a point. People will focus on your anger.

If you are asked a negative question, resist the temptation to say things such as "That's an unfair question" or "I'm not going to dignify that with a comment." Here are some example responses:

Question: Why would this former female employee accuse you of sexual harassment?
Bad example: She is lying. I never harassed anyone (adversarial).

Good example: I have been with this organization for 15 years and it is distressing to think that any current or former employees might feel this way.

Technique #17: Research your message and reach your peak through practice

As mentioned before, there are messages about the aviation industry, your organization, and your job that you can carry around with you at all times. You should be formulating what those are prior to anything ever occurring. You do not wait until something happens to formulate your message, or to rehearse and practice.

Technique #18: Prepare for the worst and do your homework

You should always try and anticipate audiences and questions from those audiences long before you get into the situation where you are asked these questions. Formulate your responses to these questions. If you can formulate responses to difficult questions, the responses to simpler questions should be easy.

Technique #19: Streamline your message

Your messages should be delivered in 20 seconds or less. There are three reasons for this. The first reason is because laypeople do not listen to you after 20 seconds. The second reason is that if you are to be edited into something, you are not going to get more than 20 seconds. The third and most important reason is because the longer you speak the more likely you are to open a door you did not want to open. This is vital when dealing with controversial audiences. If someone asks you what time it is, don't explain how to make a watch. Aviation is a multinational audience. Therefore, communication benefits from being simplistic. This avoids the possibility of being misunderstood. Although English is the international language of aviation communication, with many non-native speakers it is still safer to avoid some messages being lost in translation by ensuring the explanation doesn't go on for too long.

Technique #20: Admit mistakes

Since many of the most controversial and difficult aviation events are operational events where facts will reflect what took place, the facts could indicate that an error occurred in which your organization has a role. By the time the facts do come out, your organization, like all organizations, will have made the changes needed to improve safety. These investigations take months, sometimes years, and no one waits until that report comes out. The key is to talk about corrective action and where you are today. This also goes beyond just technical problems. It could apply to accounting problems, computer problems, staffing problems, etc.

Additionally, you may have been short-staffed six months ago or had budget constraints and no one paid attention. However, this event of today – was it a result of your budget constraints from six months ago that no one mentioned? Were you cutting corners on safety that led to what happened today? Here are some examples:

Bad example: Things were not going well and we were short staffed, so it happened.
Good example: It happened and here are the changes we have made and where we are today.

From a commercial perspective, you may, for example, have to answer to one of your customers for a delay issue: "Yes, we had a problem, but we have already put changes in place to remedy it."

Technique # 21: Be politely persistent, but do not get angry

If someone keeps asking you the same thing repeatedly even though you have given the response you intended to give, they may be trying to manipulate you into giving the response they want to hear or opening up a door. To avoid being manipulated into changing your response, use one of the following examples:

- As I said before …
- Let me clarify what I said earlier.
- Again …

Technique #22: No personal opinions

Remember that every employee at an aviation-related organization represents the fact-based perspective. All organizations know that every employee has his/her own personal opinions; the key is not to be trapped into giving a personal opinion. When someone is asked for their personal opinion, they are being asked to open doors. Do not fall into this trap. The objective would be to change a personal opinion into a fact-based response. Words like "I think," "I feel," or "I guess" reflect opinions. Do not use them and beware if you hear them. You are not there to give your personal opinion. Be particularly careful when asked "In your expert opinion …" because everyone wants to feel like an expert.

Response: My expert opinion is based on 30 years in this business and from that I can tell you … (This changes an "expert opinion" into a fact-based response.)

Even if you have not been with an organization for a long period of time, your expertise extends back to the time you entered the industry:

Good example: My personal opinion is based on 17 years in the industry and from this I can tell you …
Question: How did you feel about the issue?
Bad example: I don't think it is appropriate to ask that (adversarial).
Good example: How I felt really does not play a role as long as we were compliant with all regulations.

However, if it is an emotional issue like the aftermath of an incident or accident, you must reach out to the emotional audiences while sticking to the facts:

Good example: I am sure that anyone who goes to work every day to prevent these types of events would feel terrible, but the investigators of the host country/this country will determine what went wrong.

Consider the following exchange:

Question: Your computer system (or baggage system) at the airport malfunctioned. How do we know you have things under control?
Bad example: What went wrong can happen to anyone. We were short-staffed and someone made an error.
Good example: The problem that caused the inconvenience was resolved and operations have returned to normal.

Technique #23: No comment

There is no such thing as no comment. Do not ever say these words. There is always a reason for no comment. The words "no comment" *are* a comment. These words imply several things. First, they imply that you are guilty. Second, they imply that you are unwilling to cooperate. Third, they imply that you have something to hide. The end result will be to fuel animosity. Consider the following:

Question: What went wrong?
Bad example: We have no comment at this time.
Good example: It would be irresponsible for any of us to say anything that might jeopardize the outcome of this situation.

This still means "no comment" but you do not actually say the words. Instead, you provide the reason why. Here is a further example response:

Good example: This is still under review and I think for the sake of accuracy you might want to check back with us in 30 days.

Technique #24: Make them part of the process

The best way to defuse a situation is to make the adversary part of your process:

Question: What do you have to say about the delays you have caused?
Bad example: They are a reality of our industry.
Good example: You as a member of the traveling public should appreciate the steps we take to ensure the highest levels of safety.

Technique #25: Make yourself part of the process

People sometimes look at an organization as though they are the victims of that organization. The first thing you need to do is make yourself part of the process. This puts you on the same level as those with whom you are speaking. Consider the following:

Question: What do you have to say about the delay in the baggage?
Bad example: It is just a computer problem.
Good example: We are customers on this airline ourselves and we can understand your frustration.

Source of support points – development of a technical data sheet

Technique #2 emphasizes the need to have support points to back up messages. It is in this way that you can factualize a response and hopefully cut off a line of questions. These support points do not just have to be numbers; they can be examples as well. Since aviation is a technical industry, but it is commercially sold, it is the commercial people who are frequently called upon to sell technical information. This may not happen initially but eventually it does. That is when things become difficult. Airport operators may initially have to sell the services and capabilities of the airport, but at some point they may have to sell the safety and compliance of their operation. Tour operators and travel agents may have to sell the price and benefits of one tour over another but eventually they may have to sell the safety of one operator or piece of equipment over another. When are these organizations taught how to do that? An operator's commercial people may be taught to sell the comfort, service, and on-time performance of their operation, but when in their careers are they taught to sell the safety of their equipment or to prove the safety of their operation? Thirty years of experience working with organizations tells me never. The best way for the aviation industry to help themselves get their messages out is to provide their own employees and those who might have to answer for their products or services with a technical data sheet.

A technical data sheet contains facts-at-a-glance – simple data that users can refer to that supports their messages. It is traditionally divided into several sections.

The first section would be general information. This section would include basic background of an organization. Some of the information in the technical data sheet's general information section that I have seen includes: date organization established; number of employees with breakdown; number of operations per day/month/year; equipment; destinations; ownership; amount of turnover which would indicate a seasoned workforce; and employee programs.

The next section might include safety and operations. The safety and operations section would include, *inter alia*: employees and breakdown; training; certifications; publications; internal oversight and reviews; accident prevention proactivity; and alliance participation.

The next section would be engineering, maintenance, and quality assurance, and would include, *inter alia*: employees and breakdown; equipment including engines; radar systems; certifications; contracting; training conducted; global standing (if appropriate); quality systems in place; and awards. The next section could be security which would include, *inter alia*: procedures; international standards met; certifications; data processing systems; screening mechanisms; training procedures; and recurrent training requirements. This section would not be as detailed as the others because you would not want to tell those trying to circumvent the process how specifically to do it!

Another section would indicate checks and balances which would include, *inter alia*: regulatory surveillance – both domestic and international; certifications; audits; country competency; employee medical requirements; and contractor requirements.

The last section would be devoted to proactivity and international interface. This is the section that would show an organization's safety consciousness and would include, *inter alia*: association memberships; task force participation; safety committee participation; how organizations take advantage of lessons learned; courses taken in accident investigation; technical go-team training; participation in system design with manufacturers (if they are controllers, mechanics, pilots, cabin); contributions to publications; participation in data sharing; and any form of innovative activity.

Things you would not put on a technical data sheet are the amount of revenue you achieved and the customer service awards you received. The technical data sheet is meant to be a support point to back up aviation messages and not business messages. Sometimes I have found when you put this task in the hands of commercial people or communication departments, the objective becomes clouded. The technical data sheet is not meant to sell a product. You would not use market share to prove safety when customers are questioning equipment or an operation. A travel agent could not very well convince a customer to take a certain carrier because they are "making money." That is not a support point to back up a message. We provide a template for a technical data sheet under the following heading.

Technical data sheet template

The data that goes into this does not have to be numerical. Some of the support points and proactivity can be memberships in trade organizations which comes from the trade associations located in the terminology section of this chapter.

General information:

- Background
- When established
- How many employees (breakdown)
- Total operations (airport capacity; air traffic operations; people transported; equipment manufactured)
- Employee programs

Safety and operations:

- Employees and breakdowns
- Certifications
- Training
- Internal oversight and reviews
- Accident prevention proactivity
- Alliance participation

Engineering/maintenance/quality assurance:

- Employees and breakdown
- Global systems
- Equipment
- Certifications
- Training
- Global standing and awards

Security:

- International standards met
- Procedures
- Certifications
- Data systems
- Screening mechanisms
- Training procedures
- Recurrent training requirements

Checks and balances:

- Regulatory surveillance – both domestic and international
- Certifications
- Audits
- Country competency

Aviation terms and communication techniques 45

- Employee medical requirements
- Contractor compliance

Proactivity and international interface:

- Association membership
- Task force participation
- Safety committee participation
- Courses taken
- Go-team training
- Participation in system design
- Contributions to publications
- Data sharing

Chapter summary

1. Terminology and lingo

- 60 Minutes
- AAIB
- AC
- ADFAA
- Airworthiness Directive
- Airworthy
- ALPA
- AOC
- ATSB
- BEA
- CFIT
- Codeshare
- Corrective action
- Criminality
- EASA
- ECAC
- EEO
- EIR
- ETOPS
- FAA
- Federal Family Assistance Plan for Aviation Disaster
- Flight Safety Foundation
- FOIA
- FOQA
- GASP
- Ground handling agents
- Harmonization

46   *Aviation terms and communication techniques*

- IAM
- IASA
- IATA
- ICAO
- ISASI
- JAA
- Just culture
- LCC
- Letter of investigation
- Lip service
- LOC
- LOFT
- MAU
- MRO
- NPCA
- NPCP
- NTSB
- Pencil-whipping
- SARPs
- SAT
- SDR
- SMS
- SOP
- TCAS
- TSB
- VST
- Whistle-blower

2. Techniques

- Have a message
- Develop support points
- Low level of expertise/defer to the experts
- Establish credibility
- Give them credibility
- Use of statistics/facts
- Take the high road
- Humanize
- Turn a negative into a positive
- Bridging/closing the door
- Defuse negative words or inaccurate statements
- It is all right to disagree
- Do not get into arguments with unnamed sources
- Determine the right message for the right time
- Set the tone

- Do not get angry or emotional when the issue is emotional
- Research your message and reach your peak through practice
- Prepare for the worst and do your homework
- Streamline your message
- Admit mistakes
- Be politely persistent but do not get angry
- No personal opinions
- No comment
- Make them part of the process
- Make yourself part of the process

3. Technical data sheet

- General information
- Safety and operations
- Engineering/maintenance/quality assurance
- Security
- Checks and balances
- Proactivity and international interface

Notes

1 ICAO, Annex 13, International Standards and Recommended Practices, Chapter 1, Definitions, ABC, p. 169, https://www.icao.int/safety/airnavigation/AIG/Pages/Documents.aspx.
2 *Ibid.*
3 *Ibid.*

3 The 4-point formula – your absolute safety net

The aviation industry prepares at all times for the worst-case scenario on many levels, from family assistance to prevention through the study of past events. The worst-case scenario, being defined as a crash with deaths and/or injuries, is the easiest thing to strategize in terms of communication. Everything that can be said by any employee can be planned prior to anything ever occurring. You do not have to know what happened to cause the situation; you just need to know the process. The answer is found in the 4-point formula. This formula is a very simple, commonsense strategy and it meets the reality of the situation. More importantly, it is the truth and does not jeopardize an organization's position in an investigation or legal event. It is applicable to every part of the industry in every country. We will first learn how to use it on a large scale and then see how to use it individually for specific types of jobs, and then in the workplace for a different type of scenario.

Background

Let's just say, for instance, that an organization chooses not to communicate with the media at all. There is no regulation that says an organization is required to communicate with the media. It would be an absurd strategy to have but still no regulatory requirement. However, in an accident scenario there would be an investigation at the very least and most likely a lawsuit and other situations. Many people in an organization will be required to communicate with one audience or another, including but not limited to: regulators; investigators; lawyers; insurance companies; investors; travel agents; tour operators; customers; and their own employees. If you are a manufacturer, you will be required to communicate with: customers; regulators; investigators; attorneys; foreign governments; and others. Who makes this determination? Your reality does. What determines your reality? Variables do, and these you will not know until whatever happens does. You have no idea who the operator will be, the manufacturer, what nationalities will be involved, what countries, what locations, what the issues will be, whether it be a technical event or a human factors event, etc.

This seems to be the most difficult of all situations to handle and that is due to the shock, emotion, and logistics of what happened. For those who do not work in the organization it is shocking enough, but to work in the organization, if you have never experienced it, it is hard to imagine. It is perhaps harder to imagine if you have worked for an airline that has experienced it more than once in a short time frame.

> **Mistake #1** – Organizations think they are in control of how they are notified. Not true! You find out how you find out.

Organizations have internal notification channels to inform staff. To think that this is how employees are going to be notified and that an organization is going to be in control in today's world of social media is to have a strategy that does not meet reality. For example, the country manager of Air France for the UK learned about the Concorde crash two minutes after it happened when he was called by Sky News. The senior vice president of Air France found out about their Toronto crash when he received my all-employee condolence email.

> **Countermeasure to mistake #1** – Mandate that every employee be equipped with the 4-point formula which is the ultimate safety net in the event an employee is caught off guard. Also, understand how to communicate on the message when you are blindsided (see Chapter 2).

> **Mistake # 2** – Because the subject is communication, organizations think the lead communication strategists should be the offices of corporate communications.

If I had to pick one reason for a strategy failing, this would be it. These events are not media events. They are investigations. These events are not commercial events. Technical events are at the root. Reputation management is not the main objective, although if you go to many organizations' emergency response plans you will see that reputation management is stated as a main objective. The main objectives are not jeopardizing the integrity of the investigation, reaching out to the affected parties, and getting to the root causes of the tragedy. If your organization does that, you will have managed your reputation. Reputation management is not the product of an accident investigation, it is a by-product.

> **Countermeasure to mistake #2** – These are not public relations events. An airline is not an airline unless it has an air operator's certificate. The people who are responsible for that are the ones who should be the lead communication strategists. They are the keepers of the message. The corporate communication departments are support to the organization.

Mistake #3 – Organizations believe they are in control of who can and cannot speak to the media. Not true! Everyone who represents the organization to any audience is a spokesperson.

Because we have defined a spokesperson as anyone who is required to speak to any audience on behalf of an organization, the reality is that any person can be a spokesperson. To make matters worse and stick with the theme of having a strategy that meets reality, due to cell phones and what we have seen recently in today's world, any employee can end up on the evening news through no fault of their own. In recent times we have seen passengers or customers screaming to their fellow customers or observers "Someone record this!" Therefore, every employee needs to be considered a potential spokesperson, and if an organization does not have a strategy that takes this in to consideration, they do not have a strategy that meets reality.

> **Countermeasure to mistake #3** – Employees who may be confronted by the public should be empowered to communicate without the fear of punitive action, because they may very well end up on the news. They should know what the federal airworthiness regulations are. You do not want someone telling a family that a child who is over two years of age must be held in a parent's lap ending up on the evening news. All the regulators in the world will know that the staff is not familiar with federal airworthiness regulations.

Mistake #4 – Organizations believe that their policy determines who is the "spokesperson." Not true! The people who decide who the spokesperson is are the ones *asking* the questions.

When someone comes up to an employee and shoves a microphone in that employee's face, they have decided to make that employee the spokesperson.

They do not care in the least what an organization's policy says about who may or may not talk to the media. What comes out of that employee's mouth, or in some cases what does not, is the statement. In today's world of social media no one waits for an organization to sit around and strategize about what they will say, who will say it, organize an event, or anything else.

> **Countermeasure to mistake #4** – Have all employees equipped with the basic aviation messages that are the reality of the entire industry no matter what country or what part of the industry you operate in. You do not have to wait for something to happen to know what they are. Aviation is the product – not seat pitch. These messages should be taught during initial aviation training (see Chapters 5 and 6).

> **Mistake #5** – "Our CEO/DG/director is our spokesperson." Not true! They may be one of your spokespeople but if you think they are your only one, you do not have a strategy that meets reality.

This policy exists for different reasons. It is a large contributing factor to a strategy that will fail for several reasons:

1. Your CEO/DG/leader may be a great CEO, but may be a terrible communicator.
2. You may have more than one location where you need primary communication.
3. Many CEOs do not have the technical expertise to answer the questions in a situation like this or are not familiar with the process. Most CEOs have a background in finance, marketing, or general business.
4. Many organizations on the corporate side look toward a strategy of "reputation management" as their primary objective.

> **Countermeasure to mistake #5** – Everyone should know the 4-point formula. It is the ultimate safety net. It is better than saying "No comment" or "I'm not authorized" or "Call our office of corporate communications."

In the worst-case scenario, an organization is involved in an accident investigation whether you are an operator, manufacturer, corporation, regulator, investigator, government agency, union, or some other party to the event. I have worked with organizations for over 30 years and most of them cannot think out of the box and visualize using strategizes for more than just the worst-case scenario. However, the 4-point formula has many different applications. The following generic case studies will show three of them, but tweaked for people in different positions within industry. Each part of the industry would have a slight variation to the formula. A regulator would not say the same thing as an operator, for example.

The 4-point formula

1. *Humanize.* When something like this happens, the first words out of your mouth need to humanize. If you do not do this, you will fuel the anger of the emotional audience, and once you do that, you will never be finished. The emotional audience triggers the political audience. The emotional audience is not just relatives and friends. The emotional audience is anyone or group who identifies with the relatives and friends, and that is everyone. If it is a commercial event, it is any customer. If we are talking about a government agency and the criticism is against the government employee, all people are taxpayers, so they identify with the taxpayer and are part of the emotional audience. Because a tragedy is a human event, the word "humanize" is the appropriate way to respond.
2. *Make yourself part of the process.* People look at people in the industry for someone to blame: "you did this to my loved one." They forget that people in the industry go to work every day to prevent these things from occurring. You do not want to include this in the same sentence as the families because in some cases the families are looking to blame the operators, manufacturers, regulators, or those in authority.

    People look at those in the aviation industry and forget they are also users of the system. There is also criticism of government employees and "taxpayer fraud, waste, and abuse," but people talk to government employees as though they do not pay taxes themselves. When you do not separate this from the first group, the statement can imply that "We know how you feel" and you could provoke the response or feeling of "You can't imagine how I feel," thereby fueling the adversary's anger.
3. *Low level of expertise/defer to the experts.* There is only one reason why people in aviation cannot speak: it relates to the accident investigation, and based on the scenario given an accident investigation is what you are in. Give that reason. This is your safety net and it closes the door and protects you from any future statements. This is the only reason why you cannot speak. It is never going to be anyone other than the investigators who announce what did or did not happen, so it sets you up for expectations to say you will be providing more information when you will not.

    All the statements that organizations may mandate their employees to say in their policies (such as "I am not authorized to speak"; "Please call our office of corporate communication"; "I am waiting

for executives to get here"; "No comment"; or anything similar to these statements) are just internal corporate politics and have nothing to do with why an organization or any employee may not speak about accident investigation.
4. *Give the facts.* This refers only to the facts as you know them. Organizations may say, "How can we know what the facts are until we know what has happened." The point is that you know some things up front and the rest you know is the process you are involved in, i.e. the accident investigation process (see Chapter 4).

Rationale for the 4-point formula

The strategy should be to defuse a request for information at the lowest possible level. Organizations who have centralized corporate strategies for large organizations have a high chance of communication failure. Here are the usual responses employees are told to give and what happens:

1. *Call our headquarters.* If the organization is in country #1 and a call comes in to an employee in country #2, why would someone want to call headquarters in country #1? When they reach headquarters in country #1, will they get the information they are looking for? No. Therefore, the call has been elevated instead of being defused at the lowest possible level and they do not have the information they wanted.
2. *No comment.* No comment is a comment. It implies guilt, a cover-up, and an unwillingness to cooperate, and it fuels the adversary. If that is your strategy, use it, but I do not believe that it is any organization's strategy because it is almost guaranteed to fail.
3. *I am not authorized to speak.* If you represent an organization in some way to some audience, take customers' money, represent taxpayers as part of a government agency of one sort or another, or are responsible for budgets and personnel, people believe that you should be authorized to speak.

If a representative of an organization uses any of the above excuses for not responding, it could have negative effects on an organization and many times the entire process as well. If the above statements are made, they would be in an organization's strategy before anything ever happened. If they were to be avoided, the employees would have to be empowered with the preventative solution before anything ever happened.

The 4-point formula accomplishes several things:

1. It closes the door on answering any questions.
2. It defers to those who will answer the questions.
3. It gives the safety net and real reason why an organization does not have to answer questions.

Mistake #6 – Many organizations think that point #4 is the centerpiece of this formula. That is incorrect.

Countermeasure to mistake #6 – Remember that point #3 is the centerpiece of this formula. You need to defer to the experts before you give the facts. That closes the door.

Organizations frequently dive right into giving the facts and that creates the perception that they are the experts in the minds of those watching. Anyone can look up on the Internet what most organizations say in point #4.

Case studies – uses of the 4-point formula

Case study 1: Crash scenarios

Scenario: The case study would be where a plane crashed and there were some fatalities and/or injuries. It could also involve another aircraft. This formula is what would be followed by the parties to the event.

The crash scenario: Complete statements for various parties

Here is how the complete statement is read for the various parties to an event.

THE 4-POINT FORMULA FOR AN OPERATOR

The operator is the one who must answer for everything even though in this scenario the issues that caused it might not be operational. It is the operator who is the first to answer for manufacturing issues. Here is an example of the formula employed:

1. On behalf of this organization, let me extend my deepest sympathies to the relatives and friends of those who lost their lives in yesterday's terrible tragedy.
2. We would also like to extend our sympathies to the families of all our own employees and crew who also died, as they were like family to us.
3. However, as an operator, we are just one small part of a larger team led here in this country by investigators, so for the sake of accuracy you are going to want to speak with them.
4. In the meantime, this is what we can tell you. This aircraft was a Boeing/Airbus/Embraer, which was first certified in 19XX* by the [regulator]

and [how many other regulators] around the world through bilateral agreements. There are [how many of them] in use in the world today. We are an operator who was certified in 19XX and we fly to [how many countries]. We have [how many operations] on a daily basis, etc. (see Chapter 2)

★ This is data that can be found in an organization's technical data sheet. There is a template for how to develop this in Chapter 2, section 2.3. This is a good reference for commercial people to use for "facts at a glance." No employee should have to rely on a specific department to get back to them with this type of data regarding an organization.

THE 4-POINT FORMULA FOR AN AIRFRAME, ENGINE, OR OTHER MANUFACTURER

Anything that is manufactured may have to be answered for in this scenario. However, it is the operator who will have to answer for the equipment first. Some of the people who may have to answer for the equipment may not know how to defend the equipment. Some of those groups may be airport personnel, cabin personnel, sales personnel, and others. The first question would be, "Is this aircraft safe?" How many people during their aviation training are taught how to answer this question? The manufacturer knows how to answer the question, but do the commercial groups know? Do they know how to "prove it" to their commercial clients? The commercial clients of a travel agent are not going to call Boeing or Airbus to ask them to prove their aircraft are safe. Here is an example of the formula employed:

1. We extend our sympathies to the families and friends of the people who lost their lives in this tragic event, and to our customers.
2. Let us also extend our sympathies and thanks to all the people who are there with us, who go to work every day to try and prevent these terrible events from occurring.
3. However, as a manufacturer we are just one small part of a team being headed in this country by investigators, so for the sake of accuracy you are going to want to speak to them.
4. In the meantime, this is what I can tell you. This aircraft was manufactured in 19XX. There are [how many of them] in use in the world today, etc. (see Chapter 7)

THE 4-POINT FORMULA FOR A REGULATOR

Regulators are in the most challenging position of all. Regulators are the ones who say whether or not an airline is an airline, a pilot is a pilot, etc. If something happens, one of the first criticisms heard is "This would not have happened if the regulator had done their job." If one of the other parties to an event in this scenario does a poor job communicating, there will be a backlash against the regulator. Here is an example of the formula employed:

1. We would like to extend our deepest sympathies to the relatives and friends of those who died is this terrible tragedy.
2. We would also like to say thanks to all those people who are participating in this process to try and get to the bottom of this tragedy as quickly as possible so as to prevent it from happening again.
3. However, as a regulator we are just one part of the team assisting the investigators with their effort, and when a determination is made, they will be making that announcement.
4. In the meantime, this is what we can tell you … (see Chapter 7)

THE 4-POINT FORMULA FOR AN INVESTIGATOR

Generally, investigators are not directly related to an accident because they will not have a family member involved. However, they are personally there to get to the bottom of what happened. Here is an example of the formula employed for an investigator:

1. We would first like to extend our sympathies to all those who lost a friend or loved on in this terrible tragedy.
2. We would also like to thank everyone who is here helping us get to the bottom of this tragedy as we know it is a difficult situation for all of you who go to work every day to try so hard to prevent these things from occurring.
3. As you all may know, the accident investigation process is based on careful analysis of technical data, interviews with many people, and then careful analysis of all the information. It would be irresponsible for any of us or anyone else to try and circumvent this fact-based process. But when we do have conclusive information, it will be "our organization" who will be making that announcement and not the operator, manufacturer, or any other unrelated expert (see Chapter 4).
4. In the meantime, this is what we can tell you … (see Chapter 7)

THE 4-POINT FORMULA FOR CONTROLLERS, UNIONS, AND OTHERS WITHOUT PARTY STATUS*

Here is an example of the formula employed:

1. Let me first say that our hearts go out to all families and friends of those affected by this terrible tragedy.
2. We would also like to thank those who go to work every day to try and prevent these things from occurring and who are trying to get to the bottom of this event.
3. We are not directly involved but we can tell you one thing about the process. It is based on the careful analysis of technical data by the investigators.

The 4-point formula 57

When the cause of this tragedy has been determined, it is the investigators who will be making that announcement. In the meantime, this is what we can tell you ... (see Chapters 3 and 7)
4. All members of our association/union, before beginning their jobs, are certified by the regulators of their countries and must remain current. Our union/association is actively involved in international efforts/task forces to proactively study these events in the name of prevention.

★ Party status is explained in Chapter 2 (party system).

THE 4-POINT FORMULA FOR CONTROLLERS, UNIONS, AND OTHERS WITH PARTY STATUS

Here is an example of the formula employed:

1. First let me say that our hearts go out to all families and friends of those affected by this terrible tragedy.
2. We would also like to thank those who go to work every day to try and prevent these things from occurring and who are trying to get to the bottom of this event.
3. We are a party to the investigation that is being headed by investigators, so for the sake of accuracy you are going to want to speak with them. When the cause of this tragedy has been determined, it is the investigators who will be making that announcement. In the meantime, this is what we can tell you ... (see Chapters 3, 4, and 7)
4. All members of our association/union, before starting their jobs, are certified by the regulators of their countries and must remain current. Our union/association is actively involved in international efforts/task forces to proactively study these events in the name of prevention.

THE 4-POINT FORMULA FOR CODESHARE PARTNERS AND AFFILIATES

Many operators who codeshare or affiliates who do business with another company like third party maintenance think that they can defer to the main company and be done with it. Many times, I have clients who say, "I can't say anything about them. It's not our airline." If an airline takes the money from clients in a business relationship with another airline, customers have a way of thinking you should be able to answer for that airline with whom you are in a relationship. If there is outsourced maintenance on your equipment, you have to answer for the company who did any third-party work. Here is an example of the 4-point formula employed:

1. First of all, we would like to extend our deepest sympathy to our partner/affiliate who suffered this terrible tragedy today.
2. And to families of our passengers who were lost in this accident.
3. But in spite of this terrible tragedy, it does not alter our confidence in their safety.

4. Here is what we can tell you in the meantime: Before we enter into any relationship with any of our partners, they must pass a technical review conducted by us, have a current IOSA certification, and most importantly be certificated by the regulator of their country.

THE 4-POINT FORMULA FOR AIRPORT OPERATORS (ON SITE)

The challenge for airport operators is that if an event happens on their property, they are the on-site coordinators. However, they are not the ones conducting the investigation, though in the eyes of the lay-public, they may be thought of as the ones conducting the investigation. In addition, the airport may be in a location where the investigators are hours away, so they may be coordinating briefings in the beginning.

The next challenge, which is one not to be underestimated, is that if the operator does not have on-site personnel and does not partner with anyone on site, it is the airport staff who have to coordinate and handle the families. This can be the case when an operator does not have staff on site at a location and uses ground handling agents. It is those agents who must handle passengers and customers as the operator's representative. Many times, the customers believe that the ground handling agents are the operator. Here is an example of the 4-point formula employed by on-site airport operators:

1. First of all, we would like to extend our deepest sympathy to those affected by this terrible tragedy.
2. And we would like to thank all of the first responders and investigators who are here helping us get to bottom of this until the investigators arrive.
3. As the airport operator, we are the coordinator. It will be the investigators who will be making any announcements relating to findings of this terrible tragedy when they have that information. Our role in this event is this …
4. What we can tell you up to this point is this …

THE 4-POINT FORMULA FOR TRAVEL AGENTS OR TOUR OPERATORS

Travel agents and tour operators may have to answer for the operators or equipment they sell to their customers. These groups are generally involved in the commercial aspect of aviation but when something happens find themselves needing to defend their sales. Here is an example of the 4-point formula employed by travel agents/tour operators:

1. We are very saddened to hear of the tragedy today with X airline and we extend our sympathies to all involved.
2. We would also like to extend our support for all those working to get to the bottom of this tragedy for the rest of the industry, so we can all learn from this event to prevent it from ever happening again.

3. While we don't know what happened and we, like the rest of you, are waiting to hear from the investigators as they complete their investigation, we can tell you this in the meantime ...
4. In spite of this terrible tragedy, it does not alter our confidence in the people with whom we do business. All of the airlines we do business with are certified by the regulators from the countries in which they operate; all of the equipment they fly is certified by the state of manufacturer and other countries around the world through bilateral agreements; if a major airline codeshares with one from another country, that other airline must undergo a safety audit and remain current with their standards in order to remain in the alliance (see Chapters 2, 3, and 5).

Case study 2: Workplace scenarios

Scenario 1

A standard workplace situation would be when there is a disgruntled employee who feels they have been mistreated for whatever reason. It could be age discrimination or race discrimination, but for the sake of this scenario we will use sexual harassment. The woman feels that she was prevented from advancing through the ranks of management or not given a raise because she refused the sexual advances of her boss. She quits in protest and becomes a whistleblower for the regulator, saying the company is cutting corners on safety. Her co-workers say, anonymously, "She is a crazy nutcase." The former employee sues and the statement by co-workers fuels the anger of feminist groups who then protest in front of the company with signs saying the company is unfair to female workers.

The problem with a scenario like this is that people tend to want to defend themselves. You do not want to do this. The reason this happens is that people prepare to answer questions without having a message or formula for this type of scenario. This is still an investigation due to the lawsuit. Here is an example of the 4-point formula employed:

1. I cannot speak for what any of my co-workers may have said anonymously. I can just tell you I have been with this company X number of years.
2. It is very sad to know that any current or former colleague feels this way.
3. But, as you said, there is a lawsuit and it would be irresponsible for either of us to say anything that might jeopardize this individual's opportunity to get a fair hearing in court.
4. In the meantime, this is what I can tell you. This organization is in compliance with all the national EEO requirements. As far as cutting corners on safety, the good thing about the aviation industry is that it has an interdependent system of checks and balances, and if any of those charges are found to be true, the FAA (or EPA/Labor Department, depending on the accusation) will make that determination.

In the above scenario, everyone identifies with a disgruntled employee if management tries to make this person the culprit. The lawsuit is the investigation. The anonymous employees are the "witnesses have said …" and "sources have told us," and they fuel the anger of the emotional audience, i.e. the female groups. The whistle-blower complaint is the fact-based part of it. Depending on the stature of the case, you may have a politician or a persona as a party to an event (if they decide to take up the cause).

Scenario 2

An employee commits suicide either on company property or outside the office. Here is an example of the 4-point formula employed:

1. Our hearts go out to our employee's family.
2. And also, everyone in our workplace who worked beside him and considered him part of our family or as a friend.
3. We do not know what motivates a person to take such tragic action nor understand what went through his mind. We will need to wait for the results of the investigation for the answers to those questions.
4. In the meantime, we are making counseling available to our employees should they feel it would be beneficial.

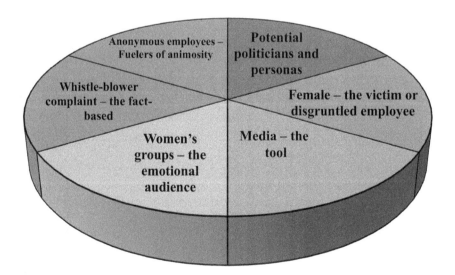

Chart 3.1 Potential parties to this event

Case study 3: Commercial scenarios

Scenario 1

A customer checked their dog into the cargo hold and when the dog was offloaded it was left in the sun and died from the heat. The customer was traumatized, and the airport operator says, "It's just a dog." This activates the animal activists who picket the airport.

THE 4-POINT FORMULA IN THE COMMERCIAL SCENARIO

Here is an example of the 4-point formula employed in such a scenario:

1. Our hearts certainly go out to this person who is grieving over the loss of their beloved pet.
2. Many of us are pet owners ourselves and can understand how a pet can be like a member of the family.
3. We cannot speak for the airport operator and why he said what he did. We are still reviewing what happened, but while we are waiting their results …
4. Here is what we are going to do in the meantime …

Mistake #7 – "We can't train everyone on the 4-point formula."

Countermeasure to mistake #7 – This is the one time when employees can get caught off guard with no time to refer to a manual or have time to make a phone call for guidance. Companies who deal with this proactively can equip all employees with the 4-point formula on a small card, which they can keep with their IDs or in their wallets so that it is readily available.

Scenario 2

A customer's property was damaged/lost, and the customer/passenger is furious.
The strategy is to defuse at the lowest possible level. Here is an example of the 4-point formula employed in such a scenario:

1. First of all, let us apologize for what has happened and for the inconvenience it has caused you.
2. Let me also say we understand how you feel because we/I fly as a passenger on this airline/go through this airport as a passenger/customer)myself.

3. While we both wait for the results of what happened to your property …
4. Let me tell you what we can do for you in the meantime …

Case study 4: Ethics scenarios

Scenario 1

It became public that a contract worker for an on-site company day care facility was caught drinking during a break. The ensuing publicity creates a firestorm. Here is an example of the 4-point formula employed in such a scenario:

1. First of all, it's a tragic situation when any workplace suffers this type of situation with our most precious of concerns – the trust of children.
2. All of us have children and can understand the concern and worries of the parents and public this brings on.
3. We are awaiting the outcome of the investigation and would not want to say anything to jeopardize the outcome of that investigation. The person in question is not in contact with children until we receive investigation's findings.
4. In the meantime, this is what we can tell you. At no time was any child in harm's way and that employee has been removed. We can say that although we are investigating, this is the exception and not the rule.

While this type of situation is not an accident, it is an investigation and the details must be kept confidential.

Scenario 2

An employee was caught selling merchandise on the black market and now an organization's [safety/integrity/environment/finances] is in question. Here is an example of the 4-point formula employed in such a scenario:

1. We are very sorry this has happened.
2. There are X number of people in our workforce and this was the exception, not the rule.
3. We, like you, are waiting on the outcome of the investigation. This is a law enforcement issue and the law enforcement officials will be informing all of us how this happened.
4. There is no workforce, whether it is in the public or private sector, who can regulate honesty, integrity or work ethic. In the meantime, what we can tell you is this: We are in compliance with the regulations of the regulating agency.

This scenario could apply to a safety issue, a workplace personnel issue, an environmental issue, a workplace health and safety issue, or anything that might have oversight from any governmental agency. It does not have to be aviation-related.

Many industries are regulated in the same way that aviation is and have the same oversight. The 4-point formula works in the same way.

Scenario 3

An employee was accused of signing off on employees' qualifications and taking money for it. Here is an example of the 4-point formula employed in such a scenario:

1. I do not know where you get your information, but I am sorry to hear this.
2. We have a workforce of many people and it is difficult in the aviation industry to do anything unethical for long.
3. The good thing is our system employs checks and balances with the regulator and if there is anything out of order, they will let us know.
4. In the meantime, let me assure you that we are in compliance in the following ways ...

Why reinvent the wheel?

When developing a communication strategy, it is nice to be proactive but sometimes you may need to be reactive. You may be reacting to various events such as internal situations, occupational accidents, or business situations, e.g. a change in company finances, a media concern, or a viral social media campaign. There have been cases where social media has been used against an organization by customers, passengers, angry employees, unions, or some other audience. The worst case would be in the face of tragedy. What strategy does an organization use? Organizations have myriad choices.

A winning strategy

There are strategies that work and strategies that do not. Why reinvent the wheel? There are organizations that are perceived to have done a good job in the aftermath of tragedy and those that have not. As mentioned in the introduction, Tony Fernandes of AirAsia is generally regarded as having done a good job in the area of communication in the aftermath of the Indonesia AirAsia Flight 8501 crash on December 28, 2014.[1] In his own words:

> Thanks to social media I was able to go directly to the audiences I wanted to reach. When I had to face conventional media, I was very conscious to not tailor my message for them, but rather making sure I stuck with and communicated the Four-Point Formula through the media to whom they were channelling the news to.[2]

Some additional steps were taken in the AirAsia communication strategy:

- Using social media to reach out directly to the audiences they wanted to reach out to and bypass those they wanted to avoid
- Developing a communication manual that encompassed all issues and recognized that emergency response was part of communication, not the other way around
- Treating the event as an investigation first and not a media event

One thing that their manual included were the messages of aviation and accident investigation, which are in this book – in Chapters 3, 5, and 6. Tony Fernandes's personal style also does not use clichés that are handed down from one company to the next:

> Fernandes has been applauded earlier for his communications style. He reacts fast, uses simple language that people can understand and is not hiding behind meaningless phrases. So, he is a great combination of speed, tone and message that reaches people and make it easier to trust and believe him.[3]

Mistake #8 – "If we do nothing and wait long enough, it will go away."

Countermeasure to mistake #8 – Doing nothing is not an option in the tragedy scenario.

Do nothing

This is certainly an option but what would happen if you did nothing in a tragedy scenario? Think back to the pie chart of those who are potential parties to an event. We will analyze in what position the fact-based party to the event would find themselves and how the other parties would react:

- *Political (including witnesses, social media, and "expert" speculators):* Look what happened; this is what happened.
- *Persona:* It may not have happened if they had listened to me.
- *Union:* We don't know what happened, but it wasn't our people.
- *Media:* The tool to get the message out.
- *Emotional:* I lost my loved one.
- *You:* Say nothing? You get what you get. You have allowed others to determine your message, which will be received as insensitive; something to hide; uncaring. Whatever they say will establish a misperception that you

will then have to work to undo along with what needed to be done initially. You won't be at ground zero. You will be below ground zero working your way up.

Have a press conference

In the worst-case scenario, which would be a crash with deaths and/or injuries, the CEO or top executive would certainly want to hold a press conference. It is important that he or she be seen. In the case of AirAsia, CEO Fernandes was en route to the crash site as soon as he heard. In the case of the Asiana Flight 214 that crashed in San Francisco on July 6, 2013, it is generally agreed by most industry experts and analysts (I did not work directly with them) that they lacked a communication strategy that dealt effectively with the reality of their tragedy.

There are ways of bypassing the fact that you are not in the actual spot, depending on the culture. An executive can issue a statement on a Facebook page, YouTube, the company website, or some other social media platform, but it could offend your audience if it does not come out personally. It also depends on the persona of the executive(s) and the global size and stature of the organization. The point is that you cannot wait until something happens; you need to have a strategy in place prior to the event happening – but remember that the 4-point formula is your safety net.

> After the accident and while still in Korea, Asiana President and CEO Yoon Young-doo made several public apologies, along with statements about the experience of the plane's pilots. But the Seoul-based carrier has issued few statements in the U.S. and declined to arrange for any media spokespeople outside of Korea. It took the airline "an inordinate amount of time" to put up a toll-free number for families to get information after the crash, a step that is required. The company's website didn't post the number until about nine hours after the crash.[4]

And, the company's website did not post the phone number for families required by the NTSB until nine hours after the crash.[5] The company's attitude toward a portion of the emotional audience and therefore the market was, "It's not the proper time to manage the company's image."[6]

How does all of this affect the results and outcome for Asiana Airlines? Let's analyze:

- *Political:* Videos went viral on social media and the crash was on show, as it could be seen from the windows of planes waiting to take off. Within one hour the fire department, the Mayor's office, and the airport authority had come forward. Passengers gave accounts and press conferences.
- *Union:* There would be unions representing the firefighters because of the issues involved, i.e. fatalities after the fact.

- *Media:* Traditional and social media were the tools. Visuals of the crash as it happened were revealed. People watched the event occur, including the regulatory authorities and the National Transportation Safety Board (NTSB).
- *Persona:* The mayor's office was involved, because it happened at the airport in a major US city. (A politician who was a persona was inevitable.) The NTSB was conducting press briefings/press conferences and using social media.
- *Asiana (fact-based):* Nothing! Perhaps in Seoul but the crash did not happen in Seoul!

Analysis: Asiana was strongly criticized for the lack of communication. The media went away, but the images that went viral on social media remained. Mainstream media was very critical of Asiana. Although they had several press conferences in Seoul, the crash did not happen in Seoul. They codeshared with United Airlines, but it is the flag carrier's responsibility to comply with US requirements. Asiana was fined $500,000 for failure to comply with the family assistance plan required of operators flying into the United States.[7]

Press briefing

The use of social media and an organization's website can take the place of a press briefing. In the case of Asiana, they had made some public apologies in Seoul, as is the Korean custom, but nothing in the United States until days later. The NTSB was conducting press briefings/interviews. Therefore, by doing nothing Asiana was left with a persona that was created for them by others.

Issue a press release

In the world of social media, this is far too slow. Organizations issue written words on their websites, Facebook pages, Twitter accounts, and other platforms. Organizations can post CEO statements on social media to reach large numbers of people instantaneously, as the CEO of Southwest Airlines did in the aftermath of their tragedy in April 2018.[8]

The clichés

There are certain recognized clichés that appear in statements and that seem to be handed down from organization to organization. When I ask an organization why they say a particular thing in their comment, the response is often, "Well, another organization used it, so we are just following what they said." This is pervasive throughout the industry. Someone wrote it the first time and it wasn't correct then; it is not correct now either. The problem is that perhaps the media has the statement they want for the moment and perhaps the laypublic do too (customers and passengers do not know the difference between something that is/isn't technically accurate), but the safety professionals, regulators, investigators, lawyers, and all the technical people will know that there were no safety people involved in the communication strategy process. They will know that you are an organization who is trying to "spin" a message. Just because the media go away quickly, it does not mean you did a good job. It's how you do with the regulators, investigators, and lawyers that will determine how you do, and the results of that will not be known for months or possibly even years. Here are some examples of clichés:

- "Safety is our number one priority" – this is a PR cliché.
- "We'll be providing more information when it becomes available" – this is a PR cliché and it is not accurate. This creates expectations that cannot be met because it is the investigators who are going to be announcing any information. The statement does not specify that the information is for families or customers.
- "We meet the highest levels of safety" – this is another PR cliché and it is not a fact-based response.
- "Our executives will be making an announcement as to what happened" – internally, organization subordinates may think executives are in charge because they do not understand the process of accident investigation, but it is the investigators who will be making the announcement. That is why safety and quality people need to be lead communication strategists. In many organizations, they do not train their staff on the process of accident investigation, so if safety and quality professionals are not an integral part of the strategy development, an organization may not have a strategy that meets reality. That is when an organization's communication strategy goes bad.

Dealing with various audiences

The following advice comes from talking with various members of each part of the industry.

Regulators on dealing with regulators

Here is some advice from regulators around the world on how best to deal with regulators:

- Establish a good working relationship before you have an issue. Court the regulators. Go see them. Develop contacts.
- The relationship should be one that is cooperative. However, we know that in some cases and in some countries, this is not possible.
- Do not ask for favors.
- Industry should adopt the attitude of "Yes, we want to make money, but we share a common objective for safety."

- Industry should convey the attitude that whatever they do has to be done safely. It must be in our mutual interest to work together. We need to operate in the name of safety or we will not make money.

Investigators on dealing with investigators

Here are some suggestions from investigators on how best to deal with investigators:

- If you do not bring technical expertise, we will not share information with you. This is a standard of Annex 13.
- Do not try and put up defenses because they become transparent.
- This is a cooperative process that involves participants. This process goes bad when one party tries to turn the cooperative process to its advantage. Beware, as the advantage is only for the moment.
- Do not suggest to investigators they should not reveal their findings, especially in an environment where there is a concurrent criminal investigation.

Insurance professionals' advice on dealing with insurance

You must sell insurance on a safety culture; otherwise you leave yourself vulnerable.

Media on dealing with the media

This is advice members of the media would give if you asked them how they would want to be dealt with:

- Never say "No comment." This means you are hiding something in the minds of your audience. That perception extends beyond the media.
- If you have no or can't give any information, point them in the right direction.
- Do not try to use the media to play games because of internal politics. This shows disorganization within an organization and unprofessionalism.
- It can fuel an adversary to be non-accessible.
- Impress upon your organization there is a give and take.
- Relationships should be established prior to anything controversial happening.
- "No comment" means something so much more than no comment. You aren't fooling anyone.
- If you don't want to talk to us, we know where to go to get our story.

Conclusion

You can see from the examples above that the safety/quality people, or the operations/technical operations people of an organization, will be required to be involved in the worst-case scenario at every level.

Table 3.1 In summary: the 4-point formula

The 4-point formula	What to say
Humanize	Identifies with the emotional audience, who is everyone that identifies with the victims – and in aviation that is everyone.
Make yourself part of the process	People forget you are users of the system yourself.
Low level of expertise/ defer to the experts	The only people who are going to be announcing what happened are the investigators. Educate the public on the process.
Give the facts	Only the facts as you know them and the facts of how the process works.

The most important point in this chapter is that you can get it right with the families and the media. However, if you cannot get it right with the investigators, regulators, and lawyers, the families and the media will turn on you. If there are regulatory and/or compliance issues with your organization, and the families and media believe, whether it is true or not, that your organization may have been able to prevent the death of their loved one, they are going to be very angry on top of being emotionally devastated. Take the crash of Swissair Flight 111 and the resulting investigation. When I ask how many people in an audience know what happened with the Swissair crash and the resulting investigation, few people are able to answer. This is because the media group no longer covers it. That does not mean that the families, lawyers, insurance companies, regulators, and investigators are no longer involved. As I have mentioned before, long after the media have gone home, there are many people left in the organization who have to answer for what happened to many different audiences.

Chapter summary

1. The 4-point formula
2. Rationale for the 4-point formula
3. Case studies – uses of the 4-point formula
    - Crash scenarios
    - Workplace scenarios
    - Commercial scenarios
    - Ethics scenarios
4. Why re-invent the wheel?
    - A winning strategy
    - Do nothing
    - Have a press conference
    - Press briefing
    - Issue a press release
    - The clichés
5. Dealing with various audiences

Notes

1 Rachel Bonello (2015) "Crisis Communication: 5 Critical Steps to Take, Modeled By AirAsia's Recent Actions," Identity, https://identitypr.com/public-relations/crisis-communication-airasia/ (accessed September 2018).
2 Tony Fernandes (2016) "A Family Affair: AirAsia Group in Light of Indonesia AirAsia Flight QZ8501," ISASI, *Forum Magazine*, p. 16.
3 Venus Hew (2017) "PR Professionals Laud Tony Fernandes for Defending AirAsia Pilot," Marketing, July 3, https://www.marketing-interactive.com/pr-professionals-laud-tony-fernandes-for-defending-airasia-pilot/.
4 Susan Carey, Rachel Feintzeig, and Kanga Kong (2013) "Asiana's Response to Plane Crash Draws Notice," *Wall Street Journal*, July 9.
5 *Ibid*.
6 *Ibid*.
7 Mike Ahleers (2014) "Asiana Airlines Fined $500,000 for Failing to Help Families after July Crash," CNN, February 26, https://edition.cnn.com/2014/02/25/travel/asiana-plane-crash-fine/index.html.
8 Mark Matousek (2018) "Southwest Says It's 'Devastated' after Major Engine Failure Leads to a Fatality," Business Insider, April 17, https://www.businessinsider.my/southwest-responds-to-fatal-flight-engine-failure-2018-4/.

4 The accident investigation process and associated scenarios

Who is *really* in charge?

The accident investigation process is an international process. In today's world of global aviation most events are multinational. There are a set of standards that the world goes by that fall under the International Civil Aviation Organization (ICAO). Many ICAO states do not necessarily have similar autonomies for accident investigation, so it can vary from state to state, especially when a state views an accident as a potential criminal event from the onset. Sometimes local laws supersede ICAO guidelines and those guidelines cannot override local judicial process. This complicates international accident investigation. Note that all acronyms in this chapter can be found in Chapter 2.

Background

ICAO is a UN specialized agency, established by states in 1944 to manage the administration and governance of the Convention on International Civil Aviation ("the Chicago Convention").

The Chicago Convention established the ICAO. This treaty also established the rights of signatory states over their territorial airspace and laid down the basic principles relating to international transport of dangerous goods by air. It provided two basic freedoms. The first was the freedom to fly over another country without landing, and the second freedom was to stop for fuel and repairs in a country without taking on or leaving cargo or passengers. It also established rules of airspace, aircraft registration and safety, detailed the rights of the signatories in relation to air travel, and specified the parameters of air accident investigation. Its continued mission is to ensure the safe and orderly growth of international civil aviation throughout the world. It has no authoritative power when it comes to enforcement.

The treaty was signed in December 1944 in Chicago. As of November 2017, the Chicago Convention has 192 state parties, which includes all member states of the United Nations except Dominica and Liechtenstein. The Cook Islands is a party to the convention although it is not a member of the UN. The convention has been extended to cover Liechtenstein by the ratification of

Switzerland.[1] It has a 36-member governing council elected from within. The ICAO works with its member states to reach consensus on international civil aviation Standards and Recommended Practices (SARPs) and policies in support of a safe, efficient, secure, economically sustainable, and environmentally responsible civil aviation sector.

Contracting states

A contracting state of the ICAO is a state which has agreed to the Chicago Convention on International Civil Aviation, whether or not it is a member of the United Nations and/or any of its other agencies, e.g. Switzerland. A non-contracting state of the ICAO is a state which has not signed and does not adhere to the Chicago Convention, but which is a member of the UN and/or any of its other agencies, e.g. the Holy See. There is a third category – states that are not signatories to the Convention on International Civil Aviation and which are not members of the UN or its agencies. Very few states belong to this category.

There are numerous important articles to the treaty that help them accomplish their mission and lay down guidelines for the aviation industry, such as rights of states, authorities for air space use, landing at customs airports, and many others.

There are numerous annexes to the treaty, but the one that provides international requirements for air accident and incident investigation is Annex 13. It not only spells out which states may participate in an investigation but defines their rights and responsibilities. It says that the states of occurrence, registry, operator, design, and manufacture may be parties to the event. It also states that a state that has a special interest to the event may participate. A special interest could be a number of citizens from a particular state who suffered fatalities or injuries, which would entitle that state to appoint a special representative to the investigation. Annex 13 is a good guideline, but states need to adapt their local laws to ensure the process is effective.

Under ICAO Annex 13 the state of occurrence is in charge of the investigation. However, if the resources or technical expertise is limited in a particular state, the state of occurrence may delegate all or part of the investigation to another state or a regional organization.

The misunderstanding here among the lay-public is that it is the operator who is in charge of the investigation. That is never the case. When the government steps in to communicate or speak in the aftermath of an event, it is sometimes misinterpreted as a political maneuver. The state of occurrence may also call upon the best technical expert to assist. An example of this was the confusion that took place in the aftermath of Malaysia Airlines MH370:

> One of the world's most perplexing aviation mysteries is casting a harsh spotlight on Malaysia's government, as a leadership unused to heavy scrutiny comes under intense international criticism for a litany of confusing messages and a perceived lack of transparency.

Frustration over the fruitless search has increasingly been directed at Malaysian officials after a series of fumbling news conferences, incorrect details given by the national airline, and a long delay in divulging details of the military's tracking of what could have been the plane hundreds of miles off course.[2]

It you look at the extract above, you will see the reason the state of Malaysia was perceived not to have handled its communication well in the aftermath of MH370. There were "incorrect details given by the national airline" which made the news conferences look "fumbling" to the public. If the state investigators are taking the lead, the national airline should not be putting out details. They are not going to have the details, and given what we know about MH370, no one had the details. Any attempt to put them out would have made the process look "fumbling," which would have had a ripple effect. This is where point 3 of the 4-point formula comes in – defer to the experts (Chapter 3). It is always the investigators in the state of occurrence who make the announcement. However, since the state of occurrence was not known, it should be the state of registry who takes the lead. The key word here is "state." It is not the "operator" from the state of registry. The operator, in this case Malaysia Airlines, could have deferred to the state investigators. If you look at Figure 4.1 below, you will see the progress and how point 3 provides a safety net and complies with the communication criteria of the international accident investigation process. Once the enormity and confusion began to surface, a large-scale international effort emerged. As of this writing, no one knows for certain what took place – but Malaysia could have avoided being much of the bad publicity resulting from their communication.

The other states that are participants through the party process (the states of registry, operator, design, and manufacture) may designate an accredited representative (see Chapter 2) to take part in the investigation. It is important to note here that it is each state which has the authority to say who participates on that state's behalf and not the actual operator or manufacturer. It is also important to note that state of manufacture can mean engine as well as airframe. All of the parameters outlined by the ICAO constitute a treaty between the member states as opposed to a contract or some other form of agreement.

Figure 4.1 Communication safety net for MH370

74 *The accident investigation process*

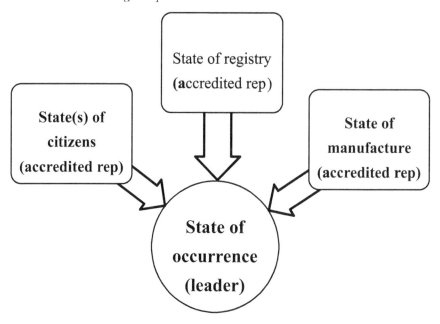

Figure 4.2 International investigation participants

Figure 4.2 shows what it might look like with the accredited representative and the other states that are parties to an event reporting to the accredited representative.

Standards and Recommended Practices

Introduction

The objective of the SARPs is to achieve international standardization by helping states manage aviation safety risks in cooperation with their service providers. They are used by ICAO member states to see that their local civil aviation regulations and standards conform to international standards and norms. This is a safety strategy developed by the members in a proactive effort to establish a strategy to address the safety risks in agreement with a safety management system that cuts across multiple ICAO annexes.

Safety is an ongoing and evolving effort that must be proactive rather than reactive due to the growth that is projected in air traffic in the future. States may choose to adopt SARPs and states may file differences. Local laws of a state usually prevail over SARPs.

A new annex dedicated to states' safety management responsibilities and processes was developed under the State Safety Programme (SSP) in a two-phase process. Annex 19 was the first ICAO annex to be adopted in over 30 years. The provisions are as follows:

- An upgrade of SSP provisions integrated with the State Safety Oversight (SSO) system Critical Elements (CEs); as recommended by the Second High-level Safety Conference, the proposed amendment
- Maintains the visibility of the eight CEs of an SSO system and their role as the foundation of the SSP is emphasized
- An enhancement of the Safety Management System (SMS) provisions to facilitate implementation, including the extension of SMS to organizations responsible for the design type and/or manufacture of engines and propellers
- An upgrade of provisions for the protection of safety data, safety information, and related sources

Investigation board formats

Introduction

There are a few investigation boards in the world who get involved assisting in international accident investigation at the request of other countries due to any one of a number of reasons. The main reasons are that many times a multinational investigation requires a large number of human resources and an immense amount of technical expertise, and few countries have these capabilities for an extended period of time. The reality of accident investigation in today's world is a pooling of resources and talents. There are a handful of first-tier countries that have the labs and human resources; they are the US, UK, France, Canada, and Australia. Others have additional expertise and make contributions to accident investigation. We briefly discuss below the backgrounds of the main five. France and the US have a strong probability of being involved in many of the investigations due to the fact that they often represent the state of manufacture.

Background – NTSB

The National Transportation Safety Board (NTSB) originated in the Air Commerce Act of 1926, in which the US Congress charged the US Department of Commerce with investigating the causes of aircraft accidents. Later, that responsibility was given to the Civil Aeronautics Board's Bureau of Aviation Safety, when it was created in 1940.

The NTSB gets involved in many international investigations for any one of a number of reasons. The main reason is because it is the accredited representative, being from the state of manufacture. Other reasons could be because it represents the state of registry, has a substantial number of passenger involvement, or smaller countries that do not have the resources – whether it be human or technical – request assistance.

The NTSB is an independent federal multimodal agency charged by Congress with investigating every civil aviation accident in the United States, and other significant incidents. Because this book focuses on aviation, we are only going to look at the NTSB in terms of aviation.

The NTSB determines the probable cause of the accidents and does not place blame. It issues safety recommendations aimed at preventing future accidents. It carries out special studies concerning transportation safety and coordinates the resources of the federal government and organizations to provide assistance to victims and their family members impacted by major transportation disasters. Its main mission is to make transportation safer by conducting independent accident investigations, advocating safety improvements, and deciding pilots' and mariners' certification appeals.[3]

The NTSB is led by five politically appointed board members. Each of these members is appointed by the president and confirmed by the Senate for a five-year rotating term.

Background – AAIB

The UK Air Accidents Investigation Branch (AAIB) is part of the Department for Transport and is responsible for the investigation of civil aircraft accidents and serious incidents within the UK.[4]

The purpose of the AAIB is: "To improve aviation safety by determining the causes of air accidents and serious incidents and making safety recommendations intended to prevent recurrence."[5] It is not to apportion blame or liability.

The AAIB has its origins in the Accidents Investigation Branch (AIB) of the Royal Flying Corps (RFC). It was established in 1915 when an appointment was made to the independent post of "Inspector of Accidents" for the RFC, reporting directly to the Director General of Military Aeronautics in the War Office. At the end of the First World War a Department of Civil Aviation was set up in the Air Ministry and the AIB became part of that department being concerned with the investigation of both civil and military accidents. The Air Navigation Act of 1920 gave the secretary of state for air the power to make regulations for the investigation of civil air accidents. The first regulations made for this purpose were the Air Navigation (Investigation of Accidents) Regulations of 1922. Following the Second World War, the Ministry of Civil Aviation was created and in 1946 the AIB was transferred to it but continued to assist the Royal Air Force with accident investigations – a situation that has continued ever since.

After having various parent ministries, the AIB passed to the Department of Transport in 1983. In November 1987, it changed its name to the Air Accidents Investigation Branch (AAIB). Following further reorganizations, the AAIB became part of the Department for Transport (DfT) in 2002. The British investigators are some of the best in the world and are frequently asked to assist those states whose resources and expertise need supplementing.

Background – BEA

The Bureau Enquêtes d'Analyses (BEA) is the French agency responsible for technical investigations into civil aviation accidents or incidents. It also acts in this capacity abroad on behalf of the French industry.

The sole objective of the technical investigation is to collect and analyze useful information, to determine the circumstances and the certain or possible causes of the accident or incident, and, if necessary, to make safety recommendations in order to prevent future accidents and incidents. However, France is one country where there is the potential for a criminal investigation running concurrently with the technical investigation.

Every year, the BEA conducts more than 400 investigations following accidents or incidents in general aviation and in public transport occurring on French territory (which includes the Departments and the Overseas Territories), acting as the state of occurrence, in accordance with Annex 13 to the Convention on International Civil Aviation. The BEA can, equally, act as an observer in an investigation conducted abroad and relating to an accident involving French passengers.[6] The BEA has high international vulnerability due to France being the state of manufacture of Airbus.

In this capacity, the BEA is involved in around 100 events every year.

Background – TSB

The Transportation Safety Board (TSB) of Canada is an independent multimodal agency that advances transportation safety by investigating occurrences in the marine, pipeline, rail, and air modes of transportation, which is much like the NTSB. The TSB is an independent agency, created by an Act of parliament (Canadian Transportation Accident Investigation and Safety Board Act), which came into force on March 29, 1990. The TSB consists of up to five board members, including a chairperson, and has approximately 220 employees. Because of that, it is often requested to assist in international events. The head office is located in Gatineau, Quebec; however, most investigation staff are located in various regional and field offices across Canada where they are better able to respond quickly to transportation occurrences anywhere in the country.[7]

Background – ATSB

The Australian Transport Safety Bureau (ATSB) is an independent Commonwealth government statutory agency. The ATSB is governed by a commission and is entirely separate from transport regulators, policymakers, and service providers.

The ATSB's function is to improve safety and public confidence in the aviation, marine, and rail modes of transport through excellence in: independent investigation of transport accidents and other safety occurrences; safety data recording, analysis and research; and fostering safety awareness, knowledge, and action.

The ATSB is established by the Transport Safety Investigation Act of 2003 (TSI Act) and conducts its investigations in accordance with the provisions of the Act. Under the TSI Act, it is not a function of the ATSB to apportion blame or provide a means for determining liability. The ATSB does not investigate for the purpose of taking administrative, regulatory, or criminal action.

Like most of the other accident investigation boards, the ATSB works according to a no-blame approach, but this does not equate with no responsibility. It simply means that disciplinary action and criminal or liability assessment are not part of an ATSB safety investigation, and should, if necessary, progress through separate parallel processes.[8]

The ATSB's commission is constituted by a full-time commissioner and three part-time commissioners.

The ATSB's staff includes approximately 100 multimodal investigators, of which some 60 are for aviation. Most are based in Canberra. Field offices are located in Brisbane, Adelaide, and Perth.

Rationale for communication

The rationale for who from an organization is to communicate is based on the levels of communication (see Tables 4.1 and 4.2). When an accident or an incident occurs, there are numerous audiences an employee of any organization must communicate with. This is not optional. The specific employee does not have a choice and the strategy an organization has in place prior to anything occurring will determine whether that organization has a communication success or failure.

Many organizations believe that the most important audiences are media and families. They believe that "crisis communication" refers to dealing with media and families, which is not the reality of communicating in a crisis, as mentioned before. Many different people must communicate with various audiences and the employees do not have a choice. However, in most cases, the people who will be involved – whether on the first line or second line – will be those from the technical departments. Table 4.1 explains the levels of communication.

Levels of communication

There are numerous levels of communication in the aftermath of an accident/incident when an investigation takes place. Organizations develop policies for communication, but it is the reality of the investigation that determines who from an organization ends up communicating in the aftermath. How closely an organization's strategy and policy for communication matches reality determines how successful their end result will be. Strategy and policy for communication in an investigation do not mean just strategy and policy for dealing with media and families, although in my experience that is how communication is

Table 4.1 Levels of communication – who will be asked?

Party	Who is allowed?	Who is the expert?
Investigators	Only those technically qualified	Safety/quality ops/tech ops
Regulators	Who will they talk to?	Safety/quality ops/tech ops
Lawyers/insurance	Who will they allow to testify?	Safety/quality ops/tech ops
Families/loved ones	Why did their loved one die?	Safety/quality ops/tech ops
Media	What happened?	Safety/quality ops/tech ops

Table 4.2 Levels of communication – what is the reality?

Levels of involvement	Who will be called?	Who has the answers?
Investigators	Safety/quality ops/tech ops	Safety/quality ops/tech ops
Regulators	Safety/quality ops/tech ops	Safety/quality ops/tech ops
Lawyers/insurance	Safety/quality ops/tech ops	Safety/quality ops/tech ops
Families/loved ones	Crisis family assistance	Safety/quality ops/tech ops
Media	Corporate communication	Safety/quality ops/tech ops

defined by many organizations. It is one of the three reasons for having a strategy that is going to lead to a negative result in many cases because it ignores many of the audiences that are instrumental in determining whether a communication strategy is a success or a failure.

Investigators

The investigators of the state of occurrence are the number one audience about whom parties to any investigation must be concerned. At the onset this sounds harsh, but it is only because they have the ultimate authority over the investigation and may remove a party to the investigation from the process. Everyone who is a party to the process will need to deal with the investigators, and those dealing hands-on with the investigators will be the first to know what is going on, at least as it relates to the cause of the tragedy.

The employees of each part of the aviation industry of a state need to familiarize themselves with the investigation process in their country so as not to jeopardize their position on the investigation team or do something that would compromise their state's position on that team. Technical employees from an organization will represent them on various organizations or aviation groups at the request of and with the permission of the state's team leader, who is the accredited representative of a team's state. Again, and I cannot say this enough because there is a misunderstanding among many organizations and the lay-public, it is not the manufacturer or the operator.

> **Mistake #1** – The operator or the manufacturer leads the investigation.

> **Countermeasure to mistake #1** – Aviation organizations should educate employees on the accident investigation process during their initial aviation training process.

> **Mistake #2** – The operator or the manufacturer can send their lawyers or other individuals who may best represent their interests.

This is not true. Lawyers or other unrelated individuals are not permitted to be parties to the investigation. The organization may have their own internal briefing team, but that has nothing to do with the investigation team itself.

> **Countermeasure to mistake #2** – Have those who could potentially represent an organization's technical interests in an investigation prepared to communicate on their behalf and understand the international process.

Employees from an organization who will represent that organization in the investigation team will be from the technical areas where their expertise is a contributing factor. Those areas traditionally are operations and technical operations, with the safety and quality concerns being the windows into the operations and technical operations areas. Cabin representatives may be a party to the event, so it is always important to keep them part of the safety operation. From the manufacturing side, participants in the investigation would be from the engineering or technical side. The investigators of a particular state have the authority to determine who participates, so it is imperative that the local employees of "our organization" communicate properly in the investigation.

Most of the aviation industry is tangible in that it is technical and based on strong and sound scientific principles. Communication, however, is intangible. It is the intangible, or those variables one cannot predict, that will get you.

In Table 4.1, the levels of communication are identified. The left-hand column shows the parties to the event. The middle column indicates those who are allowed to speak according to the accident investigation process and what question will they ask. The right-hand column indicates who is the end expert on the subject. As one can see, in each case it is the technical people who will ultimately have the answer to the question or be the ones to provide the information to the technical groups, so they can respond. The people who are the experts are those working with the issues of safety and quality. These events are technical in nature, not commercial.

Table 4.2 illustrates who will be called. Although in the last two levels the family assistance people and corporate communication people may be asked the difficult questions, it is ultimately those working hands-on with the investigation that they will need to go to for the answers.

Although the families want to know the answer to the question "Why is my loved one dead?" that information may not be known for months, years, or never – in rare cases like Malaysia Airlines MH370.[9]

The family assistance representatives are the first point of contact for loved ones.

The number one question families ask is, "Why is my loved one gone?" The family assistance representatives will not have the answer to that question. The first people who are asked that question within an organization may have a policy that mandates employees within the organization to call a legal department, human resources department, or other department, but again it is ultimately the people who are working hands-on with the investigation who will have the information first.

Regulators

The next audience an organization would have to be cognizant of in terms of communication would be a regulator. When an accident/incident occurs, a regulator will be there to look at paperwork, manuals, training, and many other things to determine if an organization was compliant and help the investigators find out what happened. An organization does not determine whom in their organization the regulator communicates with. The regulator determines this itself. Therefore, it is important that the communication skills of each employee who comes into contact with the regulator best represent the organization. If a regulator walks into an organization and asks to speak to you, you do not have a choice but to be the communicator. The exception is when regulators ask for documents that are first to be given to the investigators. However, you will still need to communicate with them about why you cannot turn over those documents.

In the event of an accident, a regulator may come into an organization and begin asking for paperwork. Whether you hand it over will depend on the country. In some countries, the functions of investigators are shared with regulators. But mostly it is the investigators who lead the investigation.

Lawyers/insurance

The lawyers and insurance companies are next because they are the group that is going to cost an organization all of the money. In the end, it will be about liability and lawsuits, especially in litigious societies. All organizations are entitled to have their own internal advisory team and your lawyers will be a part of that. That does not mean an organization can put those people forward to the investigation team to represent them.

For example, in a court of law the question may be asked, "Why was work being signed off on that was never done?" A lawyer may know how to respond for the best legal protection, but the only person who can answer the question is the person whose signature is on the document. Of course, the lawyers may advise the mechanics in internal briefing sessions, but it is only the person who signed the document who would be able to answer that question. He/she is the person who will need to respond.

Families/loved ones

Next come the families. I am not suggesting that the families are less important than the other groups. I am just saying that Tables 4.1 and 4.2 show a hierarchy of communication, which I will discuss in this chapter's conclusion.

There had been a lengthy ongoing effort by families and loved ones affected by aviation disasters for better treatment in the aftermath of a tragedy. Many of these efforts were a result of either poor or a complete lack of communication in dealing with this group at the most difficult of times. A group calling themselves the National Air Disaster Alliance/Foundation was formed and they were very effective in advocating for the development and passage of the Aviation Disaster Family Assistance Act (ADFAA) of 1996, to create the family advocate position with the NTSB.

The NTSB, which again is the government agency charged with investigating all domestic civil aviation crashes in the United States, was charged with executing the ADFAA, in response to which it issued detailed guidelines applicable to airlines and federal agencies. The ADFAA was enacted for the purpose of resolving persistent problems in the treatment of grieving families in the aftermath of commercial airline crashes. Some of the benefits that came from the ADFAA were:

- Prompt and appropriate notification
- Family support services/victim accountability
- Family receiving briefings before the media
- Consulting family members about the return of personal affects

These are not all of the benefits, but they are the ones that apply specifically to communication and are the things that were most important to family members. The fact that this group was able to accomplish this much shows the power that the emotional audience can have when they work with the political audience – with the catalyst being poor communication.

In the aftermath of the Pan Am Flight 103 tragedy, I visited the AIB in the UK. I was interviewing the then Chief Inspector, asking him, "What can I tell Americans to better help them communicate internationally?" After our interview, he asked me if I would like a tour of his hangar. I said, "Of course." In the hangar, he had the wreckage of the British Midlands plane that crashed at Kegworth, a Sikorsky helicopter that crashed in the North Sea, and, because there were still legal issues to be resolved, the partial wreckage of Pan Am Flight 103. He told me that he had recently met with about 40 families from that tragedy. I asked him, "What questions did they ask?" He told me they wanted to know where their loved ones landed, if their body had been in one piece, where their luggage landed, and things one would think they would not want to know.

When developing communication strategies to deal with this group I have found that organizations sometimes do not prepare for questions they feel are uncomfortable. They ignore the fact that this audience sometimes needs to ask these kinds of questions, as uncomfortable and gruesome as they may seem.

The questions above came long after the fact, but a number of them were associated with the fundamental concerns that families have: initial notification of involvement, which had long passed; victim accounting; access to information; and personal effects. I asked the Chief Inspector if they had anything to say about the Americans. He said, "They said that no one would talk to them." Again, lack of communication had fueled the anger of the emotional audience.

One question that almost always comes up externally is the money question. How this question is handled externally can affect the relationship with the families because the families are the emotional audience. The extended emotional audience is anyone who identifies with the families, and that will be everyone.

I ask this question in training: "How much money do you think your victims' relatives should get?" Under any circumstances this is an uncomfortable question. The standard response is, "I don't think now is the time to talk about money. Our number one concern is to care for the families." This response is such a PR cliché it makes me laugh. It is also oxymoronic in that money at a time like this is taking care of the families. In many circumstances, the survivors are wondering how they are going to make it through life without their breadwinner.

Mistake #3 – The operator should make the decision about what information is best for the families to hear.

Countermeasure to mistake #3 – Operators need to know "what lane they are in and stay in their own lane." Survivors want to hear what they want to hear. You will know what they are by the questions they ask. Be prepared to answer.

As mentioned, ADFAA of 1996 and the Foreign Air Carrier Family Support Act of 1997 indicate that all air carriers flying in the United States, including all foreign carriers flying in or out of the United States, have a fundamental responsibility for family notification and all aspects of victim and family logistical support, including communication. These Acts were revised in December 2008 to form the Federal Family Assistance Plan for Aviation Disasters. Within this plan, there are seven Victim Support Tasks (VSTs) that identify the response requirements assigned to participating organizations. VST 2 is assigned to the air carrier, stating that it must be able to provide assurance to the NTSB that it can comply with each of the items identified.

Some of the tasks within VST 2 include:

- The carrier must notify the NTSB of an incident including the place the incident occurred, the flight number, station pairs, passenger demographics, and whether the flight is domestic or international.
- In addition, they must supply the NTSB with contact information for the persons responsible for the airline's humanitarian response, manifest reconciliation, and family notification process.
- Finally, the airline must provide the name, telephone number and location of the facility designated as the Family Assistance Center and Joint Family Support Operations Center.
- The NTSB must be provided with a reconciled copy of the passenger manifest in a timely manner.
- The air carrier must provide a reliable, publicized toll-free telephone number with enough capacity to handle the high volume of calls an incident of this type is likely to generate.
- The air carrier must provide timely notification to family members. Also, the air carrier must provide notification to family members prior to releasing information to the public.

The key to all of this is "response." It is not dealing with media, but it is still communication. The question is, who needs to be doing this communication?

Organizations establish volunteer groups to be the "interfacers" with the families. Depending on the size of the organization, these could be internal or external representatives or large or small groups. The internal groups for the smaller companies could be representatives from the human resource or commercial departments. From the larger companies, the volunteer groups could be large and consist of employees that cross-cut many departments. Although organizations generally provide training to these groups, not everyone possesses the special skills it takes to deal with the audience of the families.

Media

The last level is the media. The reason for this is simple. When I pose the question in any of my classes about an event that is in the not too distant but not too recent past, "What is going on with this event?" the answer is invariably, "We have no idea." I then ask, "Why is that? Why don't you know?" They tell me, "There is no media coverage." I say, "Exactly." The media are the first to go. Therefore, the strategy should be to defuse them at the lowest possible level. The lowest possible level is going to be where the question is asked.

Many people think that the media are the problem. The media are not the problem. The problem is the people who use the media. The media are just doing their job. They are a tool. It is the strategies that organizations have in dealing with the media that cause things to go wrong.

If a multinational organization get a call from the media and the media are told, "Call headquarters," that is not resolving things at the lowest possible level. That is a strategy that will elevate the call to a higher level. When the caller gets to headquarters, they are not going to get the answer they are looking for because it is the investigators of the host country (not the organization) who will announce what happened.

Organizations generally have corporate communication people on staff. These people are prohibited from being a part of the accident investigation team by ICAO standards. They have no technical expertise to contribute. They would have to go somewhere in an organization to get the information to do their job, i.e. the technical and operations departments.

Having said all of this about the media, there is a further important point. The media do go away first. However, if you get it wrong with the media, there will be ripple effects on the rest of the audiences.

Variables for reality

We have said a number of times that a communication strategy must meet reality in order for it to be effective. We have also said that the difficult thing about communication is that it is the intangible part of aviation. The aviation industry is a very technical industry based on data, science, documentation, and many other systems and analyses. In accident investigation, there are many variables that can make a difference to your strategy. Here are some of them that need to be taken into consideration:

- *State of occurrence:* How experienced are the investigators in the state of occurrence? Where is the crash located (terrain, logistics)? Was this in international waters? Are the country's air traffic controllers unionized? How active are the media? What are the political realities of this country, e.g. do they consider it a criminal event?
- *State of registry:* Where was the aircraft registered? Is the cultural communication style of this nationality passive or aggressive? Are union issues a factor? Do they comply with international expectations of a proactive family assistance effort? Do they have an active and positive use of social media?
- *State of manufacture:* Is it Boeing or Airbus, meaning will there be American involvement? (Americans are considered a litigious society.)

- *Nationalities of victims:* Where were the victims from? Were there codeshare issues involved? What are the beliefs on litigation? What is the level of media interest? What are the religious concerns?
- *Circumstances:* What were the circumstances? Was this a human factors event? Technical? Terrorism?
- *Other countries assisting:* What other states are involved?

All of these variables make up what the reality of an event will be. You can prepare as best you can but, in many cases, you may never know what your variables will be until a situation occurs. That is why knowing the process in this chapter and the 4-point formula from Chapter 3, which is your safety net, are the two things that are of value to all employees.

Three common threads

I did not set out to do a study on why organizations get it right or wrong when it comes to communication. However, in working with organizations – in both the public and private sector – over the past 30 years, I have found there are three things in common between those who are perceived to have done a good job in communicating and those who have done a poor job in the aftermath of a worst-case scenario. All the organizations in the world who are perceived as having done a good job did so because of the strategy in place before anything ever occurred. All those who are perceived to have done a poor job did so because of the strategy that was in place before anything ever occurred.

Three common threads for getting it right

These are the things organizations who are perceived to have done a good job have in common:

1. They treat the event as an investigation and not a media event.
2. They have the right people trained to deal with the issues to speak with the audiences with whom they come into contact with, whether they will be regulators, customers, investigators, passengers, etc.

Table 4.3 Three common threads – getting it right

Organizations that have been perceived to have done a good job have done so because of the strategy that was in place before anything ever occurred.	1. They planned for an investigation.
	2. The right people are trained to talk on the issues and they plan for an investigation.
There are three common threads that organizations have when getting things right in the aftermath of an event.	3. The technical investigation was not separate from the crisis and safety and quality people were lead strategists.

Table 4.4 Three common threads – getting it wrong

Organizations that have been perceived to have done a poor job have done so because of the strategy that was in place before anything ever occurred. There are three common threads that organizations have when getting things wrong in the aftermath of an event.	1. They planned for a media event. 2. The wrong people talked about the issues. 3. The technical investigation was separate from the crisis and safety and quality people were not lead communication strategists.

3. They consider the entire event for which they prepare well in advance with a strategy and messages, and it is a team effort, with their safety and quality personnel as lead strategists.

Three common threads for getting it wrong

These are the things organizations who are perceived to have done a poor job have in common in the area of communication in the aftermath of the worst-case scenario:

1. They plan for a media event.
2. They have a policy that directs all media responses to those without the expertise to respond to the questions, and use answers that are PR clichés and inconsistent with the reality of accident investigation.
3. They separate their plan and prepare as though the crisis is just dealing with the media and families and the technical investigation/go-team is separate from the crisis. The safety and quality people are subordinate to the corporate communication and emergency response people. In their planning stages, safety people are denied training by business departments. I have been told by safety directors that they are "low men on the totem pole" within their company or they cannot get training because the corporate communication departments will not give them permission. It is very predictable how this ends up.

You can see from Tables 4.1 and 4.2 that whether an organization's strategy says so or not, it is the people in the safety and quality departments – the operations and technical operations people – who will in fact have to answer for what happened every step of the way long after the media have gone home. The weight of the organization and how well they do with the investigators, regulators, lawyers, attorneys, and the emotional audience is going to be on their shoulders. How the technical people do here will have a direct, commercial impact. I have heard so many times these people tell me that they are not allowed training because they are not official spokespeople, their business continuity manager already has a consultant they deal with, they have an external emergency response company they pay a retainer to that will handle everything, that they are part of a codeshare relationship and the "big brother" airline will take care of everything, that they are just safety managers so they are "low men" on the totem pole, and many more ridiculous statements. You can get things right with the media and families, but if you do not get things right with the investigators, regulators, and lawyers, the media and families are going to turn on you.

The emotional audience will say, "Are you telling me the regulators/operators/manufacturers knew something that might have prevented the death of my loved one?" Whose fault will that be? It will be the fault of organizations who put the strategy in place before anything ever happened. And who is an organization going to call upon within their organization to defend their position or present their facts to the regulators, investigators, lawyers, and insurance companies? They are not going to have a choice but to rely on the people who have the answers to those questions. The people who have the answers are in the operations and technical operations departments and the windows into those departments are through the safety and quality departments. The terms used may be different in different companies but generally they are the same people. When I heard employees from those departments tell me, "I'm just in the safety department so I'm a low man on the totem pole," I know that this is an organization that has a strategy in place that is destined for failure. Figure 4.5 illustrates what a successful strategy should look like. PR consultants talk about organizations having consistent "messaging," especially in today's world of social media. The reason inconsistent messaging exists is because the wrong people are doing the messaging. You can see from Figure 4.3 who in

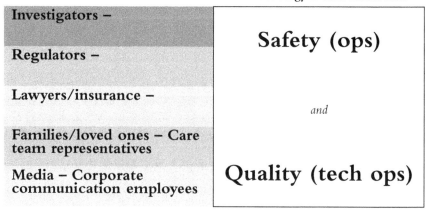

Figure 4.3 Strategy for reality

reality should be doing the messaging. Remember that the message must travel all the way up the chain and it must meet the reality of the situation. The situation we are talking about is an investigation, not a media event. The message not only has to be good for the media but go beyond the media and families to the lawyers, insurance companies, regulators, and investigators. Insurance companies are going to be looking and listening to see if there is a safety issue and rates should be raised. After a full-scale tragedy, depending on the reputation of the organization before the event, the only product an organization has to sell is safety. That is the product. No one ever asked me what kind of wine was served on the Concorde after the crash.

The CEO and their communication styles

Is the CEO always the right person to be the spokesperson? Of course, he/she is expected to say something, but different CEOs have different strengths and not all of them deal well with all audiences. Some CEOs are great with bankers and investors but are terrible with politicians and the media, while others are real showmen. CEOs also come from different backgrounds which contributes to their different styles of communication.

The technocrat

Some CEOs come from a technical background. They are usually very flat in their style of communication and talk numbers and data. They tend to gravitate toward the business side of things and do not do a good job of talking about the intangible concepts. They have a difficult time using the techniques of turning a negative to a positive, taking the high road, bridging, streamlining their message, and making themselves part of the process.

The politician

Some CEOs have a political background. They are good communicators, but their big weakness is often that they forget they are no longer in the political arena. Many times they say too much. They react like politicians when they should be diplomats and sometimes regret what they say. The techniques they have the most difficulty with are "taking the high road," not getting angry or emotional when the issue is emotional, admitting mistakes, avoiding personal opinions, etc.

The businessman

Some CEOs are former businessmen, which means they have a commercial or marketing background. These CEOs have a grasp of talking to bankers and investors but are not necessarily good at delivering a message to customers if it is not well scripted or if it is in a controversial situation. They sometimes have a difficult time not using industry clichés, because they don't know the technical or regulatory messages and don't use the techniques to deliver them, e.g. bridging or establishing credibility.

Case study

The following case study illustrates the importance of everyone in an organization understanding the reality of the international investigation process.

There was a carrier whose pilots took off on the wrong runway at a foreign airport in poor weather and crashed on takeoff. Before the accident investigators of the state of occurrence had time to decode the flight data recorder, the carrier conducted a press conference and announced that their plane had not been on the wrong runway. This statement was made by a representative of the operator's corporate communication department. There are a number of things wrong with this strategy.

First, the company pre-empted the investigators of the state of occurrence. The operator could have jeopardized the position of their technical representatives and the state of registry as representatives to the investigation team.

Second, this was not a fact-based response because there was no technical way of knowing whether or not their plane was on the wrong runway unless, of course, you take into account the smoking wreckage on the runway.

Third, and most important, it is never going to be the carrier who announces what did or did not cause the crash. It is going to be the investigators of the state of registry. This pre-empted the investigators and is the worst mistake an operator, manufacturer, or any party to an international investigation can make. (Remember, it is not a media event – it is first an investigation.)

The results of this were very bad for the company.

First, when the flight data recorder was decoded the following day, it was revealed that the plane was in fact on the wrong runway – not that anyone needed this because, as I said, the wreckage was still to the side of the runway.

Second, their initial actions offended the investigators of the host country.

Third, this fueled the anger of the families.

Fourth, it made the carrier look like they were trying to spin or lie about the issue.

Fifth, the media then turned on the carrier.

What should a person experienced in the technical issues and qualified in accident investigation have said?

This is the kind of event that the industry can look at and within minutes know what the questions are that are going to be asked. If you look at the six reasons that cause these events (see Chapter 6), you can rule out three of the subjects. No technical person has to wait for an accident report to come out to know, but no technical/safety person from an operator/manufacturer is going to answer questions because they know the process in which they are involved – an accident investigation. They know their issues are going to be operations, weather, and air traffic. However, they are only going to respond based on the safety net of the 4-point formula and what they know as the industry messages on those subjects, as they knew them prior to the tragedy.

What should an operator's strategy be? The answer is the same as any operator's strategy should be in the same situation – to preserve the integrity of the investigation, send a signal of credibility and safety to the traveling public, and reach out to the affected parties. It is not reputation management. If you do the first three, you will have the last one. Reputation management is the by-product, not the product.

Who had the most credibility within an organization to send that message of credibility to the traveling public on the subjects of operations, weather, and air traffic? Is it the office of corporate communication? What message are you sending with a person from this office to discuss this? Let's examine it this way: If an organization sends a lawyer to be a spokesperson on these issues, what perception do they create? The perception is one of unwillingness to cooperate, covering up, or something to hide. It has the effect of fueling anger. If you send a PR person to talk about technical issues in an event like this, you create a perception that you are trying to spin. The appropriate people to speak on these issues, assuming your objective is to send a signal of credibility, would be the vice president of flight operations, director of safety, or chief pilot. The performance of the operator resulted in the following editorials/articles:

Editorial: A lesson in how not to handle a disaster
Editorial: Airline must tell the truth
Article: Passengers criticize airline's post-crash service
Article: Families increase demands
Article: Kin of crash victims vent anger at airline officials

A pilot would never have said what a corporate communication person said because a pilot knows they are part of an accident investigation and they are going to have to answer for what took place all the way up the line, possibly for years to come, to investigators, regulators, and insurance companies. Depending on what country this takes place in, they could be prosecuted for manslaughter because some countries consider these events criminal investigations from day one, which run concurrently with the technical investigation.

A sample response would have gone like this:

> The events that occurred here today are certainly a tragedy. On behalf of our organization I want to extend my deepest condolences to all those affected by this terrible disaster and also to the families of our own flight crew who were like family to us [humanize and part of the process].

However, as an operator we are just one party to a larger investigation team, and they are the ones conducting the investigation. We are providing them with whatever information they need and when they have more information, they will be the ones making the announcement about what took place [defer to experts – closes the door].

In the meantime, this is what we can tell you … [give the facts]

While we don't know what caused today's terrible tragedy, we do know one thing. Whenever a tragedy like this occurs, there is always more than one contributing factor.

This is always going to be the response. This individual's response humanizes, has technical credibility, and doesn't offend the investigators of the state of occurrence. The answer is honest because it is always a chain of events that led to these events. The world has been through these events so many times that we know this is how it works.

Chapter summary

1. The investigation process and ICAO
2. Rationale for communication
3. Levels of communication

    - Investigators
    - Regulators
    - Lawyers/insurance
    - Families
    - Media

4. Reality
5. Common threads
6. CEO and their styles
7. Case study

Notes

1 "Chicago Convention on International Civil Aviation," Wikipedia, https://en.wikipedia.org/wiki/Chicago_Convention_on_International_Civil_Aviation (accessed July 2018).
2 Stuart Grudgings (2014) "Malaysia Failing Credibility Test as Flight Confusion Deepens," Reuters, March 13, https://www.reuters.com/article/us-malaysia-airlines-confusion-pictures-idUSBREA2C0A420140313.
3 NTSB, https://www.ntsb.gov/ (accessed July 2018).
4 AAIB website, https://www.gov.uk/government/organisations/air-accidents-investigation-branch.
5 *Ibid*.
6 BEA, https://www.bea.aero/en/ (accessed July 2018).
7 TSB, http://www.tsb.gc.ca/eng/ (accessed July 2018).
8 ATSB, https://www.atsb.gov.au/ (accessed July 2018).
9 Brown B. (2018) "Mystery of MH370 Only Grows after Final Report into Disappearance," *NY Post*, July 31.

5 Strategy and messages

Establishing the foundation for success or failure – the meat and the bones

There are numerous mistakes an organization can make when having to communicate in various situations. The number one mistake people make is that they do not have a message appropriate for each audience with whom they must communicate or for each issue on which they need to focus. Events involving aviation worst-case scenarios are operational events and there will be an ensuing investigation. When the investigation is complete, a report will be issued. That report will be based on careful analysis of technical data.

However, the worst-case scenario is one that, fortunately, rarely happens. There are events that occur in our workplace, both aviation and non-aviation related, on a daily basis. There are organizations, groups, and individuals we all must communicate with daily. There are aviation industry messages that are fact-based and appropriate for each issue, audience, or situation. Employees for every organization, whether it is in the public or private sector, need to have a message. This chapter provides those messages. It shows how to state those messages succinctly using the techniques learned in Chapter 2. Before you can deliver those messages, an organization must have a strategy for preparing everyone (all employees) for the possibility of delivering the messages. These are fact-based messages for the aviation industry.

Strategy for who speaks

The determination of exactly the appropriate spokesperson is based on a number of variable criteria. The spokesperson could vary between different situations. A strategy that only deals with an incident or accident as a media event will not lead that organization in the direction it needs to go. The issues at the core of these events are *not* public relations issues, but rather technical issues. An operator must think of itself not as a commercial operator with safety and quality departments but rather as selling safety and quality with commercial benefits.

The operator, tour operators, travel agents, and people in that end of the industry represent all aspects of the industry and must know their clients. After all, they are the ones who put the customer in the "product," so they are the ones who may have to answer for the product. What kind of plane am I going on? Is it safe? Is the company safe? Do tour operators and travel agents know how to answer those questions? If something happens, people head for the airport. Do the employees of an airport know how to respond before officials arrive? If ground handlers are representing an operator, are they taught how to respond to questions? So, who exactly are the appropriate people to respond? Reality decides who speaks! And, again, it is not just about the media.

More importantly, long after the media have gone home, it is the technical people who must answer for what happened. If you look at the definition of crisis communication as it is stated in this book, you will see that many audiences need to be considered, including but not limited to regulators, investigators, lawyers, communities, politicians, communities, and unions.

To determine the appropriate people for the communication strategy or team, an organization must think about who within the organization is going to be called upon to respond to the various audiences. When we say "organization," we are talking about all organizations – from airports, travel organizations, manufacturers, and unions to trade associations, etc.

This is another situation where it is not the corporation who determines who speaks. When investigators knock on your door, they are the ones who determine who speaks. When a court summons your employees to testify at an inquiry or in court, they have decided who exactly will testify. Many times, how an organization performs in these events depends on the communication skills of the employee communicating on their behalf. Therefore, you have to ask who will lend the most credibility to a situation, but yet has the technical expertise to answer the questions.

For example, if there are maintenance-related issues, you have to be represented by those from the organization who will give the most credibility in your message and lend the greatest expertise.

Of course, it is obvious that when dealing with investigators, regulators, and other legal or technical audiences, the member of an organization will put forth a technically appropriate person to speak on behalf of the organization. However, the issue becomes subjective when an organization deals with the non-technical or public audiences. The very question of who speaks becomes a dilemma for the organization. The most effective strategy is to have all people prepared because each member of the organization is vulnerable, particularly if that organization is an international organization spread over the world. If that is the case, then every employee should be prepared to communicate with one audience or another.

An organization's objective for who communicates in an accident or incident

Any organization's objective for who communicates in an incident or accident should be to resolve the issue at the lowest possible level. That responsibility will rest with the person asked the question. This book equips employees with messages, techniques, and knowledge of the process of accident investigation. While it does not encourage the seeking out of exposure through the media and other audiences, it provides the empowerment to communicate in given situations, if an organization chooses to empower its employees. Due to social media, you do not have to seek out exposure. It will find you.

I have worked with investigators all over the world and have written manuals and trained them with the same empowerment statement that is in this book (see Chapter 1, section 1.4). I find that it is not the investigators who are the issue. I have found that it is internal politics of organizations that is the real issue.

The higher up the chain the issue is sent, the greater the chance to fuel the anger of our various audiences and complicate our issues. The appropriate people to handle issues are those who are asked, if they are equipped with the appropriate information, which this book provides.

Reality decides who communicates

In today's world, any aviation employee can be unknowingly taped at any time in any country by someone with a cell phone and appear on the Internet and ultimately the evening news through no fault of their own. How many times have we seen a clip on the evening news of what it looks like in the cabin of an aircraft during an event, whether it be turbulence, a disruptive passenger situation, or an evacuation? To have an employee or manager say, "He has not been authorized to speak so he is not able to say anything" does not meet an organization's reality in today's world. This strategy could potentially fuel the anger of an audience and could cause more problems due to lack of communication.

Every statement is going to achieve a result for an organization, including saying nothing. If an employee says, "No comment," it is going to get a result. If an employee says, "I am not authorized to speak," it will get a result. If a remote employee says, "Call headquarters," it will get a result. Whichever of these statements you say will be your organization's statement because no one waits for the answer to come from "on high." The results of these statements will be negative. This will have quite the opposite effect of what a strategy is trying to achieve. These types of strategies encourage an interviewer to probe even further, which could result in an outcome that could be extremely negative in view of the confidentiality you are contracted to maintain. Everything that is said may be found in the 4-point formula designed in this book in Chapter 3, summarized in section 3.1. Therefore, the appropriate people to respond are those who are asked a question.

At an airport, there are numerous employees who will be faced with questions, including the counter and gate employees. This does not matter if they work for the airline, the airport, ground handlers, or others. Those who are asked the questions must respond. If you take the media out of the equation, these employees will most likely be asked by customers, passengers, or local officials. They cannot simply say, "I'm not authorized to speak."

If a member of a political body requests information from an organization's representative, that representative cannot tell them they are not authorized to speak. Whatever words come out of their mouths will be the statement, so why not have it be the correct one?

When a regulator or investigator walks into an organization and asks a question, they decide who to speak to. Therefore, the employees of an organization must all be prepared to speak to those individuals. They are not going to tell these regulators or investigators, "Call our office of corporate communication."

Here are some of the results you will get with the standard answers people give:

"No comment" means guilt, cover-up, and an unwillingness to cooperate. The result of this in an accident investigation when speaking to the media is to fuel anger and create negativity. Also, "No comment" *is* a comment. Perhaps people get it from watching too many television programs where the guilty party is walking away looking over their shoulder saying "No comment" to hordes of journalists. One is always left wondering who in an organization advises them of this strategy.

"I'm not authorized to speak" means *my management has no confidence in me and they have something to hide.* Saying this creates mistrust and inspires deeper investigation into your activities. It could also mean that there is an internal control issue.

"Call headquarters" means *I am too apathetic to give you an answer and I am trying to put you off.* This fuels audience anger and lets someone else set the tone/message for your organization. Most people who are calling your location are not calling you because they want to be told to call headquarters in some remote location, especially if it is halfway around the world.

Messages for potential audiences in an accident or incident

Employees

Employees are a technical audience looking for facts and information, but they are also an emotional audience, many times identifying with what took place. When speaking to them, the first thing to remember is to be humanistic. The components within any organization could be large or small entities themselves. If an organization is small, its employees are often like family. If anything happens within the organization, the employees most likely will know most of the colleagues personally.

External audiences

Events that happen to the departments, units, etc. within an organization can unfold quickly. There is not always time to check with anyone for approval or guidance. Therefore, it is probable that an employee may be taken by surprise, especially since there could be several different countries involved. The key objective is to be factual (even if you do not know the facts at that time) and humanistic, and respond without fueling the adversary.

Political audiences

Political groups have been defined as not just elected officials, but also people who communicate in a certain way. The important thing you should know is that in an aviation emergency it is not your parent organization or a particular component of the group who controls the event. Your company may be a party to an event, but only one party in a government-controlled investigation controls it and that is governed by Annex 13 and the investigators of the state of occurrence. If the location of the event is undetermined or in international waters, it is the state of registry. So, for example, in the case of Malaysia Airlines 370, it was the state of registry who was in control of everything, not Malaysia Airlines.

Depending on the enormity and/or controversy of the event, political individuals/groups may get their information from CNN, BBC, Sky News, etc. The best message for this audience is one based on the facts as you know them; and one that refers them to those who do have the information, thereby educating the political group on the process of accident investigation. Those who will have the most updated information in the case of an accident or incident would be the investigators in the state of occurrence.

Note: This is of the utmost importance. It is never going to be anyone other than the investigators in the state of occurrence who announce what did or did not occur. Any statement that says, "More details will be announced as they become available" is not accurate and cannot lead to a good conclusion.

Media

There are two key factors to remember when dealing with the media. The first is that *you* must be in control. The strategy should be that you are not there simply to answer their questions – they are there to hear what you have to say. The techniques for doing this are addressed further in the section on techniques (see Chapter 2).

The second key is not to fuel the adversaries in the media. The quickest way to fuel their animosity is to make their ability to obtain information more difficult than it needs to be. This does not mean telling them what they want to hear, but rather ensuring that things are not unnecessarily cumbersome. For example, if they want information on a particular aircraft, that information is available to you today. If the person answering your phone does not feel comfortable giving the information, there are qualified staff within an organization that are able to respond to this without making the media wait hours or even minutes for information. Providing facts that were known before an event, such as type of aircraft, age of aircraft, etc., does not jeopardize an investigation. Not providing that information to the media simply because they are the media is an internal issue.

Ways to fuel the animosity of the media include saying things like "No comment," "I'm not authorized to speak," or "You have to call another office." Every time you refer the media to another source, you elevate the issue. And you run the risk of taking something that could be resolved at a low level and expand it into a bigger issue.

Community

The most important point to remember about community groups is that they are emotional audiences and may identify with issues specific to their community that have nothing to do with aviation, such as environment or labour issues. Consequently, the community may see people from your organization as "the bad guys."

Government

The message for the government, no matter what the agency, beyond the primary message of cooperation, is one of safety, compliance, openness, and facts delivered in a forthcoming and timely manner. The last thing you want to do is generate suspicion and/or fuel animosity. By being expeditious you may be able to pre-empt questions.

Unions

The unions' objective is to protect their members. This is exactly what they are supposed to do. They may or may not have party status to an event. If they have party status, they must be careful not to issue their own analysis of that event – so as to avoid being removed from the investigation. If they do not have party status, they can comment generally on the issues.

Not all organizations are unionized. However, this does not mean organizations that do not have union members will avoid union impact issues. For example, if a non-union member plane is involved in a ground incursion, the air traffic controllers, who are highly unionized, will receive strong union support.

Another example is the outsourcing of maintenance. If the mechanics unions have an anti-outsourcing campaign and an organization is the first one with an event that may be linked to outsourced maintenance, the union could use the event to make their point, thereby giving you added exposure.

Communicating with unions can be difficult, especially when an organization is not unionized. This is because organizations that are not unionized many times do not have a strategy that takes union input into consideration. They find themselves challenged by a union and placed in a position to communicate either with or against their message.

An organization's objective in this scenario would be to stick to the facts and the message of the process of accident investigation or the fact-based message of the system of checks and balances between government and industry.

Contractor/affiliate/outsourcer

This refers to a situation where an organization may subcontract another company to accomplish a contract. Examples would be a codeshare organization or a parent company. There are two main things to say on behalf of an affiliate. Also, you will be seen as a partner of the organization and you have to communicate your confidence in its safety.

Additionally, it is a sincere and moral position to humanize on behalf of the affiliate. This is common sense, jeopardizes nothing, and reaches out to the emotional audience. Consider the following example message:

Message: On behalf of "our organization," let me offer my sympathies to the families, loved ones, and friends of those who perished. In spite of this terrible tragedy, we still have the utmost confidence in the affiliate's ability to operate safely.

Investigators

The key to dealing with investigators is to be deferential, as they are the team leaders or the accredited representatives of the investigation teams from the states of registry, manufacture, etc.

Messages by subject

Accident/incident investigation

In an accident or incident there two key messages that act as a safety net. They are accurate and fact-based. It does not matter who you are speaking to. And they serve to educate the audience you are speaking to. They are applicable to the industry and good things to know for the commercial and technical parts of the industry in particular. They serve as the responses to many questions, no matter how many times they are asked. These are two of the most important messages in this book.

The process of accident investigation

Message: I cannot speak for what he might have said. I can only tell you that the accident investigation process is based on careful analysis of technical data. When the report is issued at some future date by the investigators, it will be fact-based.

The objective of accident investigation

Message: What we do in our organization is going to be consistent with the international objective of accident investigation. We're not going to treat the symptoms; we're going to get to the root cause, so we can put procedures in place and prevent it from occurring again.

Operations

Potential pilot error

You can look at an aviation event and know within minutes the subject areas that the organization must respond to, even though, when the final report is issued at some later date, these issues may or may not have been contributing factors. Pilot error is frequently one of the first issues to arise.

Message: We do not know at this time what caused this event. However, we do know that whenever anything of this nature occurs, there is always more than one contributing factor. What we can tell you now is that all of our pilots, like all operators, are certificated to fly on their equipment and must remain current.

Pilot training

When something happens that involves potential pilot training issues, many parties posture to protect their interests. From a fact-based perspective, pilots train according to manufacturer's standards.

Message: Our organization, like all operators, follows the manufacturer's recommended standards and industry practice regarding our training. All of our training programs are certified and monitored by regulators.

Remedial training

In the aftermath of an event, remedial training may be recommended. The controversial question here is "Why don't you train your people before you put them on the job?" This could be perceived as a negative remedy, but it is really a positive remedy.

Message: The good thing about the aviation industry is that our training is never done and it is standard procedure for technical people to continually update their skills.

Unscheduled stop controversy

There have been times when passenger flights have had to make unscheduled stops for any one of a number of reasons, such as an unruly passenger, medical emergency, technical difficulties, etc. These unscheduled stops may occur in countries in which you do not fly. When this happens, the operator is under the jurisdiction of the immigration authorities in those countries and the airline has no control. Passengers may not be allowed to exit the plane, and this could go on for hours.

Message: We are very sorry for the inconvenience to our passengers; however, we are in full compliance with all international security and safety standards and it is up to the officials of this country to determine what we are permitted to do.

Pilot suicide

PILOT SUICIDE PART 1

There is the rare occurrence when a member of a flight crew commits an intentional criminal act, e.g. suicide. Of the six potential causes of events, five of them are aviation accidents and one of them is law enforcement. An intentional act such as a pilot suicide (which causes the death of all on board the aircraft) falls under the category of a law enforcement/terrorism event.

Message: This is a terrible tragedy not just for "our organization" but the aviation industry in general. It is mass murder with airplanes used as the weapons.

PILOT SUICIDE PART 2

The question raised in the aftermath of the murder/suicide caused by a flight crew is "How many others are there that might be apt to do this?"

Message: Company workforces may have employees with problems relating to alcohol, drugs or illness. That does not make them mass murderers. We have employee assistance programs that help with these issues and crew resource management programs that help identify trends and changes in behavioural issues among the crew.

Cabin and passenger issues

In an event that involves passengers, a cabin attendant may be required to communicate with many different audiences. Some of those audiences could be passengers (customers), regulators, investigators, attorneys, and media. If there is an emergency evacuation that could involve injuries, they may need to answer questions regarding training, safety culture, and other issues. An organization may think of a passenger operation and cabin attendants as primarily part of a commercial operation, but they all need to know how to communicate about safety issues. For example, they may be the first asked, "Is this aircraft is safe?"

Message: We, like all operational people, are required to maintain a level of competency in training and proficiency required by the authorities.

Unruly passenger – alcohol

The standard response of passengers who are intoxicated is one of defensiveness. Some companies refuse to fly intoxicated passengers, and in some cases ask them to reimburse the company if an unscheduled stop is required.

If alcohol is served on board, the issue becomes why the cabin attendants served the passengers alcohol in the first place which compromised the safe operation of the aircraft. Companies do not need to be defensive. The common clichéd defensive responses given are, "He may have been drinking in the airport" or "Perhaps he brought the alcohol on board."

Message: We have X number of other passengers we have a responsibility to, and every passenger is responsible and accountable for their own behavior when they board the aircraft. We have a responsibility to the rest of our industry to send a strong signal that this type of behavior is not tolerated.

Death in-flight

There have been occasions when a passenger has died in-flight due to any one of a number of circumstances. In the aftermath of an in-flight death there may be controversy. There have been situations where the family members blame the airline for the tragedy, even though the final results of an investigation have not been determined. It is necessary to remember that this situation is a tragedy scenario, and even though it involves just one passenger, it must be handled like a tragedy scenario. The mistakes an airline makes in a scenario similar to this is to suggest that food allergies, medications, health problems, allergies, or something else may have caused this event. Remember that it is never the airline that will make the determination. To suggest it is something other than the airline will fuel the animosity of the family and everyone who identifies with the family, i.e. all of the emotional audience.

The steps an airline would take are the same with a situation that required an investigation.

Message: Our hearts go out to this family who lost their loved one. It is a tragedy for all of us to lose a passenger, and we, like this family, are waiting for the results of the investigation to learn exactly what happened. Generally speaking, whenever there is food poisoning there is more than one affected passenger. However, even though we do not have the results from the coroner, we are going to conduct a quality assurance audit of our catering.

Air traffic

The problem with air traffic issues is that they often position the controllers against the pilots because it can come down to a single controller against a single pilot. In many organizations, these roles have active unions that proactively come to the defense of their members.

Message 1: The traveling public should be very confident that the system transports X number of people through the system safely on a daily basis. There are numerous safeguards built in that have reduced the number of tragedies resulting from air traffic errors to a very low level.

Message 2: Remedial training is positive because in air traffic the traveling public should feel confident that a controller's training is always ongoing. We are always training to ensure our skills keep up with technology advancements.

Technical

Potential maintenance error

A maintenance-related accident will always involve more than one contributing factor. It is a system failure. It is never one mechanic. People must sign off on work and this is all part of the system of checks and balances that exists in the aviation industry.

Message: There is always more than one contributing factor.

Expanded message: Operator maintenance is a highly refined and regulated process where we start with licensed technicians and then have them work within a system of checks and balances. When and if there is a maintenance error, of necessity it involves several components or factors. This takes an in-depth investigation, which is now ongoing, but we know that in the end there is always more than one contributing factor.

Part failure

Only the highest quality approved parts and components are used on aircraft. However, sometimes parts do fail for a variety of reasons. However, modern aircraft are built with safeguards.

Message: Modern aircraft are built with not just part redundancy, but entire system redundancy and pilots are trained in simulators to compensate for parts failure.

104   *Strategy and messages*

Aging aircraft

When the issue of the age of an airplane is raised as a factor in an event, the key is to put the aging aircraft issue in the proper perspective.

Message: Let me clear up your misunderstanding on the aging aircraft issue. It is not a safety issue, it is an economic issue. As long as it is economically possible to maintain proper airworthiness, the plane is safe.

Potential engineering/design issues

Engineering and design issues are certification issues and therefore between the manufacturer and the regulators who certify these designs. However, it is always the operator who has to answer for the equipment it owns. The equipment may include the actual aircraft, engines, components, and other systems. An operator must be able to answer for every piece of equipment it operates.

Message: Every piece of equipment we have has been certified by the "regulators of this country" and accepted by the regulators of all the states into which this equipment is used. Nothing about engineering is arbitrary. It has been tested, tried, retested, and much more before it is ever allowed into the system. However, the engineering and design aspects of all equipment are a part of the investigation.

Actual engineering/design issues

Sometimes there are engineering and design issues which present themselves after the certification process has taken place. These events were not predictable at the time of the certification process. Engineering issues are not the issue of an individual operator, but rather the industry as a whole. One thing you do not want to do is aggressively point the finger at the manufacturer because it could reflect negatively on your own internal system of quality assurance. Design is based on engineering and engineering is not arbitrary.

Message: There are rarely instances where a weakness has slipped through the certification process. When this happens, the best minds in industry internationally get together to resolve it.

Questioning design safety

In the aftermath of an event, parties sometimes question the design philosophy of a certain manufacturer. From an operator's perspective, it is not really their issue. However, it is the operator who is the first to have to answer for every piece of equipment it has. In the aftermath of the crash of American Airlines Flight 587, manufacturing issues of the A300 aircraft arose. Manufacturing

Strategy and messages 105

issues again were mentioned in the aftermath of the Air France Flight 447 crash. These are not necessarily issues for a specific manufacturer, but rather industry issues. For example, the question of the philosophy associated with computerized equipment is not being asked, i.e. whether pilots are too focused on following the computers rather than flying the aircraft.

Message: This is not a specific issue, but rather a question for the entire industry. The best minds in the world will work together on a solution or an improvement of the system, and the decision they arrive at will not be arbitrary. Pilots and mechanics will be part of that decision.

Regulatory issues

Regulatory actions

There are two parts to this issue. The first is if an affiliate of an organization received fines/actions that they are contesting. The second is if an affiliate of your organization will be paying a fine for a regulatory violation.

It is fairly standard procedure for a corporation to contest a regulatory issue. Your organization may not be a company with a record of serious violations, regulatory non-compliance, or controversy in this area. Therefore, this issue is most likely not going to bring exposure to your organization. However, if you find yourself in this situation, the strategy would be to defuse it as soon as possible. Additionally, in some countries they do not impose fines. Even if they do not impose fines in the country where an air operator's certificate (AOC) is issued, that does not mean they will not impose them in all of the countries in which you operate, or in which your equipment is operated.

Even if an organization has a regulatory episode today that brings no exposure, if a serious situation occurs at some future point, past events could potentially resurface. This could include, *inter alia*: aviation-related, environmental, workplace, health and safety, or occupational issues.

Message 1: "Our organization" has always been in compliance with all of the regulators we deal with. Our legal advisors are working with the appropriate regulators on this issue and it would be irresponsible for any of us to say anything that might jeopardize the outcome of those discussions.

Message 2: "Our organization" has worked out this situation with the regulators. This is another example of the system of checks and balances this industry has which keeps it safe. We certainly welcome all input from our regulatory process that helps strengthen our safety systems.

Message 3: Yes, we received a fine but anything that plays a role in helping enhance a system of prevention is a small price to pay and a

Safety

It is the regulator's job to say whether or not an airline is fit to operate. It is not just as an operator, but every other part of aviation, including air traffic systems, equipment, aviation professionals, systems, manuals, training programs, parts, etc. In addition, for an operator to operate in other countries, the regulators of those countries must approve that process (the process of that operator being acceptable to operate to and from the country).

Message 1: Our organization would not be operating if the regulator did not grant us an air operator's certificate.

Message 2: Our planes could not leave the ground unless they were certified as airworthy.

Message 3: Prior to getting hired, all of our pilots and mechanics must be certified by the regulator.

Cargo issues

Dangerous goods

The International Civil Aviation Organization's (ICAO) Technical Instructions has a legal requirement for the safe transport of dangerous goods by air. They require that initial and recurring in-depth training must be taken by shippers and their agents, packers, freight forwarders, cargo agents, operators (or airlines), and agencies handling operators and performing the cargo acceptance function. Awareness level training is required for staff of operators and agencies acting on behalf of operators performing the functions of ground handling, storage, and loading of cargo and baggage; and passenger handling and security staff responsible for screening passengers and their baggage, flight crew members, and flight attendants.

Message: All our staff involved with the handling of dangerous goods have the required knowledge, training, and awareness of requirements needed to handle dangerous goods. They must have this before working with dangerous goods and must remain current.

Security

Air cargo security is not just a carrier's responsibility. International attention was raised when terrorists tried to ship explosives via FedEx and UPS aircraft.[1] This is a law enforcement issue and an international issue. Joint government–industry task forces exist to work on this issue under the umbrella of international organizations like the International Air Transport Association (IATA), Flight Safety Foundation, and others.

Message: It is not just the responsibility of the carrier but the aviation community as a whole. The best experts in the world study this issue in the name of prevention. The industry is not reactionary. Government and industry work together proactively in an effort to enhance security.

Sabotage

There have been cases where disgruntled employees have engaged in sabotage of their companies. This is a rare event and fortunately difficult to see through to completion. It is a combination of ethics (a one-off event) and law enforcement messages.

Message: Yes, that did occur and fortunately it was discovered early on. The good thing about the aviation industry is its system of checks and balances. It is difficult for an act of this nature to not be detected prior to the intended result. We have X number of people in our organization and fortunately those who do these types of things are the exception, not the rule. Ultimately this is an issue for law enforcement.

Commercial issues

Lost baggage

This is an issue that only affects one or a few passengers at a time. However, the people who are experiencing this issue are acting out of emotion and anger. Your passengers and customers identify with this issue. When addressing this issue, do not forget that you, too, may be a passenger on this airline.

Message: I first want to say that I, too, fly on this airline as a passenger and I would be as upset as you are if my bag was misplaced. I sympathize with you and here is how I can help …

Delayed flight due to weather

Unfortunately, weather delays are inevitable. These are very disruptive to everyone's plans. They present not only technical but commercial issues.

Message: Unfortunately, there are weather delays that are out of our control. These decisions are out of our hands and they are safety and not commercial decisions. We apologize for the inconvenience and understand how you feel, as we are all passengers on the airline ourselves.

108 *Strategy and messages*

Codeshare

Many commercial organizations believe that they are not required to answer for their codeshare partner. However, these are business relationships and operators, tour operators, travel agents, and others take money from customers. These customers many times expect a response from the commercial people with whom they deal. Before the codeshare relationship can be made there has to be a technical justification. If the commercial people are not informed of the process upon which that technical justification is based, they will not be able to respond to their customers.

Message: While a codeshare relationship may have commercial benefits for the industry, it is not entered into without a technical justification. No airline is flying without being certified by the regulators of the countries they fly into. In addition, they must pass an IATA Operational Safety Audit (IOSA) every two years.

Financial concerns

When a company is going through a financial crisis, it is necessary to reassure not just customers, but also authorities. There is a misperception that a corporate financial crisis may not just affect reliability, but safety, too.

Message: We may be experiencing the same financial issues as others in this industry but it has no effect on our ability to exceed our past standards of reliability. As to our safety, the good thing about the aviation industry is its system of checks and balances. The authorities will ensure we are in full compliance and I would also anticipate that we experience additional scrutiny by the regulator/authorities of our country.

Reputation with public

If you have an externally exposed event, it may bring unwanted and critical public attention to your operation. When something like this occurs, you want to make sure your responses to whichever audience with whom you must communicate emphasizes the fact-based response. You do not want to create the misperception with these audiences that you are trying to spin a message at all costs. You do not want to start a statement with "In my personal experience …" You are not there to represent anything but the facts. Anything else could bring negative customer responses toward your organization.

Message: Let me correct the misunderstanding as to why we lost the contract. It was based on business decisions, not safety or efficiency as an operator. We have no safety or regulatory problems.

My personal experience is based on 20 years in this business and what I can tell you is that this might be a commercial setback, but the authorities still have confidence in the quality and longevity of our performance and I am sure we will move past this based on our long experience as a world-class operator.

Workplace issues

Personnel issues

While you may not think this type of situation would gain public exposure, it does sometimes happen. A personnel issue is still an emotional issue with which many people may identify. It should be handled in the same manner as an investigation even though it may just be part of a pending lawsuit. The "crisis" may only be one person, but the issues are of a crisis nature to that person. So you should treat it like a crisis.

Message: This is certainly an unfortunate situation for this person and our hearts go out to her, but we would not want to say anything that might jeopardize the outcome of her situation or hinder her ability to get fair hearing in court. Protecting her privacy is our number one priority at this time. If she chooses not to share these details, we will honor this.

Discrimination

Many people in a workplace feel they are unfairly treated on the basis of race, religion, or age. The key is to stick to the facts of compliance with the laws that govern an organization's requirements.

Message: We value the expertise and experience of anyone in our organization who is close to retirement. This organization values all races, ages, and cultures that contribute to the enhancement and diversity of our workforce and we comply with the regulations that support the rights of those groups.

Whistle-blower

In many organizations, employees, or former employees, feel the need to inform against, or "blow the whistle on," their employer. These claims must be investigated, and an organization cannot interfere with this investigation.

Message: It would be irresponsible for me to say anything that might jeopardize the outcome of this investigation. We certainly encourage a non-punitive effort that could enhance either aviation or workplace safety. Our operation is under constant scrutiny by many authorities at all times and if those authorities had found any of the charges to be true, we would not have an operator's certificate.

Protecting privacy

In many workplaces you may have people who become involved in compromising situations. These situations may become well-known in the workplace or even become public. The key in these situations is to protect the privacy of the individual regardless of whether you think or know that they are not correct.

Message: It would be irresponsible of me to acknowledge a situation like this because our number one objective is to protect the privacy of our employees, either current or former.

Sexual harassment

In today's world, sensitivity to harassment or discrimination is important. Whether or not the country your employees are working in is progressive or modern in its attitudes, it is imperative to protect the privacy of the individuals involved.

Message: While it would be irresponsible for any of us to say anything that hinders an employee's ability to pursue their claims and we would not do anything to violate their privacy, we can tell you that all of our employees, whether current or past, have a right to pursue whatever means they see fit to resolve issues they feel are unjust. Our objective right now is to provide an atmosphere that would allow them to do that. We will leave it to them to disclose whatever information they see fit. In the meantime, I can tell you that our policy around the issue of sexual harassment is …

Occupational accidents

Occupational accidents occur in every workplace. Remember that even if you have an event of this nature, it is for the government agencies to determine if you comply, in what areas you are at fault, etc. You must also humanize and not jeopardize the investigation.

Message: While this is a sad situation and "our organization" regrets [whatever happened], we will not pre-empt the department/ministry or any other government agency in their investigation or say anything that might hinder their investigation in any way.

Law enforcement

Law enforcement/terrorism

A terrorism event is not an aviation issue and not exclusive to aviation. It is a law enforcement issue and often the solutions are the opposite of aviation. In aviation, the industry is assumed to be proactive and preventative. Punitive measures are only taken when there is a breakdown of compliance. In law enforcement, people are intentionally trying to circumvent the law and the solutions are punitive.

The key objective is to disclose nothing since it is a law enforcement event, *not* an aviation event. It may be a mass murder with airplanes used as weapons. Law enforcement situations can include any one of a number of events and this is a template for all of them. The things that could be law enforcement or legal situations could include, *inter alia*: bomb threats, hijackings, terrorist events, personnel/workplace situations, hazardous/questionable materials, immigration, and lawsuits.

Message: We take this event seriously, but this is a law enforcement event and not an aviation event. It is a law enforcement event that happened in the aviation industry and because of that, law enforcement officials will be handling it. We will cooperate in any way we can, but it would be irresponsible of us to say anything that jeopardizes the outcome. [This message is good for airports, operators, travel professionals, and commercial people.]

Terrorism

There may be a misperception about a particular region of the world and this subject and perhaps a belief that some cultures do not take it with the same degree of seriousness as the rest of the world. The first objective of any message needs to be to clear up this misperception.

Message: This organization and the citizens of "our country" take this subject as seriously as any other country in the world. We have a responsibility to comply with all international requirements. Before we can even fly into a country, it has to clear us to do so. Our employees have families and we care about their safety and the safety of all of our passengers, their families, and loved ones just like any other airline.

Your organization's knowledge on this subject would not be more than any other organization. There may be a misperception about this due to the geographical location. This will also be one of the first questions asked of any organization from this region – accident or not. It is very important first of all not be on the defensive and second of all to correct a misunderstanding.

Message: First, let me correct your misunderstanding. Our geographical location does not mean that "our organization" has any more information on this subject than another international organization. Second, we meet and train our employees on all international security standards. Third, prior to operating in any country, we have to be cleared by that country to do so. Fourth, we are a member of "an alliance" and to be a member of that alliance we have to meet their standards.

Hijacking

A hijacking is a law enforcement event and would be handled by officials other than the airline and investigators other than traditional aviation accident investigators, although they would be assisting the law enforcement investigators. This would also be an international event. In addition, depending on the circumstances there are most likely going to be airport issues involved.

Message 1: Because this is an international law enforcement event and we are not the leaders of the investigation, it would be irresponsible of us to say anything that might jeopardize the investigation and harm the outcome of those who are in danger. I am sure if one of your family members were on board you would want us to maintain the same level of confidentiality and concern.
Message 2: It would be irresponsible for any of us to say anything that might prevent law enforcement officials from doing what they need to do to prevent this or alert those who are trying to circumvent preventative measures by disclosing what those measures might be.

Ethics

An ethics event can occur in any workplace. However, an ethics violation is the exception, not the rule. It is usually a law enforcement type of event, depending on the severity of it. This could include the inappropriate use of alcohol, falling asleep on the job, selling of unauthorized data, or any other similar incident.

Message 1: This is one person out of our entire workforce of approximately 400 employees. There is no organization that can wholly regulate integrity, honesty, or work ethic. We require that integrity and high ethical standards are synonymous with our entire workforce.
Message 2: I cannot speak for why a person may have done this. Only he can answer for why he did not comply with the standards we all choose to follow.

Message 3: This individual passed this security screening and what happened subsequent to that only he can answer for.

Environmental issues

When dealing with environmental issues, remember that you are dealing first and foremost with the emotional audience, and everyone is potentially a concerned party. Environmental issues come in many forms. They can include, *inter alia*: noise, fuel spills, harm to animals and wildlife, hazardous materials, etc. A recent example of a company that did not have a strategy to deal with these types of events is BP. The BP event (the oil spill in the Gulf of Mexico) was a tragedy, but it was also an environmental disaster. Remember the the pictures of birds covered in oil? It was a tragedy after the initial tragedy.

The key is to first make yourself part of the process when addressing this type of group or issue.

Message 1: We do work for an operator, but we, like you, are still citizens who are just as upset by things that hurt our environment as you are.
Message 2: We have environmental regulations we must comply with. We must undergo periodic regulatory reviews for our procedures.
Message 3: Although we are part of the aviation industry, we are also under the jurisdiction of other regulators. One of those regulators is the Environmental Protection Agency.

Fuel issues

Environmental concerns relating to fuel usage cover the entire industry. It is not just a matter of what we are doing, but what the industry, of which we are a part of, is doing.

The key is to make yourself a proactive part of the process through your participation with industry working groups. Even though you may not participate in a working group, through your membership in safety trade groups and participation in their conferences you make yourself part of the process.

Message: We in the industry are all concerned with this issue. Our industry has the best international experts working together to determine a solution that is good for the environment while preserving aviation safety.

Wildlife issues

Many times, anything harming wildlife evokes an emotional response. A recent example of this would be the BP disaster in the Gulf of Mexico. Indeed, the public may be more engaged with environmental issues than a tragedy involving

114   *Strategy and messages*

loss of life. Again, you want to make yourself part of the process. Another example would be when an aircraft part inadvertently injures or kills an animal.

Message: We are all concerned with wildlife and we enjoy our natural resources – just like you.

Cultural differences

An organization may not envision dealing with other cultural issues to which they are not accustomed and in which they find themselves involved. The problem with any industry is that one cannot predict the exact variables that may be involved. However, when you are up in the air or on the ground, it is possible that you could come into contact with another organization that has foreign interest. In this rare instance, an organization needs to take into consideration cultural differences. The key is to remember that you are in an industry that is international in nature, and that you adhere to international standards without jeopardizing an investigation. Some cultures expect you to apologize for what occurred. It is extremely important not to say anything that implies guilt. It is not for any organization other than the investigators in the state of occurrence to apportion blame. Lawyers, investigators, families, and regulators all over the world will be listening to everything you say. However, you also do not want to run the risk of offending another culture. How do you accomplish both? Consider the 4-point formula once again, which will educate you on the process through point number 3 (see Chapter 3).

Message: We at [this organization] are always sorry when something like this occurs and we certainly sympathize for any distress this has caused. We are all part of an international industry and investigators from around the world will be making a determination as to what occurred.

Losing face/saving face/gaining face

In some cultures, it is very important to make sure someone does not lose face, or lose respect; instead, help them save face or even gain face. There are ways you can say the same thing, but instead of potentially insulting someone, you can cause them to gain face. Here are examples of how to cause someone to lose face, save face, and then gain face.

Lose face: You are wrong.
Save face: Let me provide some more details that might help clarify the picture.
Gain face: Please forgive me for not being clearer in my communication.

Religious issues

There may be a question about whether a particular airline or country allows customers of a particular religion to fly to their country. Since passports do not indicate a customer's religion, you need to focus on the fact-based response.

Message: All passengers who present the proper documentation and are able to accurately complete the paperwork are welcome to fly any airline they choose.

Chapter summary

1. Summary of audiences

    - Employees
    - External
    - Political
    - Media
    - Community
    - Government
    - Contractor/affiliate/outsourcer
    - Investigators

2. Summary of messages

    - Accident/incident
    - There is always more than one contributing factor
    - Tragedy – humanistic/emotional
    - Ethics – exception, not the rule; one-off situation
    - Engineering/technical/regulatory – nothing is arbitrary; there is proof of everything you do; system of checks, balances and oversight
    - Security/Terrorism/sabotage – law enforcement
    - Community/environmental – "We, too, are members of this community, industry, group, environment"
    - Industry situation – this issue applies to all the industry (or workforce), not just us

    Many of these messages are the basic messages or combinations thereof.

Note

1 Vikram Dodd, Richard Norton-Taylor, and Paul Harris (2010) "Cargo Plane Bomb Found in Britain Was Primed to Blow Up Over US," The Guardian, https://www.theguardian.com/world/2010/nov/10/cargo-plane-bomb-us-alqaida.

6 Controversial questions and answers – situational awareness – *dos* and *don't*s

Help to back out of that corner!

Now that you have the messages of aviation from Chapter 5, you may wonder how you get yourself out of difficult situations. This chapter will describe uncomfortable situations for individuals whom I have had the opportunity to work with throughout the world. Studying how to handle these situations beforehand might have eased the situation for professionals who were confronted by one audience or another, but not necessarily the media. It also contains actual questions that have been asked of individuals in every area of the aviation industry around the world, along with some *do*s and *don't*s. The guidance in these responses is not intended to be directed towards the media but rather any audience. Most of them could be used with community groups, political groups, or internal groups. In Chapter 1 we discussed that communication is a thought process. You have a pool of messages and a pool of techniques. You need to figure out which best serves you for a particular situation.

Leaving a situation

You may find yourself caught in an uncomfortable situation★ with a number of audiences. You may also find yourself addressing an emotional audience over an environmental issue. You may want to remove yourself from a situation like this as quickly as possible, but doing so could fuel the animosity of the emotional audience. You would then be creating the exact situation you are trying to defuse.

The way to avoid this would be to say the following.

> Guidance: I really appreciate the fact that you came to hear me, but I am sure you can understand that our number one priority right now is to get to the bottom of this situation, so I will have to go and assume my responsibilities with this situation as soon as possible. Therefore, please excuse me.

★ The situation does not have to be an accident or incident. It just means a more pressing situation that requires your attention. It could be a personnel or workplace situation.

Don't know the answer

Many times, the answer to a question is "I don't know." This is the truth. There is nothing wrong with saying that. The issue seems to be that people feel like they are not giving a response when they say they don't know. Those who work in a technical industry where people's lives are at stake feel they owe those people a response and therefore search for a response. They sometimes feel that "I don't know" is a non-response. However, the opposite is true.

The worst mistake you can make is to try and accommodate a question with an answer – especially if you do not know the answer. This guidance works with regulators, investigators, family members, and media. Do not be intimidated into saying something because you think it is what another party wants to hear.

> Guidance: I would really like to respond but the truth is I do not know. Since this is a fact- based situation, it would be irresponsible to tell you something that might not be accurate just because I think it is what you want to hear.

Don't know the answer but would like to respond

Guidance: I really do not have that information at my fingertips at this minute, but I would be happy to get back to you with it.

Know the answer, but don't want to respond

There are many reasons why one would not want to respond other than just not wanting to respond. You may be contractually compelled to maintain privacy. There may be a lawsuit pending. There may be another legal reason such as a Privacy Act. This is a difficult situation because to know something and not want to say could imply guilt, cover-up, or unwillingness to cooperate. The result of that could be to fuel the audience's animosity, which could complicate the problem you are trying to avoid. Inside the workplace it could cloud a personnel situation.

Guidance: If there is a legal/investigatory issue:
> It would be irresponsible for me to say anything that might jeopardize the outcome.
> Or
> I would not want to say anything that would compromise the privacy of the individual/case/investigation.
> Or
> The document is still in draft form so for the sake of accuracy you may want to check back with me in 30 days.
> Or
> It is under investigation and would be irresponsible for any of us to say anything that might jeopardize the outcome.

Or

It would be irresponsible to do anything that might prevent this individual from getting a fair day in court.

Guidance: If the situation is protected by a Privacy Act:

All cases are protected by the Privacy Act and I am bound by that.

Another form of this situation would if there is a contract of confidentiality between an organization and a customer. This is a legal issue between the group and a customer as opposed to an investigation or an issue due to national security. You may know something about what is being asked, but, in this case, you would want to stick to the fact-based response concerning only that which you have hands-on working knowledge of, which is your job.

Guidance: *I do not have hands-on working knowledge about that, but would like to stick to a fact-based response about what I do know, and my role, which is the safe operation of an aircraft from point A to point B or the maintenance or supervision of maintenance of the aircraft.*

Realize you are in trouble and want to get out of it

Many times, people go into situations with not just the wrong strategy but no strategy at all. It is not long before they realize they are in a situation and think, "How do I get out of this," or they realize they are completely out of control. This is a very difficult situation to get out of if you have no message. The best thing you can do is not get into that situation in the first place! However, if it is too late for that, then you can try to establish a low level of expertise, close the door, or change the subject, if possible.

Guidance: *That's an important issue★ but what is more important to realize is★★ …*

★ Closing the door
★★ Bridging

Or

I am really not the best person to respond to this★ but in the meantime what I can tell you is★★ …

★ Low level of expertise
★★ Bridging

Sometimes there is no winning – realize it!

Sometimes there is just nothing you can say. There is no amount of facts that are going to change the theme of the story. This is what people call the witch hunt. The character of the audience will determine how you handle things. If it is a politician, you cannot excuse yourself and walk away. You simply must try and politely correct their misunderstanding. If it is with a member of a group comprised of the emotional audience, you need to be careful not to fuel their animosity. It is the emotional audience that motivates the political audience.

Guidance: Let me provide some more details that might help clarify the picture.
Guidance: We, too, utilize the system ourselves. We, too, are employees like you.

Law enforcement vs aviation

An aviation event is a situation where the parties are trying to comply in the name of safety and prevention and an inadvertent violation takes place. A law enforcement event is a situation where parties are trying to circumvent the law. They are investigated by different agencies and you may or may not be a party to the investigation. The objectives may be very different. In an aviation investigation, the objective is not to lay blame but rather to get to the root cause in the name of prevention. In law enforcement, the objective may be to lay blame.

It does not really matter what sort of investigation it is – whether terrorism, dangerous goods, environmental violation, or health and safety. There is very little that you can communicate, and you cannot use any of the aviation messages you might use in an aviation event. You would use the system of checks and balances message with the technique of a low level of expertise. Again, stick to the facts.

Guidance: It is up to the law enforcement officials to determine what took place. What I can tell you is that we are an operator/manufacturer/airport operator, etc. in compliance with all international standards. It would not be responsible to announce what measures we take because we would be alerting those who are trying to circumvent those measures.
Guidance: This is not an aviation event. This is a terrorist event with airplanes used as the weapon.

Personnel event

This could involve a disgruntled employee or whistle-blower, an accusation of sexual harassment, discrimination, or similar. You do not want to say anything to jeopardize any personnel event. To do so could lead to negative workplace consequences. If there is an investigation or lawsuit pending, you cannot say anything to shed light on the outcome, even if you have personal feelings about what is going on. Sometimes these events are the result of a former disgruntled employee, a whistle-blower, or some other situation where you do not feel the situation has merit.

Guidance: I would not want to say anything that might preclude this individual's opportunity to have their day in court. I am sure you would not want to encourage bias in your case if you were in the same situation as this individual.

Ethics situation

This situation could include a pilot who drank alcohol prior to a flight, an employee who was dealing drugs in the workplace, an employee who was stealing parts or money, or other similar events. If they have been discovered and the accusations have been proven true, you cannot deny it. You need to acknowledge that it is the exception, not the rule, and that in "our organization," as in any workplace, there are people whose work habits are not what they should be.

Guidance: This is one person out of a workforce of 100 employees. No organization can wholly regulate integrity, honesty, or work ethic.

Insurance question

Many questions asked may not be comfortable to answer. One of these is in the area of insurance or compensation. The question would be something similar to the following:

- How much money should the relatives get?
- How much compensation will you give to the community for your error?
- How much will the employee receive as a settlement?

The answers to these questions are probably made at a level other than yours. Your objective with a question of this nature should be privacy protection. There is therefore a legitimate reason why you would not disclose this information.

Guidance: First, this will be a decision made at a level other than mine. Second, we recognize that there is no amount of money that can restore these people to the lives they knew before. However, our number one objective is to protect the privacy of these individuals. It would not be for us to communicate this information; we will let them decide to share this if they so choose.

Humanizing vs apologizing

Many aviation-related events are of an emotional nature. Many workplace situations can also be of an emotional nature, especially to the individual affected. There are various audiences who are parties to the events who are looking at them emotionally. What you do not want to do with these audiences is fuel their animosity. However, as there could be pending legal action, attorneys may recommend saying nothing because it may imply guilt if you apologize. On the other hand, you do not want to seem insensitive by saying nothing.

The key is to show humanism in a general sense without accepting specific responsibility for the event.

Guidance: We are always sorry when a situation/event/inconvenience like this occurs.

The causes

There are six main causes or combinations of causes of an aviation event. We discuss each of them below.

Operations

This refers to flight operations and ground operations. Whenever this happens, it is a system failure. There are many stopgaps in place to prevent an event that has operations as a contributing factor. When they all fail, it is considered a system failure.

Guidance: Whenever something like this occurs, there is a system failure.

Engineering (design)

This includes not just the aircraft, but all the systems of the aircraft such as the engines and avionics. It is the operator who is the first to have to defend the equipment. The good thing about aviation is that nothing is arbitrary. It is really up to the regulators to say whether or not an aircraft is safe. They are the ones who certify the designs.

Guidance: Since engineering is not arbitrary, this plane is safe because it is maintained properly. Any aircraft certified by the regulators is safe. Before an aircraft is certified, it is tested and retested by experts from government and industry.

Maintenance

This includes maintenance done by outside organizations. There is a system of checks and balances in maintenance. When work is done, it is signed off by someone, but it is not just one person who is responsible.

Guidance: To answer your first question, "our organization's" maintenance program (or those of our suppliers) is both approved and carefully monitored by the regulators. Scheduled maintenance inspections are specified and this airplane had undergone every required maintenance inspection. I want to underscore that because of the required checks that are built into every maintenance inspection program, it is very unlikely that a single event or error would result in an accident. Whenever something like this occurs, there is always more than one contributing factor.

Air traffic control

If there is an event with air traffic involvement, the operator will have to answer for this because flight operations issues will surface. Air traffic controllers are a unionized group and the union will defend its controllers. They can become very vocal in a situation like this.

Guidance: I cannot speak for what the controllers are saying, but I can tell you that the cause of this event will be determined by the investigators and not the controllers. This conclusion will be based on careful analysis of technical data. I am sure the investigators will have taken into account everything that the parties have to say.

Weather/environment

This concerns not just weather conditions, but many miscellaneous occurrences such as bird strikes, debris on the runway, and similar items.

Guidance: These events are often unpredictable; however, our pilots and crews train in simulators for these types of events.

Security/terrorism

Security/terrorism issues can encompass many factors, including the traditional definition to sabotage, dangerous goods, smuggling, customs, immigration issues, and anything similar. The important thing to remember is that they are law enforcement issues, and/or the exception and not the rule.

Guidance: This was mass murder using airplanes as weapons.
Guidance: This was an individual, one person out of a workforce of X number of people, and no workforce, whether it is in the public or private sector, can wholly regulate honesty, integrity, and work ethic.
Guidance: Law enforcement is an area where we cannot arbitrarily enforce the law. We cannot make an exception for one and not another. Our hope is that we have compliance, but in the event that there is a breakdown, we have enforcement.

Confidentiality

Many organizations in aviation contract or affiliate with other organizations and ultimately may have to answer for their contractual partners.

Guidance: "Our organization" (or the organizations we use) is involved in the business of transporting passengers and cargo from point A to point B and is in a commercial relationship with our client. Beyond that, it is not for any employee of this organization to explain the specifics of a contract. It is only for our employees to explain the business of this organization, which is the safe operation of an aircraft from point A to point B in compliance with regulations in this (their) state and ensuring no one is engaging in any illegal activity. This is the fact-based response an employee should give and maintains the confidentiality required of us by our customer.

Questions in an accident

What can you tell us about the pilot?

We have already discussed that every employee in aviation should always represent the fact-based perspective. This is what should be done in this case. Most press releases and statements provide many details about pilots that are items of curiosity but not necessary to the event, such as where the pilot is from, how many flight hours he/she has, and his/her age. These points imply that a pilot's number of flight hours is an issue. As far as your response goes, that has no point. As far as the facts go, here this is an industry answer: All pilots are certified by the regulators before they can fly. All first officers are certified to operate the aircraft in lieu of the pilot. This is what matters. It does not matter whether they have one hour or 1,000 hours. If the regulators have certified them to operate the aircraft, that is what counts. The downside of pointing out flight hours is that the lay-public sometimes believes that the pilot with fewer hours is less qualified. Then it falls back on a regulator as to why they allow lesser qualified pilots in the cockpit.

In addition, when the question is first asked about the flight crew, an airline employee may not have the exact details. A travel or tour professional certainly would not. Therefore, it is imperative to understand the process and refer to the process.

> Guidance: I do not have all the details at my fingertips at this moment, but I can tell you one thing. All the pilots of this operator, like the pilots of every operator, are certified by the regulators of the country in which they operate and must remain current on their equipment.

This type of aircraft was first manufactured in 1997 and certified by the FAA (or whatever regulator) and many other regulators around the world. All the countries in which this type of aircraft operates have certified this aircraft.

What can you tell us about the aircraft?

Every aircraft or aircraft system is certified by the regulators of the state of manufacture *and* by all the states in which it operates through bilateral agreements. Pilots and mechanics are part of that process.

> Guidance: This aircraft design, like all aircraft, was certified before it went into commercial use by the regulators of the state of manufacture and

by all the regulators where it operates. Its design is based on sound engineering principles.

How old is the aircraft?

This is another aviation question. It does not matter how old the aircraft is, but this question is always asked. The lay-public think that the age of an aircraft could be a contributing factor in an incident, but in reality, it has nothing to do with it.

Guidance: This aircraft is X years old. We took delivery of this particular aircraft in 19XX. This aircraft has had X flights and X cycles (see Chapter 2, section 2.3.1).

When did this aircraft undergo its last maintenance?

You may not know exactly when this particular aircraft underwent its last maintenance, but this will always be a question as it is one of the potential causes of an aviation event. However, all of the aircraft this operator flies are certified airworthy before they leave the ground.

Guidance: I don't have that information at my fingertips at this moment, but I will be happy to check on that and get back to you. In the meantime, I can tell you one thing and that is that all of our aircraft are certified airworthy before they leave the ground.

Do you suspect terrorism?

Terrorism or criminal acts of any kind are law enforcement events, not aviation events. The investigation is not going to be done by the regulators or investigators but rather the state law enforcement officials, local police, or some other law enforcement entity. The operator may be a party to the investigation, but only to provide information to the proper law enforcement officials.

Guidance: It would not be for us as the operator (or travel professional) to make that determination, but we are assisting all the appropriate authorities with any information to aid in their investigation.

What are you doing for the families?

What an operator would be doing for the families would be in their emergency response plan. This could vary depending on whether it is an aviation event, environmental event, etc. It should be the objective to not disclose anything except in a very general way.

Guidance: We are working individually with each family on a case by case basis to meet their individual needs. However, our number one objective is to protect the privacy of these individuals/groups.

Potential controversial questions

Why did you allow this to happen?

This question implies that you "allowed" it to happen. It needs to be defused. The responder needs to take control by not playing into the question.

Guidance: We did not allow it to happen. There are many situations that occur in spite of the best precautions taken.

Why did you kill my loved one?

The question is looking to lay blame. Many times in a tragedy the emotional audience is looking to lay blame. It sometimes cannot be helped.

Guidance: The people died as a result of a tragic accident. It is a terrible thing when a tragedy like this occurs, but they occur for more than one reason. Many people in the industry work very proactively to try and prevent these tragedies, but in spite of all the efforts by the industry, combinations of situations occur that we are unable to prevent.

How much money are you going to give the victims of this accident/incident/environmental event/lawsuit?

In a situation like this the money question always comes up. This is a very uncomfortable question no matter the situation and the best thing to do is prepare for it long in advance. There are a couple of different ways to handle this. It depends on what you want to accomplish with your answer, and that is very important. If you want to close the door, give the response in guidance #1. If you want to take a chance on a follow-up question, give the response in guidance #2.

Guidance #1: We know there is no amount of money that will return these people to the life they knew before, but this is a decision made at a level other than mine. Our number one objective at this moment is to protect the privacy of those relatives who are grieving, so it would not be for us to share. We leave it to them to share whatever details they wish to share. (This response closes the door.)

The clichéd response: I don't think this is the time to be talking about money.

Guidance #2: We comply with the European requirement for an initial amount to handle immediate expenses for survivors. (Caution: You could be asked to expand on the door you just opened.)

Will your employee/employees be fired?

In some cultures, it is standard procedure for executives to resign in disgrace or for employees to lose their jobs over an incident. That is why the question is sometimes asked.

Guidance: We are going to do what is consistent with our employment standards. However, we are not going to jeopardize the outcome of a personnel situation.

Will your managers/executives resign in disgrace?

Guidance: Our executives/managers/company will do what is consistent with the international objective of accident investigation, which means not just treating symptoms but getting to the root cause so that we can put procedures in place to prevent this from happening again.

Do you agree with your politicians?

An individual is in a difficult position when a political persona comes forward and espouses a view or position. It is imperative to be diplomatic while maintaining a fact-based perspective.

Guidance: It is not for "our organization" to agree or disagree with our politicians. Accident investigation is based on facts and on careful analysis of technical data. When the cause of this terrible tragedy has been determiend, we are going to do what is consistent with the international objective of accident investigation [see above answer]. I really cannot speak for what our politicians might have meant, but I can tell you that we are an operator/our client is an operator who is certified and audited by regulators and outside organizations in order to ensure we have the best system of checks and balances possible.

Whose fault is it?

Many cultures and countries consider events, incidents, and accidents crimes from the onset due to their legal systems. It is important to understand the differences if your organization is doing business in other countries.

Guidance: It is not for "our organization" to say whose fault it is. We are just one small part of a larger investigation that is being headed by the investigators of this country. It is they who will announce what caused this tragedy/event. However, we can tell you we know from accident investigation history that there is always more than one contributing factor.

Why do you wait until something happens to fix it?

It is a common accusation in industry. If you can figure it out after the fact, why didn't you figure it out beforehand and prevent it from happening?

Guidance: We do not wait until something happens to fix it. When something like this occurs, it is an event for the industry as a whole. The industry studies these events and the reasons they happen to try and prevent them from happening again. In addition, it tries to predict causes and collaborates (task forces, information sharing, and other means) to find preventative solutions.

What do you have to say about the animals you killed?

Guidance: It is tragic when any animal dies in this manner. In "our organization," we appreciate animals/wildlife of all types. Many of us are animal owners ourselves.

What do you have to say to the community in response to this environmental event?

Guidance: We want to point out that we are also members of this community and it brings distress to all of us to see something like this happen. What we want to focus on as much as possible is the best solution to this problem.

Will your present financial situation affect your reliability?

Guidance: Our financial situation will not affect our reliability. It will only affect our profits. In good times and bad we work with the same business objective in mind. If necessary, what we will do is figure out ways to do more with less, but that is an internal issue.

How will the current economic situation affect your reputation with your customers?

Sometimes a customer is apprehensive to use your organization if they believe it is having financial difficulties. This could be for various reasons such as their misperception that your organization could be cutting corners on safety, offering a lesser product, providing poorer quality service, or the potential of it failing altogether.

Guidance: The current economic situation will affect the entire industry. In a situation like this where no one is getting any more money or people, the only variable over which we have control is the way we do business. That is why we are improving the way we do business in order to deal proactively with this global situation on behalf of our customers without jeopardizing our safe operation.

How do you manage to offer such a low fare? Can you make a profit?

Guidance: Low fares are only one component that allows an organization to be profitable. Low fares can be seen as a win-win benefit of an excellent business plan and a vision for profitability that includes keeping control over the variable of how we do business. This is a result of being able to best utilize our human resources.

I am interested in your financial reports, company information, and anything relating to your marketing strategy. What can you tell me?

Guidance: As a matter of policy, we do not produce information packs. We do this as a tangible way of cutting costs by making our information available on our website. This strategy is consistent with our CEO's business philosophy of keeping costs down and product value up. This also helps with paper reduction, which helps the environment. Anyone interested in information on "our organization" can go to our website and click on the menu item "Reports" to access our financial reports. The website also provides comprehensive information such as press releases, management profile, history, industry overview, etc.

If you are so safe, why did you have a whistle-blower?

There are often people in workplaces who come forward with information about a company or organization, whether it is in the public or private sector. This should not be a surprise. There are various reasons for people doing this.

Guidance: We had a whistle-blower because the aviation industry is an open industry with an effective system of checks and balances. Whistle-blowing is part of that system and we welcome anything that enhances that system.

What do you have to say about crashing into a shopping center?

The "shopping center" is just an example. It can be any type of structure, such as a school, bus stop, etc. It is always going to be a community event. If there are victims involved, it is going to complicate matters. It will expand the questioning. What are you going to do for the victims; for the community?

Guidance: We offer our prayers and sympathies to the people who are suffering because of this terrible tragedy. We are also offering our help and assistance to the victims on an individual basis. As for the community, we are offering our services, planning for a memorial service, and establishing a task force to see what would be most appropriate.

What do you say about your lack of security procedures at some airports?

Just because someone implies that something is true, it does not mean that it is. Airport procedures have a system of checks and balances just like the other parts of the industry and indeed other modes of transportation.

Guidance: I do not know where you got your information, but I can tell you we are in compliance with all international law enforcement authorities. It would be inappropriate to disclose specific details of any airport security procedures. We have not been prohibited from flying into any airport.

Why was one of your pilots (staff) drinking before the flight?

Aviation has very strict rules about alcohol use, and employs random drug and alcohol testing in many parts of the industry around the world. All too often we have heard about personnel being detained at security checkpoints on suspicion of alcohol use.

Guidance: While I cannot speak for what the pilots did, I can say that we have strict prohibitions about alcohol use and flying. We do not allow pilots to drink before a flight period. This individual is one person out of a workforce of approximate 100 and this is the exception, not the rule. Every workforce, whether it is in the public or private sector, has people whose work habits are not what we would like them to be. No one can wholly regulate integrity, honesty, or work ethic.

Isn't it a danger to aviation safety to have pilots who are less experienced?

Some organizations have employees in positions of authority, particularly in regional airlines; however, it is important to understand that technical employees are all certified.

Guidance: It is for the regulators to say whether flight times are enough to ensure the safety of the system. This is an issue for the entire industry and we will certainly comply with what the industry decides.

130   *Controversial questions and answers*

We attend the industry conferences to study this issue and others in a proactive way.

Why don't you train your employees fully before you put them on the job?

In many parts of the industry there is on-the-job training. There is sometimes remedial training in the aftermath of an operational error. These are not negative things but rather positive things.

Guidance: You as a member of the public should appreciate the fact that in the aviation industry our training is never done. We are always looking to update our skills to keep up with technology.

What was your biggest mistake?

This type of question is a manipulation to try and get someone to open a door. If you try to answer a question like this, you could be manipulated into opening a door you did not want to open.

Guidance: In aviation, whenever something occurs, there is always more than one contributing factor. It is considered a system failure when all the stopgaps put in place to prevent a tragedy fail.

What do you do for a job?

Guidance: I fly planes for "this organization."
I do maintenance for "this organization."
I conduct air traffic for "this organization."

Will I lose my job as a result of this event?

An event could be the result of a mistake an employee made in their daily work or a large-scale company-wide concern.

Guidance: "Our organization" has a policy of just culture in place, which means we do not consider a tragedy, incident, or accident to be an event which warrants punitive measures. We therefore do not take punitive actions against any employees.

What is going to happen to me as a result of this event?

An event can be anything that happens in a workplace from the mundane to the worst-case scenario which could affect an employee or cause them concern over their job.

Guidance: "Our organization" is a family and as such we will support each other throughout "the situation." We have trained as a team and each department is dependent on others. We work together to ensure that we maintain continuity throughout to be able to survive "this situation."

What does this mean for business continuity?

Guidance: "Our organization" has a plan to continue with business in spite of any tragedy. We will continue with sales as usual and advertising will resume as normal after an appropriate, respectful time of mourning as stated in our contingency plan and policy. We have trained as a team and each department must work together as a team to support one another in order to maintain the optimum continuity.

What will this do for our sales?

Guidance: We cannot predict what will happen with our sales, but in studying the effects of these events on other organizations and understanding why some organizations have seen better outcomes than others, we have chosen to model our strategies after those organizations that have seen better outcomes.

Dos and *don'ts*

Dos

- Do remain in control of your communication. Go to a situation prepared to deliver your message. If you go into a situation just to answer questions, you can easily be sidetracked and may end up saying something you do not want to say.
- Do teach all incoming employees about aviation and the issues, most importantly safety. After all, that is your business. You have to be able to answer for them.
- Do take control of your message when communicating with anyone.
- Do begin in the hiring phase to educate your employees about your organization's communication strategy and policy to ensure that communication means any audience an employee may be required to interact with due to the reality of their position, whether it be regulators, investigators, customers, passengers, internal audiences through human resources, any type of authorities, or the general public.
- Do have a communication and emergency response plan that meets the reality of the country's specifics, where your business is being conducted, and not just the theory based on a manual that sits on a shelf.
- Do try to communicate in a crisis at the lowest possible level – i.e. when and where the question is asked. If it is asked of a station manager, that is where the response should be given.
- Do have all appropriate people within "our organization" who communicate with various audiences aware of "our organization's" aviation and

safety messages and trained to effectively deliver those messages to their perspective audiences, whether they are regulators, customers, or some other part of the industry.
- Do provide employees of "our organization" with the techniques to help maintain "our organization's" confidentiality when you encounter a situation where it is warranted.

Don'ts

- Don't be manipulated into saying what you think someone wants to hear, whether it is the media, investigators, or attorneys.
- Don't go just to answer questions. Have a message.
- Don't treat communicating as *just* dealing with the media.
- Don't believe that crisis communication refers only to an accident.
- Don't have the wrong people talking about technical issues, otherwise they may end up saying something completely inaccurate or ridiculous, such as, "We never have bird strikes because our planes fly too high." Everyone will then know (including the media) that they are totally inept.
- Don't exclude technical people from communication training or strategies just because your policy says they are not allowed to speak to the media. A policy like that is based on internal politics. Technical people will be required to speak to regulators whether your policy says they are allowed to speak or not. "Our organization's" ability to deal with this audience is only going to be as good as their ability to communicate on "our organization's" behalf.
- Don't think that because you believe headquarters has not "authorized" you to talk, you are relieved of that responsibility. When someone walks up to you and sticks a microphone in your face, *they* have decided that you are the one to talk. They do not care about your corporate policy. They could be recording you on their mobile phone as you speak.
- Don't ever ask an airport official or an authority to paint over the logo on the tail of the plane. You could be accused of trying to tamper with evidence in an investigation.
- Don't think that there is a holding statement. In an aviation event, there is no such thing. Who do you think you are "holding" for in this world of instantaneous communication on social media?
- Do not say, "We will be back with more details as they become available."

English as a second language

English is the international language of aviation. No one in aviation is expected to be a media star. However, because of your position or expertise you may be thrust into a position where you'll need to communicate in the most public of forums. In addition, you may not have any control over the backdrop or location. You may be caught off guard and not dressed in an ideal manner. There is a very important point that needs to be remembered. It is the message that will carry you through. If you do not have a message or the right message, there is no amount of articulation, beautiful clothes, or any nice scenery that will help you. In addition, a lot more is forgiven of those who are not native English speakers compared to those who are.

Chapter summary

1. Situational awareness
2. The causes
3. Questions in an accident
4. Potential controversial questions
5. *Dos* and *don'ts*
6. English as a second language

7 Communication response worksheets – learning to plan it all *before* something happens

Chapter 5 showed the messages and Chapter 6 the questions along with the messages. Chapter 7 now shows how to pre-think a strategy with a template worksheet based on the subject area. It then gives hypothetical questions and both incorrect and correct answers, with an explanation and analysis of each. The questions are based on actual questions people around the world have faced. These scenarios and some responses have all been used/given in training.

Because the worksheet is designed as a "think sheet" when preparing and brainstorming how to communicate on specific issues, it is not just for oral communication but may be used when preparing a written statement. These are not examples, with the idea in mind that the audience would be just the media. The messages would not change as the audiences change.

Communication response worksheet template – how to fill it out

Basic template

Scenario: This section will establish the scenario, such as accident, incident, workplace event, law enforcement event, environmental event, or anything else.

Strategy: This section describes your strategy. For example, a strategy may be to say something but actually say nothing, defer to the experts, expand on a subject, use the 4-point formula, etc.

Messages: Once you decide what your strategy will be, you then determine what your messages are. They should be short. They should not be long paragraphs. After you have your messages, you will know where to go to get your support points.

1. Message
2. Message
3. Message

Support points: As we said in Chapter 2, technique 2 (develop support points), you must have support points to back up your messages because a message alone does not mean much. Once you know what your messages are, you can start researching your support points. The majority of your support points would come from your organization's technical data sheet. You would learn how to develop the technical data sheet in Chapter 2, section 2.3.1.

Message 1:

- Support point 1
- Support point 2

Message 2:

- Support point 1
- Support point 2

Message 3:

- Support point 1
- Support point 2

Opposition questions: Once you have your strategy and messages, you anticipate your questions based on guidance in Chapter 6.

Sample question:
Intended answer:
Sample question:
Intended answer:

Template 1 – accident with deaths and/or injuries

Scenario: Yesterday, ten minutes after takeoff, a plane crashed and there are no survivors. A [local official, investigator, persona] came out publicly and said, "The preliminary information looks like it might have been the same thing that caused an incident with the industry a year ago and if this organization had taken recommendations made at that time, it might have prevented this accident."

Strategy: To use the 4-point formula.
Messages:

1. Humanize
2. Make yourself part of the process.
3. Defer to the experts.
4. Give the facts.

Statement: First of all, on behalf of this organization, let me say that our hearts go out to those who lost a loved one in yesterday's terrible tragedy (point #1).

Our thoughts are also with the families of our own crew and staff who were on that flight or affected by it, as they are like family to us (point #2).

But as an operator, we are just one small part of a larger investigation team headed by the investigators of this country, so for the sake of accuracy you are going to want to speak with them (point #3).

In the meantime, what I can tell you is the following: This was a Boeing/Airbus which was first certified in 19XX/20XX by [regulators]. There are X of them in use in the world today. The flight departed from X en route to Y, etc. (point #4).

Opposition questions follow below:

Question: What do you think about what this [politician, local official, persona] said?
Answer: I can't speak for him/her, but I can tell you that the international accident investigation process is based on careful analysis of technical data. When the report is issued by the investigators at some future date, it will be fact-based [the message of the process of accident investigation].
Question: What do you think caused this crash?
Answer: *As I said before*, when the investigation is complete, which will be sometime from now, it will be the investigators who will be making that announcement – not us.
Question: What is "our organization's" policy for taking safety recommendations?
Answer: *I do not work in the department* that works hands-on with those decisions, but I can tell you *we are certified airworthy prior to departure*.
Question: How much money do you think your victims' relatives should get?
Answer: We at "our organization" recognize that there is *no amount of money* that will return these people to the lives they knew before this tragedy. Also, that will be a *decision made at a level other than mine*. Our *number one objective* here is to *protect the privacy* of these people who are grieving so much, and it would not be for us to infringe on that privacy. We will leave it to them to share what information they choose to share.
Question: Will you be attending your victims' funerals tomorrow?
Answer: *Once again*, our sympathies are with the families of those affected, including the families of our own crew, whose funerals we will certainly be attending. But we weren't personally acquainted with the individuals involved so we wouldn't want to intrude on any of the families' privacy at a time like this. However, we will be attending a memorial service when one is organized.

Analysis of a proactive strategy – template 1 – accident, part 1

This scenario begins as a stated tragedy scenario. Immediately, political input is interjected in the scenario in the form of a local official, politician, or someone else saying that the event may have been prevented had the operator taken advice given a year before. You can tell if the person answering the question has gone there with a message to deliver or has just gone to respond to questions. If an individual has gone just to respond to questions, which is generally what people are trained to do, they will begin to respond to the suggestion that this event could have been prevented. Due to the fact that the investigation has just begun, there is no way to know what may or may not have been a contributing factor to this event. This can also come in the form of "Witnesses have said," "Sources have told us," because that input always plays into large-scale events. There are experts on television offering their analysis of what may or may not have occurred. A responder should close the door on all of that and address the tragedy with the 4-point formula.

When an individual makes the mistake of just going to answer questions, based on my experience with putting people through these scenarios, they begin by trying to respond to the accusations of the politician (meaning a style of communicating as opposed to an elected official). That question/answer exchange could go on for quite some time. Participants who go this route ignore the humanizing that needs to be done and go straight to the speculation as to what the politician may or may not have meant. There can be no positive outcome to engage in an exchange of this nature. A responder would use the message of the process of accident investigation to close this statement down. ("I can't answer for him/them.")

The second part of the scenario brings up one of the most difficult, but always included, issues – that of money. Traditionally, people are put off by this question, as it is uncomfortable and overwhelming to the point of causing their common sense to abandon them. It is necessary before you get into any situation to figure out what you want to do with your answer. A question like this is a negative question and a negative question is designed to make someone look bad, but it is "entertainment." With a question like this, I ask students if they want to expand on this subject, change the subject or close the door on the subject. Of course, they say close the door on the subject. Most of my students do not work hands-on with payouts. Therefore, their objective should be to close the door on the subject. However, just because they say something but actually say nothing, it does not mean that nothing is accomplished with the response. The standard clichéd responses I have people give in workshops are:

- "I don't think now is the time to be talking about money."
- "We will comply with the Geneva Convention."
- "There are state requirements that will dictate what they will get."
- "We will have to wait to see what the insurance says or the investigation if finished." [This could take years.]
- "I suppose it will be up to the lawyers." [You do not want to bring the word lawyer into the scenario.]
- They just make up a number and hope it will satisfy.

Analysis of a reactive strategy – template 1 – accident, part 1

The responses below are evasive, unsympathetic, or reactive open doors.

The last question about the funerals is just a continuation of the scenario in general. It requires the same response as the first part of the scenario, which is the four-point formula. Those who just responded to questions are caught by making up responses because they feel backed into a corner, and are caught off guard by the *nastiness* of another question.

This is a difficult scenario emotionally, but from a communication perspective it is one of the easiest because of the investigation. Here is how the questions go (based on the mistakes made by students over the course of more than thirty years):

Question: What do you think about what this [politician, local official, persona] said?
Answer: He may have meant ... [Student goes on to speculate what the person meant rather than close the door.]
Question: What is your policy on taking recommendations from safety people throughout the world? [Student usually does not have hands-on working knowledge but has already opened the door on this subject from the response above.]

This could continue for as long as the person asking the questions wants it to because the responder has given him/her control.

Question: How much money do you think your victims' relatives should get?
Answer: We'll have to wait until the investigation is finished and see what the insurance companies say.
Question: So, what you are saying is you are going to make these families wait possibly years?
Answer: I don't think now is the time to be speaking about money.
Question: The families think it is the time to talk about money because they don't know how they are going to raise their children from here.

Analysis of a proactive strategy – template 1 – accident, part 2

With something like the money question, your objective should be to close the door and say something but actually say nothing. It's an opportunity to achieve something by humanizing, using a low level of expertise and taking the high road to accomplish something after the negative question – but really saying nothing in terms of providing information. Consider how it would go if you provided a dollar amount.

There is another part to this. There is a requirement in parts of the world for initial payment to family members. Some people may tell you to quote the legal requirement of a government entity. That is certainly a fact to provide, but the problem with it is the possibility of follow-up questions. The follow-up question might be, "Will your organization go beyond what the government requires? Company A paid more." Then you are stuck because the initial question has opened a door. Think about your organization and how many people within your organization you would feel comfortable opening a door to discuss that subject. Do you want to have that as a strategy? If not, then the strategy needs to be to close the door with your response. Perhaps you have one or two people in your organization who can handle the subject. But they would be the exception, not the rule.

Question: How much money do you think your victims' relatives should get?
Answer: $1,000,000.
Question: Is that all you think a life is worth?

Any amount you say will not be enough, so this type of response will be a lose-lose answer. No matter how you respond with a dollar amount, using an insurance maximum, a maximum from the Geneva Convention, or anything else, people will take offense. Some countries may consider it generous because of their culture, but with more litigious cultures it will not work, as you can see from the potential follow-up questions. It is the follow-up questions you want to close the door on.

Question: Will you be attending your victims' funerals tomorrow?
Answer: Yes. [They are generally not attending, but they say this because they are usually there to answer questions only and this is a reactionary response.]
Question: All 200 from 30 countries?
Answer: No but we'll send flowers. [There is no good recovery from a bad first answer here.]

Analysis of a reactive strategy – template 1 – accident, part 2

The 4-point formula is the ultimate safety net to avoid some of the responses that have been seen here. A response like the one above shows a reactionary response. It's impossible for many organizations to attend funerals due to the logistics of a large event, but just following the question above causes the responder to lose the common sense of what takes place in this scenario. That happens when they do not have an advance strategy. Whether or not a responder knows it, because their organization has not been through the experience, there are numerous examples in the world of what does take place. Family members will require there to be a memorial service in the aftermath of a scenario of this nature.

Template 2 – incident, part 1

Scenario: An incident occurred at an airport involving a nose gear collapse. The plane skidded off the runway on takeoff and there was an emergency evacuation with no deaths or injuries. The preliminary information suggests it may be a maintenance error at your headquarters and it is now under investigation.

Strategy: To put the event in perspective and defer to the experts in order to make the external focus go away as quickly as possible so the organization can get to the immediate necessary technical business.

Messages:

1. "Thank goodness no one was injured."
2. "We can credit great actions by our crew."
3. "We are just one part of an investigation."
4. "There is always more than one contributing factor."

Statement: First of all, on behalf of this organization let me say that we are thankful that no one was injured or worse and we can credit the great emergency evacuation training procedures and training followed by our crew. But as you said, the event is under investigation and it would be irresponsible of either of us to do anything that might jeopardize the outcome. However, we do know one thing. Whenever something like this occurs, there is always more than one contributing factor.

Question: It looks like there was a maintenance error. How many incompetent mechanics do you employ?

Answer: None. They are all certified.

Question: In your expert opinion, what could have happened? We know it could only be one of a few things.

Answer: As I said, it is under investigation so for the sake of accuracy you are going to want to check with the investigators. They will be announcing what happened once it has been determined.

Question: The passengers who made the emergency evacuation are very angry for the inconvenience. How do you apologize to them for this?

Answer: We are always sorry when passengers are inconvenienced for any reason but as I said before we are very thankful no one was injured or worse.

Question: When the investigation is finished, and it is determined that your mechanics were a contributing factor do you think the mechanics who made the mistake should be fired?

Answer: At "our organization" we are going to do what is consistent with the international objective of accident investigation. We're not going to treat the symptoms but rather get to the root cause, put procedures in place, and prevent it from happening again.

Analysis of a proactive strategy – template 2 – incident, part 1

The statement puts the scenario in perspective by pointing out that no one was injured or worse and closes the door by saying that it is under investigation.

That is the ultimate safety net here. The general statement for an event is that "there is always more than one contributing factor." "In your expert opinion" asks the responder to speculate when there is still an investigation going on. The commercial element is then brought in, which gives the opportunity for the responder to bring the subject back to the original message of "Thank goodness no one was injured or worse." As far as punitive action goes, in terms of firing an employee, the message to be given is that of the objective of accident investigation.

The objective of responses in an incident scenario is to close the door as quickly as possible and defer to the experts because it goes away quicker than with a crash with deaths and injuries. You do not want to elevate the event to a higher level. The reason these events disappear quicker than an accident is because they are "not entertaining enough." That may sound callous, but it is not as newsy as a large-scale disaster. The key is to separate it out from the kind of event with deaths and/or injuries. You can see the differences in strategies illustrated in Figure 7.1.

The major mistake that organizations make in an incident is that they communicate with the same strategy they would for an accident. They issue the same information in an effort to give details and end up opening doors and elevating the event. They use industry clichés that have been passed along by other organizations preceding them. Here is the basic anatomy of a template notification, given in order, after an incident, and an analysis afterward:

- "We confirm that there was this incident."
- "The aircraft was manufactured by X."
- "We understand that these were the conditions that existed at the time. This particular part appears to have failed."
- "We have informed our investigators."
- "We were carrying this type of load."
- "The captain was this old from X and had this many flight hours. The first officer was this old from X and had this many flight hours."
- "The plane was this old. It had its last maintenance on this date. It was going from point A to point B."
- "Further information will be released as it becomes available."
- "We apologize for any convenience."

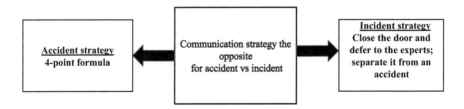

Figure 7.1 Communication strategy difference for an accident vs an incident

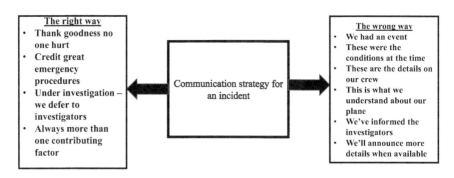

Figure 7.2 Right and wrong communication strategy for an incident

Analysis of the right and wrong strategies. If the objective is to close the door and not elevate the event, then the above information is doing the opposite. In an incident described in the scenario, the details given are irrelevant. The aircraft would have been certified airworthy prior to takeoff, so when it had its last maintenance would not matter. The flight crew were certified on the aircraft and would have had to be current, so it does not matter how old they were, where they were from, or how many flight hours they had. If the events unfolded the way the scenario described, the investigators would have already known. This statement suggests in the minds of the lay-public that the operator is in charge, with the statement the investigators have been informed. It says that further information will be released as it becomes available, which can only be done by the investigators. This also suggests to the lay-public that the operator is in charge. The biggest problem with this is that all the investigators, regulators, safety people, lawyers, and technical aviation people in the world will know that no safety person was involved in the process of developing this communication strategy.

Let's see what happens when the responder is reactionary:

Question: How many incompetent mechanics do you employ?
Answer: All of our mechanics are trained.
Question: Your training must not be very good; otherwise this would not have happened.
Answer: We do not know what happened.
Question: There are not that many things that can cause a nose gear to collapse. We know it can't be an air traffic mistake. Generally speaking, what goes wrong that allows these things to occur?
Answer: Well it could be a lot of things, such as part failure, structures, or other things.
Question: You mean your quality assurance system might have failed?
Answer: It's hard to say.

Question: The passengers are very angry over the inconvenience. How do you apologize?
Answer: We're activating our emergency response center and trying to meet all of their needs.
Question: And how much money does that translate into?

Mistake #1 – "If the media goes away quickly, I did a good job."

> **Countermeasure to mistake #1** – It is a mistake to think the media goes away in this case if you did a good job. That is not always the case. Sometimes it is because it is just not entertaining enough. The key is to close the door and not elevate it into a large-scale event with your strategy.

Analysis of a reactive strategy – template 2 – incident, part 1

As you can see, all the responses that are based on a strategy to just answer questions lead to a negative outcome for the responder. The important thing about mechanics and proving they are competent is to say they are certified. To say they are trained is not enough, as training is also certified. The objective should be to give the strongest response and that would be the one that shows the system of checks and balances. Since training is also certified, the strongest response is to say your mechanics are certified. To respond to "Generally speaking …" about the cause with a strategy to just answer questions leads a person to open doors rather than close them. When commercial issues get into these events, you want to bring the strategy back to the original one to put it into perspective.

Template 2 – incident, no deaths or injuries, part 2

Scenario: An incident occurred with a nose gear collapse. The plane skidded off the runway and almost caused an accident with Japan Airlines. There were two emergency evacuations with no deaths or injuries. The investigation was completed, the final report issued, and it did indicate that "our organization's" maintenance was a contributing factor.
  Strategy: To talk about corrective action and where you are today.
  Messages:

1. "It gives me the opportunity to point out we did not wait for a report to come out."
2. "Any recommendations that affect safety were made immediately."

3. "We are going to do what is consistent with the international objective of accident investigation."

Statement: I'm glad you brought this up because it gives me the opportunity to point out that we did not wait for the report to come out. We went in immediately to review our systems and any changes that needed to be made that might improve safety were made right away. We strive to do what is consistent with the international objective of accident investigation, which is not just treat symptoms but get to the root causes so that we can put procedures in place and prevent it from happening again.

Question: The Japanese are very angry and are demanding the resignations of your top executives. How high up in your organization do you think the resignations should go?
Answer: I can't speak for the Japanese but in "our organization" what we do is consistent with the international objective of accident investigation. We want to put procedures in place in order to prevent this from happening again.
Question: What do you think of the recommendations that were made based on the findings?
Answer: We did not wait until the report came out. Any changes that needed to be put in place that enhanced our safety were done immediately after the incident, so any recommendations that affect safety are things that were already put in place.
Question: Do you think your mechanics who made the mistakes should be fired?
Answer: As I said before, our objective here is consistent with the international objective of accident investigation. We want to be proactive in the name of prevention.

Analysis of a proactive strategy – template 2 – incident, part 2

The presence of the Japanese introduces a cultural issue into the scenario. In some countries, it is part of their culture that executives resign in disgrace over an event of this nature. In some countries, a system of just culture is not practiced and an event may be considered a criminal event, with punitive action being a way of dealing with the issue. If you stick to the process of the objective of accident investigation, you never have to get involved with the parties to it, whether it be the issue of Japanese cultural expectation or the firing of mechanics. See how some of the questions and answers have gone in classes I have conducted with those who go into this situation with a strategy to just respond:

Question: The Japanese are very angry and are demanding the resignations of your top executives. How high up in your organization do you think the resignations should go?
Answer: I do not know. I suppose that is up to our management.

Question: You mean it is a possibility that your executives would resign in disgrace as the Japanese expect?
Answer: That is not how we do things here.
Question: Are you saying you disagree with the Japanese?
Answer: That may be how they do things in their culture, but we don't.
Question: Whose culture is right?

Analysis of a reactive strategy – template 2 – incident, part 2

As you can see, this strategy gets into a cultural back and forth that does not have a positive outcome. If you look at it in terms of firing mechanics, it is the same strategy. One is not going to get into a discussion that discusses a personnel decision in any sort of a public arena.

Template 3 – safety

Scenario: "Our organization" needs to defend/prove its safety.

Strategy: To give a fact-based approach and not meaningless public relations clichés.

Statement: The traveling public should appreciate the fact that the industry never wants to consider itself 100 percent safe. The entire industry is always looking to improve on its past performance because we all consider safety a marathon with no finish line, but we are 100 percent safety-conscious.

Messages:

1. "We [or a product] are certified."
2. "We are part of an intricate industry-wide system of checks and balances."
3. "We have numbers to indicate our records."

Messages with support points:

1. "We are certified."
    a. "We cannot leave the ground unless we are certified airworthy." [operator, travel agent]
    b. "We cannot operate until we have an AOC." [answer for operators, travel agents]
    c. "We are required to be certified by a regulator in the state we manufacture in and every state where we are in use by an operator." [answer for manufacturers, travel agents]
    d. "All pilots, mechanics, and controllers are certified before they are employed and must remain current." [answer for anyone in aviation]
2. "We are part of an intricate industry system of checks and balances."
    a. "Notifying each other when there are issues that affect the industry." [answer for anyone in aviation]

b. "Ongoing task forces with experts in the industry who proactively study issues." [answer for anyone in industry]
c. "The X number of operations/aircraft/functions; how many countries you fly to around the world; or transport X number of people through the system through the system on a daily/monthly/annual basis." [answer for anyone in aviation]
d. "Regulators have the ability to audit foreign regulatory authorities and if they find that those regulators are not doing business according to ICAO standards, they have the ability to downgrade those regulators to a Category 2 status."

Question: Are you safe?
Answer: If you look at the fact that we have X number of operations/aircraft certified or fly to X number of countries on a daily/monthly/annual basis, you would know we were safe.
Question: Are you 100 percent safe?
Answer: You as a member of the traveling public should appreciate the fact that we don't ever want to consider ourselves 100 percent safe because that would be the first sign of complacency. We are always looking to improve on our past performance because to us safety is a marathon with no finish line, but we are 100 percent safety-conscious.
Question: What do you mean by safety-conscious?
Answer: We mean that we take every opportunity to learn from where others made mistakes, so we can take advantage of lessons learned and prevent ourselves from making the same mistakes.

Analysis of a proactive strategy – template 3 – safety

One of the most difficult challenges for the industry is to prove safety. Organizations tend to use meaningless public relations clichés. The key is to give a fact-based message and back it up with support points. Support points do not have to be numbers. They may also be examples. It should be the easiest thing to do, but experience has taught me it is surprisingly the most difficult – and I am referring to the technical people. Imagine how difficult this could be for the commercial side of the industry, including travel professionals.

The most difficult question is whether or not an organization or a product is 100 percent safe. The technique is turning a negative into a positive. The big mistake the industry makes is to base safety on the number of incidents and/or accidents an organization may have had. This is not a measurement of safety but rather a trend. Safety is really based on the cultural mentality of an organization. We will see where it leads to use this strategy, i.e. trying to measure a safety record by numbers of incidents or accidents, with the line of questions and answers below. The problem is that safety cannot be quantified. The expectation of the traveling public is that safety should be 100 percent, but everyone knows that is not possible. However, the perception is that anything less than 100 percent is a negative. The strategy is to turn a negative into a positive with a message of being 100 percent *safety-conscious*. See the common mistakes with a reactionary strategy below:

Question: Are you safe?
Answer: Safety is our number one priority.
Question: Please explain what that means and tell me if you think there is a company who would say something different. Please prove you are safe.
Answer: We have not had any incidents or accidents in many years.
Question: Then the companies who may have had incidents or accidents are less safe than you, based on your standards? Is that what you are saying?
Answer: No. But we are safe. We have Program A, Program B, etc. in place.
Question: Are you 100 percent safe?
Answer: I don't think any organization is 100 percent safe.
Question: OK, so by your own admission you are not 100 percent safe. What percentage of safety are you at? Are you 95 percent safe?

Analysis of a reactive strategy – template 3 – safety

There is a tendency to be accommodating when saying "I don't think any organization can be 100 percent safe." Once you have established that you are not 100 percent safe, you have set yourself up to quantify what you are. The follow-up would be, "OK, if you're not 100 percent safe, what are you? Are you 95 percent? 97 percent?" Then you are stuck. This is a question that cannot be answered, but once you try and accommodate, you have picked a losing strategy as a message as opposed to a winning strategy of turning a negative into a positive.

Template 4 – ethics, part 1

Scenario: Two of your employees were caught selling used aircraft parts on the international black market. There was an investigation. They were found guilty and they are now in jail.

Strategy: To put this in perspective and show that this is the exception and not the rule.

Statement: We are very sorry to hear about this incident, but this is one person out of a workforce of over 400, and no workforce is immune to individuals who a lack of integrity, honesty, or work ethic.

Messages:

1. "This is the exception, not the rule."
2. "The important thing is we caught them."
3. "This shows that our internal system of checks and balances is working."

Messages with support points:

1. "This is the exception, not the rule."
    a. "These are two employees out of a workforce of X number of employees."
    b. "This is not reflective of the ethics of our workforce."
2. "The important thing is that they were caught."
    a. "The episode is behind us."
    b. "No organization can wholly regulate integrity, honesty, or work ethic."
3. "This shows that our internal system of checks and balances is working."
    a. "The important thing is we caught them."
    b. "They are in jail."

Question: How many "crooks" (unethical people) do you employ?
Answer: These are two people out of a workforce of X number of people, so it is the exception, not the rule.
Question: What went wrong with your hiring practices that allowed these people to be hired in the first place?
Answer: Nothing went wrong with our hiring practices. What went wrong is that two individuals exercised a complete lack of integrity, and no workforce, whether it is the public or private sector, can wholly regulate integrity, honesty, or work ethic.
Question: I understand that it took five years to find these people. If they are so unethical, why did it take you five years to find them?
Answer: The point is, we found them.
Question: If there are sellers on the black market, there have to be buyers. If a member of the traveling public were about to board an aircraft that might have one of these parts on it, should they be afraid the plane might crash?
Answer: You may not be aware of this, but modern aircraft are built with not just part redundancy but with system redundancy, and in addition pilots are trained in simulators to compensate for part failure.

Analysis of a proactive strategy – template 4 – ethics, part 1

In an ethics scenario, when it was conclusively determined that the parties in question have committed the act, it cannot be denied. That is when you use numbers to put things into perspective. Also, in an ethics scenario, it is important not to be defensive but rather to remember that it is the exception and not the rule. No one can wholly regulate honesty, integrity, or work ethic. You can put measures in place to prevent this type of event, but there are those who will try and circumvent those measures. That is the problem with law enforcement issues and the question of compliance vs enforcement.

Question: How many crooks do you employ?
Answer: I have no idea. I did not know about these two.
Question: Could you possibly have others you do not know about?
Answer: I do not know.
Question: What went wrong with your hiring practices that allowed these people to be hired in the first place?
Answer: I don't know what went wrong. We will have to investigate and try and improve things.
Question: I understand it took you five years to find them. If they were so unethical, why did it take you five years to find them?
Answer: It took us a long time to uncover what they were doing. Or, they were good at hiding what they did. Also, we have to ensure they are treated fairly.

Analysis of a reactive strategy – template 4 – ethics, part 1

When you try and be accommodating or remain far removed from the event, it opens up questions instead of establishing that this is the exception and not the rule, which is the message of an ethics event. Two individuals should not be allowed to taint an entire workforce.

Unfortunately, it sometimes brings on an investigation of an entire workforce or the entire industry. When one wrong issue in an audit of one operator by the regulator is found, it frequently brings on an audit of the entire industry for the same issue.

Template 4 – ethics, part 2

Scenario: Pilots going through a security checkpoint are caught by security with the scent of alcohol on their breath.

Strategy: To show this is the exception, not the rule, and defend the system of checks and balances. However, some of the questions will be different.

Messages:

1. "This is the exception, not the rule."
    a. "We've been in business for X number of years and we have not had this before."
2. "This is one out of a workforce of X number of people."
    a. "We have a workforce of X number of people."
3. "This employee has chosen to not comply."
    a. "We have employee assistance programs to help people with problems."

Question: Why do you allow drunk pilots to fly?
Answer: We do not allow drunk pilots to fly. This employee chose not to comply with industry standards.
Question: Will this pilot be fired?
Answer: We are not going to say or do anything to jeopardize this employee's opportunity to get a fair hearing in court. However, let me point out what "our organization" does to provide employees with assistance programs for issues such as alcohol …
Question: How many other pilots do you have that may fly drunk?
Answer: "Our organization," like all companies in this industry, complies with mandatory random drug and alcohol testing. However, no company, whether it is in the public or private sector, can regulate a lack of integrity.

Analysis of a proactive strategy – template 4 – ethics, part 2

The key is in the beginning, with the question "Why do you allow drunk pilots to fly?" This question implies that you employ drunks. It is the same type of question as "Why did you allow this to happen?" or "Tell us about something." If your strategy is just going to answer questions, you will be manipulated into responding to this type of question. Of course, when something like this happens, it is the exception and not the rule, and you want to focus on the fact that there are employee assistance programs to help individuals with issues like drugs and alcohol. With specific workforce roles like pilots, employees are going to be unionized in most countries, so you are not going to say anything to jeopardize a labour management situation.

Question: Why do you allow pilots to fly drunk?
Answer: Well, someone was not paying attention.
Question: Will this pilot be fired?
Answer: I have no idea, but should he be?
Question: How many other pilots do you employee who may potentially fly drunk?
Answer: I have no idea.

Analysis of a reactive strategy – template 4 – ethics, part 2

In this response you taint the entire pilot workforce, though the reality of this scenario is it was just one individual's behaviour. You also fuel the animosity of the union, which you do not want to do.

Template 5 – commercial, part 1

Scenario: A passenger has lost a bag and is very angry.
  Strategy: To use the 4-point formula.

Messages:

1. "We are very sorry for the inconvenience."
2. "We fly on this airline as passengers ourselves and I would be upset if my bag were lost."
3. "We are at this time waiting for the outcome of what happened to your luggage."
4. "In the meantime, this is what we can do."

Question: What is the procedure at this point?
Answer: You will copy this number and call, and they will give you updated information. In the meantime, we'd like you to know that we have a very high success rate and we're sure you have nothing to worry about.

Analysis of a proactive strategy – template 5 – commercial, part 1

With this scenario, it is a one on one between an agent and a customer, so it is not a public communication. The main point is to make yourself part of the process because customers look at employees like they aren't customers themselves.

Template 5 – commercial – part 2, codeshare

Scenario: A customer was on a codeshare flight, and upon landing there was an incident with some injuries. Now your customer wants to know why you partner with an unsafe airline.
  Strategy: To show that your codeshare partner is safe.
  Messages:

1. "We are thankful it wasn't worse."
2. "All of our codeshare partners are certified by the regulators of their countries."
3. "Before we enter into an agreement with them we do an analysis of that operator."

Messages with support points:

1. "We are thankful it wasn't worse."
    a. "We are sorry this happened but thankful it was not worse."
    b. "We all fly on codeshare flights ourselves."
2. "All of our codeshare partners are certified by the regulators of their countries."
    a. "In addition, our partners are certified by the regulators of the X countries into which they fly."

b. "This is true for all airlines who codeshare anywhere throughout the world, not just our alliance."
3. "Before we enter into an agreement with them, we do an analysis of that operator."
   a. "Our technical employees do an audit of anyone before we enter into an agreement with them."
   c. "All members of a codeshare relationship must pass an IOSA audit every two years."

Question: Why do you partner with an unsafe airline?
Answer: We do not partner with an unsafe airline. Every airline we partner with is certified by the regulator of their state and of all the countries into which they fly.
Question: You accept them because you want the commercial profit of the expanded routes – isn't that correct?
Answer: No, that is not correct. Before we enter into any agreement our technical people review that operator and make sure they meet our technical standards. In addition, they must pass an IOSA review every two years.

Analysis of a proactive strategy – template 5 – commercial, part 2, codeshare

Often organizations believe that if something happens to a codeshare partner, they do not have to say anything. They believe that it is the codeshare partner's responsibility to do all the talking. The problem is that passengers and customers pay you, buy the ticket from you, and they expect the people who sell the ticket to answer the question. They may expect a tour operator to answer the question. There are industry answers to these questions, because in order to form a business relationship there is a process one must follow.

Question: Why do you codeshare with an unsafe airline?
Answer: It is not for us to answer for another airline.
Question: But you put us [this passenger] on this airline!
Answer: Yes, but it is not our responsibility to answer for it. You'll have to call that airline.

Analysis of a reactive strategy – template 5 – commercial, part 2, codeshare

The responses to this type of question sound defensive, as though you have something to hide regarding your codeshare partner. Putting off a customer fuels their anger. There is no reason not to answer questions about the process of entering into a codeshare relationship. People on the commercial side of an operation should know that process. In addition, tour operators and travel agents who sell the tickets should know the how and the why. They take the money and make the recommendations.

Template 6 – finance

Scenario: Your organization has recently been having financial difficulties. There have been questions asked publicly about various issues related to your financial situation.
    Strategy: To turn a negative into a positive.
    Messages:

1. "Financial issues are not an issue specific to one organization."
   a. "These things happen to the economy in general."
2. "Financial issues are one thing, but the technical side of the industry is bound by a system of checks and balances that govern the entire industry."
   a. "We are still required to comply with a number of government agencies, not just the aviation-related ones."
3. "I can't speak for the rest of the industry, but we comply with international standards." [This can be adapted to travel, airports, air traffic, security.]
   a. "We undergo periodic audits, both internal and external, at regular intervals."

Statement: While financial considerations are always a concern on the business side of an industry, we must always remember that our product is safety and quality, with commercial benefits, and because of that we have an interlocking system of checks and balances with an international network of governments. No one in industry is getting any more money or any more staff, but the demand for safety is as high as ever, so the only variable over which we have control is the way we do business. And on a daily basis, we are looking for ways to improve the way we do business.

Question: Will your current financial situation affect your reliability?
Answer: No. You may not be aware, but we are, as anyone in aviation, still bound to comply with the same standards and certifications regardless of our financial situation.
Question: Will your present financial difficulties affect your business?
Answer: That is difficult to predict, but we are a team, and this is something that is being felt industry-wide. Our competitive spirit is still the same as it always was and that will carry us through.
Question: Will your present financial difficulties affect your safety?

Answer: Not at all. You may not be aware of this, but, if the regulator is aware of an organization with financial challenges, they keep a watchful eye on it to ensure that those difficulties are not an issue. That is the power of checks and balances in the aviation industry.

Analysis of a proactive approach – template 6 – finance

The financial soundness of an organization should have no bearing on the technical side of the business due to the fact that the technical side is highly regulated. Regulators pay close attention to an organization if they think there are financial issues or if they believe a company may be cutting corners to save money. If an organization ties their safety and technical operation to tightening finances, they could be sending up red flags.

There is a tendency to confuse business issues with technical issues. No matter what happens on the business side, it should not affect the technical side of an organization. All aviation organizations are still bound by the same requirements.

Question: Will your current financial situation affect your reliability?
Answer: We hope not. We plan to be able to offer the same on-time service we have in the past.
Question: Will your present financial difficulties affect your business?
Answer: We believe our customers will maintain their loyalty.
Question: Will your present financial difficulties affect your safety?
Answer: We have a reputation for safety and we do not see that our difficulties will have any effect on that.

Analysis of a reactive approach – template 6 – finance

A reactive approach will focus on just the questions, and responders will be drawn into the business side of an organization as opposed to the aviation side. The danger is that the lay-public sometimes think that finances will cause the industry to cut corners on safety.

Template 7 – workplace

Scenario: One of your managers was accused of sexually harassing a former female employee, who quit and claimed she was also denied salary increases. She is now a whistle-blower. People in the workforce say she is a liar. She is suing. Women's rights groups are now picketing your company.

Strategy: To maintain confidentiality and remember it is a lawsuit.
Messages:

1. "We do not speak about unnamed sources."
2. "It's a legal matter."

3. "We comply with EEO requirements."
4. "Regulators will audit us."

Support points:

1. "We do not speak about unnamed sources."
    a. "Anyone can say anything but that does not make it true."
2. "It's a legal matter."
    a. "We do not want to jeopardize this individual's opportunity to get a fair trial."
3. "We comply with all EEO requirements."
    a. "Anyone has the opportunity to file a complaint with the EEO."
    b. "We have X number of females in our management workforce."
4. "Regulators will audit us."
    a. "Anyone can make a complaint to any regulator and they will come in and audit us."
    b. "We go through periodic audits."

Question: What do you have to say about what these sources are claiming?
Answer: I can't speak for who might have said anything. Anyone can say anything. That doesn't make it true. We need to give the investigation [lawsuit] time to gather the facts on behalf of the former employee.

Analysis of a proactive strategy – template 7 – harassment

The key is to not jeopardize the potential court case and fuel the animosity of the interest groups. In this scenario, the adversary could be the women's rights groups, but it could be any interest group. Issues of regulatory compliance are grouped together. First, there is the issue of EEO compliance, and then there is the issue of the whistle-blower complaint. That complaint could be with any regulator, including aviation, environmental, labour, etc. This is a sexual harassment scenario but could also work with discrimination.

Question: What do you think about what your employees are saying?
Answer: They are correct.
Question: So, you are confirming your former employee is a liar?
Answer: Well, I didn't do it, so she must be.

Analysis of a reactive strategy – template 7 – harassment

Once you get away from the facts, you can see you are in trouble. This is the last thing you want to do with a workplace scenario.

Template 8 – technical

Scenario: Technical issues arise over a series of engineering concerns.
 Strategy: When it comes to engineering, nothing is arbitrary.
 Messages:

1. "Nothing is arbitrary."
2. "Everything is tested."
3. "Everything is certified."

Support points:

1. "Nothing is arbitrary."
   a. "Design is based on engineering and science."
   b. "Many years of trial and error go into it."
2. "Many years of testing go into the design before certification is granted."
   a. "Pilots and mechanics are part of the process."
   b. "Pilots train in simulators for part failure."
   c. "Aircraft are designed with not just part redundancy but system redundancy."
3. "Everything is certified."
   a. "By the state of manufacturer."
   b. "Through all states where the planes operate."

Question: How does the traveling public know an aircraft is safe?
Answer: The best minds in the world come together to build what is the latest in technology, based on lessons learned and trial and error.
Question: Will a part failure cause an airplane to crash?
Answer: Modern aircraft are built with not just part redundancy, but entire system redundancy and pilots are trained in simulators to compensate for part failure.
Question: It is true that the older the plane is, the more unsafe it is?
Answer: No. As long as it is certified airworthy, the plane should be technically sound.
Question: What is the safest airplane out there?
Answer: Anything certified.
Question: When something happens, why don't they ground the fleet until they figure out what went wrong, like they did with the Concorde?
Answer: Design and certification is based on sound engineering principles and rarely does it warrant the grounding of an entire fleet.
Question: When a regulator issues an airworthiness directive, why don't they ground a fleet until the directive is completely complied with?
Answer: Rarely is a situation so dire that this occurs.

Analysis of a proactive approach – template 8 – technical

The response should be fact-based with no opinions given. This should be one of the easiest scenarios to strategize because nothing about engineering is arbitrary. All the issues that may be of concern are addressed in the certification process.

Question: How does the traveling public know an aircraft is safe?
Answer: They should have confidence in the experts.
Question: Will a part failure cause an airplane to crash?
Answer: I guess it depends on which part it is.
Question: Is it true that the older a plane is, the more unsafe it is?
Answer: Older aircraft certainly are prone to more airworthiness issues than newer aircraft.
Question: What is the safest plane out there?
Answer: You would have to look at the statistics and the cycles.

Analysis of a reactive strategy – template 8 – technical

These responses are not fact-based responses. They do not show a confidence in the process or the system. The equipment is the most tangible part of the industry and the easiest part of the industry to defend. This is the easiest subject to pre-strategize and you can see the difference between the questions and answers of template 1 and template 2.

Chapter summary

1. Template 1 – accident with deaths and/or injuries – parts 1 and 2
2. Template 2 – incident – parts 1 and 2
3. Template 3 – safety
4. Template 4 – ethics – parts 1 and 2
5. Template 5 – commercial – parts 1 and 2
6. Template 6 – finance
7. Template 7 – workplace
8. Template 8 – technical

8 Sample press statements

The accident and beyond with the how *and* the why

While the following statements can stand as either statements or press releases, they are not meant to be taken verbatim. They have the "guts" of the message, but each case could mandate specific introductions and closings. The key to issuing a statement, whether written or verbal, is to make it sound natural. Remember the various techniques, utilize them to fit the situation, but have the main message, and you will achieve your communication goal. There is no excuse for waiting until something happens to begin preparing what you are going to say. The templates are first given as basics and then repeated, including the techniques, to show which ones were used in the templates. These can be good training tools. All of the support points and data could be obtained from an organization's technical data sheet.

There are various categories of events and each falls under one of the following templates. The subject areas of the templates included in this section and their examples are:

- Event with deaths and/or injuries extending outside of "our organization." This could include, *inter alia*: a crash; mid-air collision; or fire
- Event with deaths and/or injuries limited only to the staff of "our organization."
- Incident with no deaths and/or injuries. This could include, *inter alia*: a ground incursion; an excursion; smoke, fire, emergency landing, in-flight event; or anything necessitating an emergency evacuation.

Statement/release #1 – event with deaths/injuries external

Introduction: This is a template tragedy scenario. There is a standard safety net for handling a tragedy scenario.

"Our organization" or [executive name] [position] is very sad to confirm that a [company tragedy] has occurred with the loss of our aircraft in [location]. We/I would first like to extend, on behalf of this organization, our deepest sympathies to the families, loved ones, and friends of those who perished in this tragedy.

We also extend our sympathies to the families of our own colleagues, who were like family to us.

As an operator, we are just one small part of a larger investigation team that is being headed in this country by [local investigation board] and we are doing everything we can to provide information in this investigation as requested by the team leaders. They will be the ones announcing what the contributing factors to this terrible tragedy were.

What we can tell you at this time is this:

This aircraft was an A320 [example] which was first certified in 1988 by the French and Italian authorities and [how many] other countries around the world through bilateral agreements. The aircraft was en route from [departure location] to [arrival destination]. There were two pilots on board. This plane was [how old] and had its last maintenance on [date]. Our maintenance is conducted by [name of outsourcer], but oversight of all maintenance of our aircraft is followed through by our own staff and we are subject to various audits at any time. All of our aircraft, like all operators, are certified airworthy prior to departure.

While I cannot give you any specifics on our pilot at this time, I can tell you that [refer to your technical data sheet] the average experience level of our pilots is [how many years] and all of our pilots are not only certified by the regulators of this country but must remain current in accordance with civil regulations.

While it would be irresponsible for us to say anything that may jeopardize this investigation, and it is not "our organization" that will be leading this investigation, we refer you to the investigators as they will have the most up-to-date details when they become available.

Explanation of statement/release #1 – event with deaths/injuries external

Humanize (technique #8): "Our organization" or [executive name] [position] is very sad to confirm that a [company tragedy] has occurred with the loss of our aircraft in [location]. We/I would first like to extend, on behalf of this company, our deepest sympathies to the families, loved ones, and friends of those who perished in this tragedy.

Make yourself part of the process (technique #25): We also extend our sympathies to the families of our own colleagues, who were like family to us.

Low level of expertise/defer to the experts (technique #3): As an operator, we are just one small part of a larger investigation team that is being headed in this country by [local investigation board] and we are doing everything we can to provide information in this investigation as requested by the team leaders.

They will be the ones providing additional information and making any announcement when something has been determined.

Bridging/closing the door (technique #10): What we can tell you at this time is this:

160 *Sample press statements*

Give the statistics/facts/use of support points (techniques #6 and #2): This aircraft was an A320 [example] which was first certified in 1988 by the French and Italian authorities and [how many] other countries around the world through bilateral agreements. The aircraft was en route from [departure location] to [arrival destination]. There were two pilots on board. This plane was [how old] and had its last maintenance on [date]. Our maintenance is conducted by [name of maintenance company], but oversight of all maintenance of our aircraft is followed through by our own staff and we are subject to various systems of checks and balances/audits at any time. All of our aircraft, like all operators, are certified airworthy prior to departure.

While I cannot give you any specifics on our pilot at this time, I can tell you that [refer to your technical data sheet] the average experience level of our pilots is [how many years] and all of our pilots are not only certified by the regulators of this country but must remain current in accordance with civil regulations.

While it would be irresponsible for us to say anything that may jeopardize this investigation, and it is not "our organization" [Low level of expertise/defer to the experts – technique #3; Use of statistics/facts – technique #6] that will be leading this investigation, we refer you to the investigators as they will have the most up-to-date details when they become available.

Statement/release #2 – event with deaths/injuries internal

Introduction: The template is the same for a tragedy that is internal, whether one person or 100 people. An organization does not have to wait for something to happen to draft a response.

"Our organization" or [executive name] [position] confirms that one of our aircraft was involved in an event in [location] that resulted in fatalities. In "our organization," like many organizations, every one of our employees is like family to us, so we extend our deepest sympathies to the families of the members of our team.

As an operator, we are just one small part of a larger investigation that is being headed by the investigators of this country, although we are trained to be technical advisors to the investigators, should they need our help. When the outcomes of this tragedy have been determined, it will be the investigators who will be making that announcement.

In the meantime, what we can tell you is this. This aircraft was an A320, which was first certified in 1988 by the French and Italian authorities and is used in many countries throughout the world.

Explanation of statement/release #2 – event with deaths/injuries internal

"Our organization" or [executive name] [position] confirms that one of our aircraft was involved in an event in [location] that resulted in fatalities. In "our organization," like many organizations, every one of our employees is like family to us [Make yourself part of the process – technique #25] and we extend our deepest sympathies to the families of the members of our team [Humanize – technique #8].

As an operator, we are just one small part of a larger investigation that is being headed by the investigators of this country, although we are technical advisors to the investigators, should they need our help. When the outcomes of this tragedy have been determined, it will be the investigators who will be making that announcement. [Low level of expertise/defer to the experts – technique #3].

In the meantime, what we can tell you is this [Use of statistics/facts – technique #6]. This aircraft was an A320, which was first certified in 1988 by the French and Italian authorities and is used in many countries throughout the world.

Statement/release #3 – incident with no deaths or injuries

Introduction: There is a standard template for an incident and the objective is to make it go away as quickly as possible so you can get to the business of the investigation.

On behalf of "our organization" or [executive name] [position] I can confirm that one of our aircraft was involved in an event in [location]. We would first like to say that we are thankful that no passenger, crew, or bystanders were injured or worse and we can give credit for that to the great actions taken by our flight crew.

As an operator, we are just one part of the larger investigation team and therefore will defer to the investigators of this country who will be announcing what did or did not contribute to this event at the end of their investigation. What we can tell you in the meantime is:

- We are [what kind of operator].
- We have been in existence since 1972.
- This aircraft was an A320.
- It is [how old].
- The last maintenance was done on [date], and it was certified airworthy.

Explanation of statement/release #3 – incident with no deaths/injuries

On behalf of "our organization" or [executive name] [position] I can confirm that a Boeing/Airbus aircraft was involved in an event in [location]. We would first like to say that we are thankful that no passenger, crew, or bystanders were injured or worse and we can give credit for that to the great actions taken by our flight crew [Set the tone – technique #15].

As an operator, we are just one part [Low level of expertise/defer to the experts – technique #3] of the larger investigation team, and therefore will defer to the investigators of this country who will be announcing what did or

162   *Sample press statements*

did not contribute to this event at the end of their investigation. What we can tell you in the meantime is [Use of statistics/facts – technique #6]:

- We are [what kind of operator].
- We have been in existence since 1972.
- This aircraft was an A320.
- It is [how old].
- The last maintenance was done on [date], and it was certified airworthy.

Statement/release #4 – security scrutiny

Introduction: A security incident could be any sort of breech. It does not mean that there was a terrorist act. If there was a security breach, it would mean it was a law enforcement event as opposed to an aviation event. It could even be a workplace-related event. The same type of template would be used for each.

On behalf of "our organization" or [executive name] [position] I can confirm that there was an event involving our company that has resulted in a security breech. While it would be irresponsible to disclose details that might prevent those officials working so hard to resolve this situation from doing so, what we can tell you [or "our organization" does confirm] is that "our organization" and its employees are certified according to regulatory standard requirements and complies with all international security standards.

This aircraft was en route from [departure location] to [arrival location]. It was an A320, etc.

Explanation of statement/release #4 – security scrutiny

On behalf of "our organization" or [executive name] [position] I can confirm that there was an event involving our company that has resulted in a security breech. While it would be irresponsible to disclose details that might prevent those officials [Low level of expertise/defer to the experts – technique #3] working so hard to resolve this situation from doing so, what we can tell you [Bridging/closing the door – technique #10] [or "our organization" does confirm] is that "our organization" is certified according to regulatory standard requirements and complies with all international security standards [Have a message – technique #1].

This aircraft was en route from [departure location] to [arrival location]. It was an A320, etc. [Use of statistics/facts – technique #6].

Statement/release #5 – regulatory event

Introduction: Every organization can have a regulator event of one sort or another. It does not have to be an aviation event. It could be an environmental, workplace, or labour incident. It could be local or national.

On behalf of "our organization" or [executive name] [position] I can confirm that the regulatory authority of this country [or other regulatory agency such as our environmental or workplace ministry] is visiting our facility. However, I would also point out that the regulator, along with other regulatory agencies, makes periodic spot audits on all aviation organizations. We always make all records available to the appropriate agency, as well as other organizations, and are happy to do so. It is this system of checks and balances that helps keep the aviation industry the safest transportation system in the world.

For the sake of accuracy, it is going to be the regulator, not our organization, who will ultimately have the information you are looking for.

Explanation of statement/release #5 – regulatory event

On behalf of "our organization or [executive name] [position] I can confirm that the regulatory authority of this country [or other regulatory agency such as our environmental or workplace ministry] is visiting our facility. *However* [Bridging/closing the door – technique #10], I would also point out that the regulator, along with other regulatory agencies, makes *periodic spot audits* on all aviation organizations. We always make all records available to the appropriate agency, as well as other organizations, and are happy to do so. It is this *system of checks and balances* that helps keep the aviation industry the *safest transportation system* [Have a message – technique #1] in the world.

For the sake of accuracy, it is going to be the regulator, not our organization, who will ultimately have the information you are looking for [Develop support points – technique #2].

Statement/release #6 – regulatory fine

Introduction: Any part of the industry that is regulated for not just aviation but environment, labour, health, and energy on a national or local level must be compliant.

On behalf of "our organization" or [executive name] [position] I do confirm that we have received a fine from [regulator, environmental regulator, labour regulator, etc.]. This fine, in the amount of [currency amount], resulted from an audit that was conducted over the course of [time frame, e.g. six months]. We are happy to report that the findings by the [regulatory agency] have already been addressed by "our organization" and do not call into question the safety of our operations. We are always happy to have a regulatory authority who effectively does their job. This audit system is part of a system of checks and balances in the aviation industry and these audits are issued in the name of prevention. That is ultimately our goal.

Explanation of statement/release #6 – regulatory fine

On behalf of "our organization" or [executive name] [position] I do confirm that we have received a fine from [a regulatory authority] [Use of statistics/facts – technique #6]. This fine, in the amount of [currency amount] resulted

164 *Sample press statements*

from an audit that was conducted over the course of [time frame, e.g. six months]. We are happy to report [Turn a negative into a positive – technique #9] that the findings by the [regulatory agency] have already been addressed by "our organization" [Admit mistakes – technique #20] and do not call into question the safety of our operations [Have a message – technique #1]. We are always happy to have a regulatory authority who effectively does their job [Set the tone – technique #15]. This audit system is part of a system of checks and balances in the aviation industry and these audits are issued in the name of prevention [Have a message – technique #1]. That is ultimately our goal.

Statement/release #7 – security/terrorism concern

Version for alliance member: The concern for security is the same for "our organization" and is taken as seriously as it might be for any airline from any country in the world. Because we are members of an international alliance, geographical borders have no influence on the seriousness we place on this issue. It is all the same, no matter the location. In order for us to be a member of that alliance, we must undergo and pass regular alliance audits in addition to meeting all required international standards we are required to meet to fly into these countries. Our audits are not just one-time audits; they are recurrent. We do this for our passengers and we understand everyone's concerns as we are passengers on this airline ourselves.

Version for non-alliance member: The concern for security is the same for "our organization" and is taken as seriously as it might be for any airline from any country in the world. Although we are not members of an international alliance, geographical borders have great influence on the seriousness we place on this issue. It is all the same, no matter the location. As an operator, we must pass regular audits that meet all required international standards in order to fly into these countries. Our audits are not just one-time audits; they are recurrent. We do this for our passengers and we understand everyone's concerns as we are passengers on this airline ourselves.

Explanation of statement/release #7 – security/terrorism concern

Version for alliance member: The concern for security is the same for "our partner" and is taken as seriously as it might be for any airline from any country in the world [Make them part of the process – technique #24]. Because we are members of an international alliance [Establish credibility – technique #4], geographical borders have no influence on the seriousness we place on this issue. It is all the same, no matter the location. In order for us to be a member of that alliance, we must undergo and pass regular alliance audits in addition to meeting all required international standards we are required to meet to fly into these countries [Give the facts – technique #6]. Our audits are not just one-time audits; they are recurrent [Use of statistics/facts – technique #6]. We do this for our passengers and we understand everyone's concerns as we are passengers on this airline ourselves [Make yourself part of the process – technique #25].

Version for non-alliance member: The concern for security is the same for "our organization" and is taken as seriously as it might be for any airline from any country in the world [Make yourself part of the process – technique #25]. Although we are not members of an international alliance, geographical borders have great influence on the seriousness we place on this issue. It is all the same, no matter the location. As an operator, we must pass regular audits that meet all required international standards in order to fly into these countries. Our audits are not just one-time audits; they are recurrent. We do this for our passengers and we understand everyone's concerns as we are passengers on this airline ourselves.

Statement/release #8 – safety issue

Introduction: Safety is not arbitrary. There are numerous systems of checks and balances in aviation that help to ensure the safety of the system. This could be regarding an audit, inspection or an incident. It could be a workplace event or involve an airport, air traffic facility, or any other operation.

I am here as the [state position/responsibility] representative of "our organization" and I'm happy to report that even though we are under scrutiny for [a particular issue], we are glad that there were no injuries as a result of this issue. The investigators/regulators are leading the investigation into this and we are doing what they ask to assist them in getting to the bottom of this. We look forward to their conclusions. In the meantime, whether or not there are any findings, we are going to carry out an internal audit of all of our systems, which we do on a regular basis as a matter of standard practice.

"Our organization" is an operator that engages in commercial operations and our employees come under the jurisdiction of the regulators of this country. In addition, we are compliant with all workplace and environmental regulatory requirements.

Explanation of statement/release #8 – safety issue

I am here as the [state position/responsibility] representative of "our organization" and I am *happy to report* [Take the high road – technique #7] that even though we are under scrutiny for [a particular issue], we are *glad that* [Set the tone – technique #15] there were no injuries as a result of this issue. The investigators/regulators are leading the investigation into this and we are doing what they ask to assist them in getting to the bottom of this [Make yourself part of the process – technique #25]. We look forward to their conclusions [Take the high road – technique #7]. *In the meantime* [Bridging/closing the door – technique #10], whether or not there are any findings, we are going to carry out an internal audit of all of our systems, which we do on a regular basis as a matter of standard practice [Have a message – technique #1].

"Our organization" is an operator that engages in commercial operations and our employees come under the jurisdiction of the regulators of this country [Develop support points – technique #2]. In addition, we are compliant with all environmental and workplace requirements.

Statement/release #9 – workplace event

Introduction: Any workplace can have a workplace event and require this guidance. This goes beyond the aviation industry.

I am here on behalf of "our organization." I am [name and position]. Because of the sensitive nature of the situation, it would not be fair to the employees involved to say anything that might jeopardize their position further. However, it is always a sad situation when something of this nature occurs and we are doing everything we can as an organization to help the affected parties. We look forward to seeing our employee/former employee having their day in court.

Explanation of statement/release #9 – workplace event

I am here on behalf of "our organization." I am [name and position]. Because of the sensitive nature of the situation, *it would not be fair* [Take the high road – technique #7] to the employees involved to say anything that might jeopardize their position further. However, it is always a *sad situation* [Humanize – technique #8] when something of this nature occurs and we are doing everything we can *as an organization* [Make yourself part of the process – technique #25] to help the affected parties. We look forward to seeing our employee/former employee having their day in court.

Statement/release #10 – loss of aircraft component

On behalf of "our organization," I want to say that although this unfortunate event occurred, we are thankful no one was injured, or worse. We are providing information as requested by the investigators of this country and they will be making a future determination as to what the cause of this event was.

In the meantime, what I can tell you is that all of our maintenance has internal and external oversight. We do regular in-house audits and, in addition to the regulators of this country, we organize outside organizations to come in and audit us on a regular basis. Our pilots, like all of the industry, train in simulators to deal with these types of scenarios.

Explanation of statement/release #10 – loss of aircraft component

On behalf of "our organization," I want to say that although this unfortunate event occurred, we are *thankful no one was injured, or worse* [Have a message – technique #1]. We are providing information as requested by the investigators of this country and *they* [Low level of expertise/defer to the experts – technique #3] will be making a future determination as to what the cause of this event was.

In the meantime, what we can tell you is [Bridging/closing the door – technique #10] that all our maintenance has internal and external oversight. We do regular in-house audits and, in addition to the regulators of this country, we organize outside organizations to come in and audit us on a regular basis. Our *pilots, like all industry pilots, train* in simulators [Have a message – technique #1] to deal with these types of scenarios.

Statement/release #11 – inaccurate or speculative statement/political posturing by outside party ("Witness has said" or "Sources have told us")

Introduction: In many controversial situations a "persona" may come forward immediately and say something that may or may not be true. It is the fact-based audience who has to answer for this (see Chapter 1). In the case of an investigation/worst-case scenario, there will often be witnesses who provide input. This could apply to any workforce. It could be a lawsuit or a situation involving a whistle-blower.

On behalf of "our organization," I do not have any idea to what [this outside party] is referring. I can only tell you that the accident investigation/judicial process is a long process based on careful analysis of technical data/facts. When the report is issued by the investigators/courts at some future point, it will be fact-based.

In the meantime, this is what I can tell you. "Our organization" [which could be an airport, airline, manufacturer, etc.] has been in business [how many years], we have [how many] operations on an annual basis, etc.

If the statement is in response to "Witnesses have said" or "Sources have told us," then add this:

> And I am sure all witnesses' accounts will have been taken into consideration by the investigators.

Explanation of statement/release #11 – inaccurate or speculative statement/political posturing by outside party ("Witness has said" or "Sources have told us")

On behalf of "our organization," I *do not have any idea* [Low level of expertise/defer to the experts – technique #3] to what [this outside party] is referring. I can only tell you that *the accident investigation/judicial process* [Message of the process accident investigation] is a long process based on careful analysis of technical data/facts. When the report is issued by the investigators at some future point, it will be fact-based.

168 *Sample press statements*

In the meantime, this is what I can tell you [Have a message – technique #1]. "Our organization" [which could be an airport, airline, manufacturer, etc.] has been in business [how many years] [Use of statistics/facts – technique #6], we have [how many] operations on an annual basis, etc.

Statement/release #12 – environmental event (non-living)

Introduction: Environmental events happen to all industries every day. They may be living or non-living. Examples of non-living would be a brush fire while fueling, the aftermath of the Gulf oil spill, and a pipe leak. Examples of a living event would be a pet dying in transport, a part falling on a pasture and killing livestock, and an animal on a runway.

I am here on behalf of every employee of "our organization," extending our concern and regret over this environmental [accident, mistake, disaster, tragedy].

We are all citizens of [this/a] community, and as citizens we have the same concerns as you about our environment. At "our organization," preservation of the environment is one of our key objectives. This affects all of us, not just as employees, but as citizens.

While we are not conducting the investigation, we are providing whatever information we can.

Explanation of statement/release #12 – environmental event (non-living)

I am here on behalf of every employee of "our organization," extending *our concern and regret* [Humanize – technique #8] over this environmental [accident, mistake, disaster, tragedy].

We are *all citizens* [Make them part of the process – technique #24] of [this/a] community, and as citizens we have the same concerns as you do [Make yourself part of the process – technique #25] over our environment. At "our organization," preservation of the environment is one of our key objectives and this affects all of us, not just as employees, but as citizens.

While we are not conducting the investigation [Low level of expertise/defer to the experts – technique #3], we are providing whatever information we can.

Statement/release #13 – environmental event (living)

Case 1 – personal pet

On behalf of "our organization," let me first extend our sympathies to the family who lost their beloved pet. We recognize that pets are part of a family.

Many of us have pets ourselves, and we consider our pets to be part of our families.

When this investigation is over, and the investigators have issued their report, I am sure there will be answers as to why this occurred.

We are doing everything we can to cooperate with authorities in order to get to the bottom of this situation as soon as possible to ensure that it does not happen again.

Explanation of statement/release #13, case 1 – personal pet

On behalf of "our organization," let me first extend *our sympathies* [Humanize – technique #8] to the family who lost their beloved pet. We recognize that pets are part of a family.

Many of us *have pets ourselves* [Make yourself part of the process – technique #25], and we consider our pets to be part of our families.

When this investigation is over, and the investigators have issued their report, I am sure there will be answers as to why this occurred [Low level of expertise/defer to the experts – technique #3].

Case 2 – general livestock

On behalf of "our organization," let me say how sorry we are to have this event with wildlife/prized animals involvement occur. No one wants to see wildlife/prized animals come to any harm for whatever reason.

At "our organization," protection and preservation of the environment and animals of all types is one of our primary objectives.

When this investigation is over, and the investigators have issued their report, I am sure there will be answers as to why this occurred.

Explanation of statement/release #13, case 2 – livestock

On behalf of "our organization," let me say how *sorry* [Humanize – technique #8] we are to have this event with wildlife involvement occur. *No one* [Make yourself part of the process – technique #25] wants to see wildlife/prized animals come to any harm for whatever reason.

At "our organization," protection and preservation of the environment and animals of all types is one of our primary objectives [Have a message – technique #1].

When this investigation is over, and the investigators have issued their report, I am sure there will be answers as to why this occurred [Low level of expertise/defer to the experts – technique #3].

Statement/release #14 – something happened, and it was your fault

Introduction: Things happen, and your organization may end up being a contributing factor to it happening. For that you could be required to respond to some audiences.

On behalf of "our organization," let me say we are thankful to see the report by the [regulators of various agencies] completed and happy to be a part of the solution. The issues that were identified in the report were issues identified by us at the onset of this process and the recommendations made today were put into place by us shortly after the process began.

Here is where we are today with the changes we put in place a number of months ago.

Explanation of statement/release #14 – something happened, and it was your fault

On behalf of "our organization," let me say *we are thankful* [Set the tone – technique #15] to see the report by the [regulators of various agencies] completed and happy to be a part of the solution [Take the high road – technique #7]. The issues that were identified in the report were identified by us at the onset of this process and the recommendations made today *were put into place* [Admit mistakes – technique #20] by us shortly after the process began.

Here is where we are today [Admit mistakes – technique #20] with the changes we put in place a number of months ago.

Statement/release #15 – ethics scenario

Introduction: Every workplace, whether it is in the public or private sector, can experience ethics scenarios. This is not an issue limited to the aviation industry.

We regret that an employee was discovered engaging in [unethical behaviour]. This was one [or another small number] employee out of a workforce of over [how many] employees. The important point is that it was discovered, so we are happy that our internal system of quality assurance worked effectively.

It is never a good thing for a workforce to discover this behaviour among its employees; however, there is no organization in the world that has the ability to wholly regulate integrity, honesty, or work ethic.

The important thing is we found it, dealt with it, and it is in the past.

Explanation of statement/release #15 – ethics scenario

We regret that an employee was discovered engaging in [unethical behaviour]. This was one [or another small number] employee out of a workforce of *over* [how many] *employees* [Use of statistics – technique #6]. The important point is that it was discovered [Negative into a positive – technique #9], so we are happy our internal system of quality assurance worked effectively [Admit mistakes – technique #20].

It is never a good thing for any company to discover this type of behaviour among its employees; however, there is *no organization* [Make yourself part of the process – technique #25] in the world that has the ability to wholly *regulate* [Have a message – technique #1] *integrity, honesty, or work ethic.*

The important thing is we found it, dealt with it, and it is in the past [Admit mistakes – technique #20].

Statement/release #16 – whistle-blower

Introduction: Any organization can have a whistle-blower. This is not an issue specific to the aviation industry or to the private sector. It could also apply to government.

We at "our organization" are aware of these charges. While it would be irresponsible of us to say anything that would hinder the investigation, we can say that this is the positive part about the aviation industry which helps to keep it safe. It is the interlocking system of checks and balances which allows for everyone to share the responsibility of ensuring that the system is safe.

We can also tell you that "our organization" works with our regulatory authorities and undergoes periodic, required audits, so our regulators do not wait for this type of information to be brought to them. They constantly have us under scrutiny. The good thing about this industry is that we would not be operating today if we were not conducting business according to the highest safety standards.

In addition to regular checks by our own authorities, we submit to audits by outside organizations. Potentially, "our organization" flies to [how many] countries, and if we were not a safe operator, we would not be allowed to do so.

Explanation of statement/release #16 – whistle-blower

We at "our organization" are aware of these charges. While it would be irresponsible *of us* [Make yourself part of the process – technique #25] to say anything that would hinder the investigation, we can say that this is the positive part about the aviation industry that helps *keep it safe* [Have a message – technique #1]. It is the *interlocking system of checks and balances.* [Develop support points – technique #2] which allows for everyone to share [Make them part of the process – technique #24] in the responsibility of ensuring that the system is safe.

We can also tell you that "our organization" works with our regulatory authorities and undergoes periodic, required audits, *so our regulators do not wait for this type of information to be brought to them* [Turn a negative into a positive – technique #9]. They constantly have us under scrutiny. The good thing about this industry is that we would not be operating today if we were not conducting business according to the highest safety standards [Setting the tone – technique #15].

In addition to regular checks by our own authorities, we submit to audits by outside organizations. Potentially, "our organization" flies to [how many] countries [Use of statistics/facts – technique #6], and if we were not a *safe* operator, we would not be allowed to do so [Develop support points – technique #2].

172   Sample press statements

Statement/release #17 – financial troubles

Introduction: Any employee in any organization could have to answer for perceived financial troubles, cutbacks, or layoffs in an organization. There are perceptions that financial troubles could ultimately have an impact on safety and service.

"Our organization" has confirmed that they have recently experienced a drop in profits. This is due to the overall global economy and is proportional to what the entire industry is experiencing.

Fortunately for the aviation industry, economic challenges do not translate into safety concerns, as we are still required to meet the same regulatory standards at all times and the industry has a great system of checks and balances and oversight to keep the industry safe.

The concern in any market such as this is our continued customer reliability standards, and we are working individually with our customer to ensure that we continue to meet their specific needs.

Explanation of statement/release #17 – financial troubles

"Our organization" has confirmed that they have recently experienced a drop in profits. This is due to the overall global economy and is proportional to what *the entire industry* [Make them part of the process – technique #24] is experiencing.

Fortunately for the aviation industry, economic challenges *do not translate into safety* [Have a message – technique #1] concerns, as we are still required to meet the same regulatory standards at all times and the industry has a *great system of checks and balances and oversight* [Develop support points – technique #2] to keep the industry safe.

The concern in any market such as this is our *continued customer reliability* [Set the tone – technique #15] standards, and we are working individually with our customer to ensure that we continue to meet their specific needs.

Statement/release #18 – defense of a regulator (if a regulator is in a Category 2 status)

Introduction: This is for a regulator in a country that has received a downgrade to a Category 2 status from the FAA. The industry of the country may have to defend the safety integrity of the entire industry as a result.

It is unfortunate that "our regulator" has received a Category 2 status downgrade, but for the traveling public it is this international system of checks and balances that protects the safety of the system of which we are all a part. It does not mean that the system is unsafe but only that our regulator is working closely with their international regulatory counterparts to address whatever items need to be enhanced.

As far as "our state" is concerned, our operation is unaffected, and we continue our operation as usual. We continue to be audited as normal by not just our regulators but our partners and the regulators in all the environments in which we operate.

Explanation of statement/release #18 – defense of a regulator (if a regulator is in a Category 2 status)

It is unfortunate that "our regulator" has received a Category 2 status downgrade, but for the traveling public it is this international system of checks and balances that protects the safety of the system of which we are all a part [Take the high road – technique #7]. It does not mean that the system is unsafe but only that our regulator is working closely with their international regulatory counterparts to address whatever items need to be enhanced [Turn a negative into a positive – technique #9].

As far as "our state" is concerned, our operation is unaffected, and we continue our operation as usual [Take the high road – technique #7]. We continue to be audited as normal by not just our regulators but our partners and regulators in all the environments in which we operate [Develop support points – technique #2].

Statement/release #19 – misperception that our industry is "third world"

Introduction: Some organizations are from countries that are located in controversial areas of the world. Although the aviation industry is governed by international standards, there could be misperceptions an operation would need to respond to.

We at "our organization" need to correct a misunderstanding about "our organization." Geographical location of an operation does not necessarily determine its safety. "Our organization" flies into all areas of the world and in order to do so we must be certified to do so by the regulators of all the countries we fly into. When we fly into those countries, it allows their regulators to conduct ramp checks on our flights at their will.

In addition, we are certified to carry out maintenance work on foreign-registered aircraft, and in order to do so we must be certified by the regulators of the countries whose aircraft we are certified to work on.

Explanation of statement/release #19 – misperception that our industry is "third world"

We at "our organization" need to correct a misunderstanding about "our organization." Geographical location of an operation does not necessarily determine its safety [Defuse negative words or inaccurate statements – technique #11]. "Our organization" flies into all areas of the world and in order to do so we must be certified to do so by the regulators of all the countries we fly into [Develop support points – technique #2]. When we fly into those countries, it allows their regulators to conduct ramp checks on our flights at their will.

In addition, we are certified to do maintenance work on foreign-registered aircraft, and in order to do so we must be certified by the regulators of the countries whose aircraft we are certified to work on [Develop support points – technique #2].

How to educate

Educating

This is the very straightforward type of situation, which is presented in a question and answer format. It may be regulators, investigators, or lawyers. The important thing is to have your messages and stick to them, while always backing them up with facts. This is the type of situation where the people asking the questions may not know what they are looking for. They may throw out subjects to see what you do with those subjects. They are looking for you to open up doors.

Example

Question: What was the mood of the pilot community at the time?

Someone asking a question like this is trying to bait you. They are trying to get you to open up a door. This is an example of an investigator asking questions of a regulator. A regulator cannot possibly know what the mood of a pilot or pilot community is without speculating.

Objective: Closing the door
Answer: I cannot speculate on what other pilots may have been thinking.

This is a fact-based, non-speculative response that closes the door.

Objective: Expanding on the subject
Answer: Well, I have been told that the pilots were angry because they weren't getting a raise and shorter hours.

This response opens up a door and is based on secondhand information at best.

Objective: Changing the subject.
Answer: I was not a pilot for that company, so I can't begin to speculate, but what I can tell you is this: Regardless of their mood, from my oversight, these pilots were conducting themselves according to regulations.

This response closes the door and then gives a fact-based response.

Objective: Correcting a misunderstanding.
Answer: Let me clarify something. I work for the regulator so if you want a fact-based response to your question, you need to talk to the chief pilot of that organization.

This response closes the door and provides an alternative person to speak to. It tells the person asking the question that the interviewee knows what he/she is trying to do.

Conclusion

Templates are just for guidance. They are not to be take verbatim. If they seem to be written for an operator, they can easily be adapted for a regulator, manufacturer, or another part of the industry. A tragedy scenario can be adapted to any form of a tragedy, whether it is in respect to 200 fatalities or the death of a single person. Regardless, it is the same template.

Chapter summary

1. Sample press statements – templates with explanations
    - Statement/release #1 – event with deaths/injuries external
    - Statement/release #2 – event with deaths/injuries internal
    - Statement/release #3 – incident with no deaths or injuries
    - Statement/release #4 – security scrutiny
    - Statement/release #5 – regulatory event
    - Statement/release #6 – regulatory fine
    - Statement/release #7 – security/terrorism concern
    - Statement/release #8 – safety issue
    - Statement/release #9 – workplace event
    - Statement/release #10 – loss of aircraft component
    - Statement/release #11 – inaccurate or speculative statement/political posturing by outside party ("Witness has said" or "Sources have told us")
    - Statement/release #12 – environmental event (non-living)
    - Statement/release #13 – environmental event (living)
    - Statement/release #14 – something happened, and it was your fault
    - Statement/release #15 – ethics scenario
    - Statement/release #16 – whistle-blower
    - Statement/release #17 – financial troubles
    - Statement/release #18 – defense of a regulator (if a regulator is in a Category 2 status)
    - Statement/release #19 – misperception that our industry is "third world"
2. How to educate

9 Social media and aviation communication

When and when not?

It is perhaps fitting that the first on-scene report on the Asiana airplane crash came not from a traditional correspondent but via social media in the form of a Samsung executive and one-time online media boss who was also a passenger on the ill-fated plane. In his first tweet, David Eun, the former president of AOL Media and Studios, calmly laid out the dramatic story for a quickly growing worldwide audience:

"I just crash landed at SFO. Tail ripped off. Most everyone seems fine. I'm ok. Surreal …"

He was even cool and collected enough to include a photo of the smoking Boeing 777 and even the handle for San Francisco International Airport (@flySFO), on whose runway he stood.

The tweet quickly ricocheted across the social media landscape, getting retweeted 32,700 times. His 2,000 pre-crash Twitter following soared almost tenfold within hours.[1]

The above event was shot as it occurred on a cell phone from the window of another aircraft. You can't get any faster than that! This chapter covers the basics of social media and then compares two examples of how companies used social media in the aftermath of large-scale and small-scale tragedies and how social media was used external to them in the aftermath of their tragedies. The two companies are BP in the aftermath of the Gulf oil spill and United Airlines in the aftermath of a passenger's pet dog dying after being placed in an overhead bin during a flight at the insistence of a flight attendant. This is not a comparison of actual events but rather the communication and social media aspects of the events, and I am not suggesting that the Gulf oil spill and the death of a passenger's dog are in any way comparable as events in and of themselves. I did not work hands-on with either BP or United on either of these cases.

Forms of social media

Social media is defined as "forms of electronic communication (such as websites for social networking and microblogging) through which users create online communities to share information, ideas, personal messages, and other content (such as videos)."[2] By 2019 it is estimated there will be 2.77 billon social media users worldwide.[3] Because of social media, events are broadcast as they occur and every passenger, customer, or passer-by can become a journalist.

This is the way it is today. Eyewitness reports play an important role in anything that happens in aviation. Social media reports share their views and videos before mainstream media and investigators reach the scene. Everyone is now a reporter. Social media videos many times play an important role in accident investigation, and as everyone now knows it is changing the way we get our news. Therefore, any employee can end up on television, YouTube, or another online platform, through no fault of their own, at any time. A message posted on a social media account can travel around the whole world within seconds. Social media is like a window on an event. This makes it even more important for organizations to have a strategy where all employees know the messages of aviation. That way if they are caught off guard on someone's cell phone and end up on a social media site, at least they will know a little about the subject or the process. According to Smart Insights, there are 3.196 billion social media users in the world, up 13 percent year on year.[4] Since this is not a book on how to write either a communication plan or an emergency response plan, it is not going to focus on how to use social media but rather touch on it in a general sense.

Mistake # 1 – Social media is a new phenomenon.

While social media is a relatively new phenomenon, the concept of information coming out as soon as something happens is not. It's the "as soon as" that is the variable here.

You will recall that the example of Swissair Flight 111 was used in Chapter 1 to illustrate that even as early as 1998 experts were appearing within an hour of an event occurring to speculate on what caused an event. Many lessons on crisis communication talk about the "golden hour" and instruct readers to "draft a holding statement" to share on social media, among other audiences. In today's world, things are broadcast as they occur, but a policy in the late 1990s that required an organization's representative (who might have been positioned half a world away) to seek permission to respond to a query would have been equally absurd. Not only does an organization not have time to seek permission in today's world, but they do not even have time to sit down and draft a response. What to say in any given situation is provided in the templates, with a few customizations.

This isn't a chapter on how to use social media but rather one that discusses its impacts.

> **Countermeasure to mistake #1** – Recognize that a successful strategy is one that needs messages and empowerment prior to an event to communicate on the spot.

Any organization whose strategy requires employees to wait for headquarters to approve their response to a query is not aware of the reality of today's world. The world can instantaneously have more information than the company. How can "headquarters" approve a response when the information is already out there due to cell phones posting on Instagram, YouTube, and elsewhere? An unfortunate employee is then left hanging, waiting for approval. The reality of today's world is that due to social media organizations are not in control of who becomes a spokesperson (see Chapter 3, mistakes #3 and #4, definition of spokesperson). Communication and messages are many times delivered in short sound bites on social media. For example, if you consider the 20-second rule on traditional media (Chapter 2, technique #19), you never want to run on with your message, but on Twitter you only have 140 characters. If an organization wants to have a plan that meets reality, they have to include social media in their plan.

In order to have a communication strategy that meets reality, an organization's messages for social media for particular events need to be consistent with traditional media and be in place prior to anything ever occurring. Those who may be in a position to deliver them need to be empowered to do so without fear of punitive action. Organizations can talk about social media all they want, but if this one issue is not part of the plan, they do not have a strategy that effectively takes the reality of social media into account. In addition, outsiders using social media can have a stronger impact on your organization than your own social media program, as we will see in the examples of BP and United Airlines below.

It is easy to have a strategy for social media in the commercial area of an organization. It is proactive, and you can reach a large number of people to generate an activity or reaction.

There are many forms of social media to use. In times of crisis, some may be used proactively, some reactively, some for notification. Social media can alleviate the pressure on an operator or airport in the aftermath of an emergency. Generally, in the aftermath of a major international aviation event, the phone lines of an airline are overwhelmed with calls.

If an accident occurs with deaths and/or injuries and an investigation begins, the standard website and Facebook page should immediately go to a predesigned dark site. All advertising should cease. Whatever social media an organization uses should be linked to the official statement (see Chapter 8, Statement/release #1 – event with deaths/injuries external; Chapter 8, Statement/release #2 – event with deaths/injuries internal; or Chapter 3, the 4-point formula).

Facebook

As of 2017 there were close to two billion Facebook subscribers.[5] Facebook is a good source of marketing, and is also used as a branding tool, and for general information and messaging. It is used to advertise and send messages to customers and the public regarding sales, promotions, news, and general information about an organization. It is one of the fastest and most efficient ways of marketing to our publics, and is used for internal communication. It is a good way for an organization to set the record straight and correct misunderstandings. It's a great way to communicate with large numbers of customers and possibly tell them about your processes in a very cost-effective way.

There are a number of contexts in which to use Facebook:

- To market a product – an organization can reach a wide number of people with one post.
- To correct a misunderstanding – BP CEO made an apology for a statement, although it was too little, too late.
- To standardize a message – it needs to be the right wording, because if it's not, and it's a mistake, everyone knows you messed up. If you call it an incident and it was an accident, you will look like you are trying to "spin" something and make an investigation a media event.
- To reach a large audience.
- To target an audience – if there is an accident and you are trying to get a message out about details for loved ones, briefings, etc., you can use this.

Facebook can also be used in an emergency:

- It provides a mechanism to communicate important information to large numbers of people, such as the fact that there are counselors, volunteers, etc. available.
- It provides accurate information in the context of rumors. Within a short period of time, experts unrelated to the event or witnesses come forward making statements about the event. There can also be videos on social media left open for interpretation by "experts." Social media provides a way to correct inaccuracies or misperceptions created by uninformed speculators.
- It provides information such as a contact number(s), briefing time(s), and location, and anything else an organization would like audiences to know. An organization can receive thousands of phone calls within the first hours of an event. If it is an internal event such as a fire or lockdown, this can stop a run on the facility.
- It provides status but not about the investigation. Should this be an internal situation in a facility, this could alleviate a run on the facility.
- It provides an opportunity to educate a large number of people about the process. However, those developing the strategy and messages need to

know about the process. So many times I have read a statement issued and it repeats PR clichés. These clichés set up expectations about what information the organization will be delivering in the future. Those clichés are not consistent with the reality of the accident investigation process and it is apparent that no safety person was involved in the development of these statements. For example, they may say, "We will be providing more details as they become available." Or, "Further information will be released as it becomes available." They are never clear about what details they will be providing. While they may be providing details regarding the coordination of the families, they will not be providing details regarding the investigation or the event. However, these statements do not say that. The public then expects the organization to bring them updates on the investigation.

The downsides of using Facebook include the following:

- Once a message is out there, it is out there. If the information is not accurate, it is impossible to "unscramble the eggs."
- If someone, such as an employee, puts something on Facebook as an individual regarding a situation that involves an investigation or lawsuit, the employee could end up in that lawsuit, and the company or organization may not provide them with legal counsel. Many people in the industry feel they are experts because they are in the industry, but that does not mean they have any knowledge of what takes place in these events.

In some countries, an event is a criminal event from the onset. Although you may come from a country where there is just culture (see Chapter 2), your company may have an event in a country where it is involved in a manslaughter case, as was the case of Continental Airlines in the aftermath of the Concorde tragedy. Although an event in the United States is not considered a criminal event, a part from a Continental aircraft fell on the runway in Paris. That part was found to have been a contributing factor to that crash. Because in France an aviation crash is a criminal investigation from the onset, Continental Airlines and some of their employees were involved in the subsequent manslaughter trial.[6] You do not want to be part of a manslaughter trial because of something you put on YouTube, Twitter, or Instagram.

- Experts on television generally have no hands-on working knowledge of the event in question and are only speaking generally about their knowledge of aviation procedures.

Instagram

Instagram is a photo and video sharing social networking service owned by Facebook, which was launched on February 4, 2004. It was designed to be multifunctional, with camera and telegram capabilities rolled into one. Individuals can instantly upload photos and videos, follow newsfeeds and connect to other social networks. This makes news instantaneous. Organizations whose policies require those in management positions to "call headquarters" or something equally time-consuming do not meet the reality of today – due to this phenomenon more than anything else. It is best used as a marketing tool, as it has 500 million active users daily.[7] Users can upload photos and videos to the service, which can be organized with tags and location information. Posts can be shared publicly or with preapproved followers. Users can browse other users' content by tags and locations, and view trending content. Users can "like" photos, and follow other users to add their content to a feed.

Twitter

Twitter is a no-frills, straightforward social networking platform. It is a way to communicate immediately and briefly, bypassing normal media and going directly to the audience with whom you want to communicate. It is not so much a way to communicate as a way to bypass others and communicate directly with your intended audience. In order to be effective, you have to have followers.

Many people use Twitter, but not everyone – it depends on the demographics of your passengers or customers. For example, if your customer base is older, it may not reach the customer base you are looking for. (The Twitter demographic is younger.) While it takes a company a period of time to issue a press release, it takes minutes to send a tweet. When something happens, even if you do not have the details, a tweet provides quick information and allows an organization to immediately own a situation. This is a way of taking a news leadership position. It is fast and immediate, but not everyone tweets. Tony Fernandes from AirAsia used Twitter to connect directly with family members in the aftermath of the tragedy of Indonesia AirAsia Flight 8501. He communicated with families several times a day, which meant they were updated on recovery efforts. At the same time, he expressed concern and rallied employees' spirits, bringing him and the airline positive reviews for his communication strategy in the aftermath of the tragic event.[8]

It cannot be expected that all CEOs will tweet to employees and affected family members. Because Tony Fernandes falls into the category of a persona (see Chapter 1, section 1.2.3), it would be expected of him to tweet. However, it would not work the same for another type of CEO.

On the other hand, if something is tweeted and it is technically inaccurate, such as calling an accident an incident, customers and families may not recognize the inaccuracy, but the technical professionals of the world will. They will know two things immediately. First, they will know that this is an organization whose safety/quality people are not involved in the communication strategy; and second, this is an organization who planned for a media event, not an investigation, and their message reflects it. (ICAO describes the difference between an incident and an accident – see Chapter 2.) It may not mean something at that moment, but it helps set the safety persona of that organization in the minds of the regulators and investigators and could work against it in a future situation.

Here is an example of a problematic tweet: A passenger tweeted a joke about a flight crew possibly having partied late the night before. It was not true, but the flight crew saw it. They did not find it funny and delayed the flight until they could test the flight crew's blood alcohol content.

Hashtags

Hashtags (#) are a community-driven convention for adding additional context and metadata to your Tweets. They are used to categorize Tweets by highlighting key words. You create a hashtag simply by prefixing a word with a hash symbol, e.g. #hashtag.

This has the ability to provide people with real-time information in emergency response situations. The list of hashtags that can be found for emergency management have been identified in the Social Media 4 Emergency Management blog, "Active Hashtags". This provides a good reference tool for those writing plans.

YouTube

YouTube is a video sharing website. YouTube operates as one of Google's subsidiaries.

It allows users to upload, view, rate, share, add to favorites, report, comment on videos, and subscribe to other users. Most of the content on YouTube is uploaded by individuals, but media corporations including CBS, BBC, Vevo, and Hulu offer some of their material via YouTube as part of the YouTube partnership program. Many videos from within the cabin are uploaded on YouTube. For example, videos of the passengers stopping to grab their bags during an emergency evacuation appeared on YouTube, which generated some controversy about cabin safety and training. Then again, investigators can use these videos to determine what happens and use them in training and prevention initiatives.

YouTube can be used instantaneously in a positive way and a CEO does not have to be at the location. Here is an example of a statement, which went out on YouTube, from the CEO in the aftermath of a fatality on Southwest Airlines: "This is a sad day, and on behalf of the entire Southwest family, I want to extend my deepest sympathies for the family and the loved ones of our deceased customer."[9]

Blogs

Weblogs ("blogs") are online journals people create to write about whatever interests them. People catch on to them and millions of people can participate.

When an event occurs, many "alleged experts" give their opinions on blogs and analyze what happened. These people rarely have hands-on working involvement in the event. It is best not to participate, because blogs are public and what you say can become part of a legal or criminal case.

When to use blogs

If an employee of an organization wants to blog about non-aviation-related issues, that is their personal business.

When not to use blogs

Organizations generally do not authorize any employee to comment on any aviation-related blogs in the aftermath of an event. Sometimes organizations will monitor blogs for trends and determine if and how to respond as a company.

It must be pointed out that if any employees comment on a blog, they generally are not authorized to identify themselves as a representative of a specific organization. Comments made on blogs can have legal consequences. Personal opinions on blogs where employees of companies have identified themselves as employees of a particular company could jeopardize those employees' chances of getting jobs with future employers. Part of the reality of candidate screening in today's work is employers following prospective employees' social media to see if they are responsible and how they interact with social media.

Case studies

Case study 1 – BP

I have not worked with BP at any time, so I have no hands-on working knowledge of the organization. However, the opinions reflected were well documented at the time and remain to this day. I base my opinion of the handling of their communication on what was said and the ripple effects of that, which remain to this day. When I ask my classes to name organizations that have done a poor job handling of their communication in the aftermath of a disaster, BP is always named. They may have done an excellent job with their social media, their handling of claims, their advertisements-after-the-fact, and many more things, but they will always be remembered for their several brief statements.

On April 10, 2010, a BP offshore oil rig exploded, killing 11 workers on the rig and spilling tens of thousands of barrels of crude oil into the Gulf of Mexico. BP's Deepwater Horizon oil well, located 5,000 feet below the ocean's surface, leaked five million barrels (205.8 million gallons) of crude oil along the Gulf Coast, with devastating consequences for nearby communities, wetlands, bayous, and coastal waters. There was a major economic impact on residents of Louisiana, Alabama, Mississippi, and Florida. Besides being a human tragedy, it was a major environmental disaster, which affected fish and wildlife. The pictures published all around the world on social media of birds covered in oil and dead fish washing up on shores were heart-wrenching.

The disaster was tragic enough, but then the CEO, Tony Hayward, was caught making an impromptu statement to a reporter. Commenting on the disaster, he said, "I'm sorry. We're sorry for the massive disruption it's caused their lives. There's no one who wants this over more than I do. I'd like my life back."[10]

The following day Hayward used Facebook to issue an apology: "I made a hurtful and thoughtless comment on Sunday when I said that, 'I wanted my life back.' *When I read that recently, I was appalled.* I apologize, especially to the families of the eleven men who lost their lives in this tragic accident. Those words don't represent how I feel about this tragedy, and certainly don't represent the hearts of the people of BP – many of whom live and work in the Gulf – who are doing everything they can to make things right. My first priority is doing all we can to restore the lives of the people of the Gulf region and their families – to restore their lives, not mine."[11] This reached an extensive number of people, but everyone's eyes were on BP regardless.

When the words from an impromptu statement go out, the result is to fuel the anger of the emotional audience (see Chapter 3, section 3.1 – Humanize). If you fuel the anger of the emotional audience, they will fuel the anger of the political audience, and then you have a ripple effect. This is exactly what happened in this case. The emotional audience here was not just the families of the 11 people who perished in the tragedy, but all the people of the Gulf region and those who identify with them. In addition, the images of the environmental disaster were being broadcast around the world as they happened.

To make matters even worse, the chairman of BP, Carl-Henric Svanberg, had a meeting with then US President Obama in which he made some financial commitments on behalf of BP. Upon emerging from that meeting, the chairman made a statement in reference to the citizens of the Gulf: "And we are about the small people. I hear comments sometimes that large oil companies are greedy companies or don't care. But that is not the case in BP. We care about the small people."[12] The public was tweeting like crazy as of a result of this statement. One example was, "Did $BP Chairman Svanberg really just call people of the gulf – fishermen and hotel owners 'small people'?!!"[13]

A day later Tony Hayward had to testify on Capitol Hill. Some of the criticisms that were levelled at him were:

- "It's clear to me you don't want to answer any of our questions."
- "You're kicking the can down the road. I find that irresponsible."
- "I think you are copping out."
- "BP's top leadership was 'apparently oblivious' to the design and safety of the ruptured well."
- "Your corporate complacency is astonishing."

These are not questions from the media, but very difficult questions from an audience you cannot say "No" to.

One of the sharpest criticisms from politicians as a result of both Hayward's and Svenberg's statements regarding the event came during the testimony on Capitol Hill from Representative Bart Stupak, D-Mich: "We are not small people. But we wish to get our lives back," he told Hayward. "I'm sure you'll get your life back, and with a golden parachute to England."[14]

BP committed to financing a $20 billion fund to compensate victims for their losses and establish a $100 million fund to compensate unemployed oil rig workers affected by the president's moratorium on drilling and the closing of oil platforms.

In the aftermath, BP came out with an advertisement in which Hayward gave a statement that began, "The Gulf spill is a tragedy that never should have happened." In the advertisement he said everything he should have said. His main message to everyone watching was, "We will get this done, we will get this right."[15] This campaign was promoted through all media with Tony Hayward being the main deliverer.

It was followed up with almost the same message, but this time delivered by a local employee. In the follow-up video, the employee said, "I was born in New Orleans. My family still lives here." By saying this, she made herself part of the process (see Chapter 2, technique #25). This reinforces the importance of cultural styles of communication and their impact. In comparing both ads in class and asking the students (all international groups) which one was more effective, I received the same answer each time: the one delivered by the local BP employee.

There were a couple of other examples of quotes from Tony Hayward that fueled the anger of the emotional audience, saying that he "pledged to honour all legitimate claims," and, when asked what was an illegitimate claim he said, "I could give you a lot of examples. This is America – come on. We're going to have lots of illegitimate claims. We all know that."[16]

Another example of how cultural differences worked against BP in the Gulf was the use of the word "scheme," which is used interchangeably with the word "plan" in Britain. In the United States, the word "scheme" can be equated with the word "scam." So now we had the people of the Gulf being called small people and schemers looking to file illegitimate claims.

Years later, BP is still remembered for the job they did in communication. They did reach a lot of people in a short period of time whom they would not have been able to reach through the use of social media. However, a lot of people saw the images and heard the gaffes of both the CEO and the chairman *because* of social media.

Chart 9.1 shows the parties to this event. The fact-based party is BP. The emotional parties are the families and those who identify with the environmental disaster. The political audience is the US Congress. The persona is President Obama. The union-type audience are the environmental groups and the media need no explanation.

BP started using Twitter to reach out and inform the public and provide updates about volunteer efforts and links to video clips and procedures.

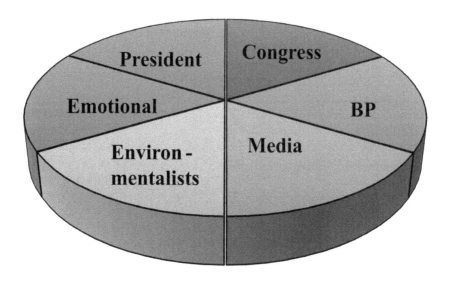

Chart 9.1 Parties to this event

Unfortunately for the company, a fake Twitter account was developed which spoofed its public relations effort and attracted more than four times the number of followers as the real BP Twitter account at the time.[17] This reflects the anger the public had toward BP. To read an after-the-fact analysis of how they communicate one could deduce this was a contributing factor. Their social media effort was good in that Tony Hayward used Facebook to apologize and BP used Twitter to inform. In fact, some analysts commend BP. But, in the end, it was the words that came out of their mouths – first the impromptu phrases of "I'd like my life back" and "We care about the small people" – that cannot be forgotten. You can send out all the tweets you want or post all you want on Facebook, but if the people testifying before Congress, talking in court or to investigators or regulators don't get it right, all the great tweets in the world aren't going to make it right. Remember the lesson about the levels of communication from Chapter 4? You can get it right with the media but if you don't, it will have effects all the way up the chain.

The lesson learned is that long after the media have gone home, if you don't get it right with them, you'll be answering to the other groups for years to come.

Mistake #2 – If you have a social media plan in your communication strategy, you can assume you have a plan that meets the reality of today's world.

> **Countermeasure to mistake #2** – In order to have a sophisticated social media strategy, you need to take into account a strategy to counteract the "fake" social media campaign (as in the BP case).

Case study 2 – United Airlines

I did not work with United Airlines on this issue, so I have no hands-on working knowledge of what they did, but my opinion of how they handled this is consistent with others in the industry who analyze these events. Some of what happened to United in the aftermath is a lesson to the rest of the industry about the power of social media. It was out of United's hands and a further lesson to take is that a corporation is not in control of who does what, nor necessarily in control of the message itself.

On March 13, 2018, a woman and her 11-year-old daughter and infant son boarded a United Airlines flight in Houston en route to New York with their ten-month-old French bulldog, Kokito, in a TSA-approved carrier. During the boarding process, a flight attendant insisted the family stow the bag in the overhead bin, although, according to other passengers, the woman and her daughter informed the flight attendant that there was a dog inside. She was insistent that she did not want her dog in the overhead bin. Other passengers nearby could see that there was a dog in the carrier. However, the flight attendant was insistent that she put the dog in the overhead bin.

Reportedly during the flight, the dog barked several times until approximately 30 minutes into the flight when it went silent. After the plane arrived in New York and the woman discovered her lifeless dog, she reportedly cradled it on the floor in tears. Her daughter was distraught.

Two passengers utilized social media. One of them began to tweet and posted on Facebook, tagging travel blogs and news organizations. She tweeted, "I want to help this woman and her daughter. They lost their dog because of an @united flight attendant. My heart is broken."[18] News organizations began to reach out immediately to the two passengers. No one knows what impact the story would have had if the passengers had not utilized social media to the extent they did to tell the story, but the exposure to this event was rapid and vast. It was not a good story for United, and the problem was that one year prior to this they had had another experience which was bad in and of itself, but was then made worse by a terrible communication strategy. When something like that happens, every bad story is going to surface.

For example, the next day's stories began to report on United's record of pet fatalities. The story that came out, which is a matter of record, was that United had the most animal deaths of all US airlines in 2017 for the third year in a row on scheduled domestic and international passenger flights, according to the latest Department of Transportation data.[19]

188 *Social media and aviation communication*

The following day the young girl and her mother appeared on *Good Morning America*. The girl was crying about having told the flight attendant that her dog was in the carrier and reported that the flight attendant had said, "It doesn't matter, you still have to put it up there."[20]

In the aftermath of all of this, the following measures were to be taken by concerned parties:

- Political – bipartisan senators filed the Welfare Of Our Furry Friends (WOOFF) Act to prohibit putting animals in overhead compartments on flights following the United Airlines event.
- Regulatory – the US Department of Transportation examined events that led to the dog's death.
- Legal – the district attorney's office in Harris County, Texas, which includes the Houston airport where the flight originated, planned to investigate the case through its animal cruelty task force.
- People for the Ethical Treatment of Animals (PETA) – they stated: "If reports are true that a United Airlines flight attendant insisted that this dog's guardian put him in the overhead bin, then he or she should be fired and charged with cruelty to animals for this dog's horrific, terrifying death."[21]
- United settled with passenger.

In Chart 9.2, you can see that the emotional audience is the child and her mother along with all the passengers on the plane and everyone else who

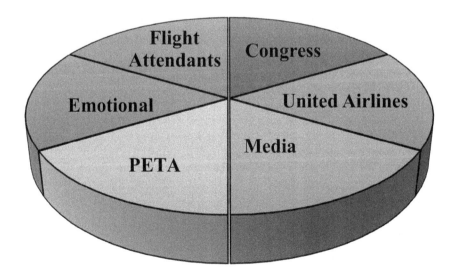

Chart 9.2 Parties to the United Airlines event

identifies with them. The fact-based audience is United Airlines. The political audience are the members of Congress who are threatening legislation (WOOFF Act) as a result of what occurred. The union are those representing all the flight attendants, and this is not just for United Airlines but for all flight attendants. The persona in this case would be PETA.

Communication comparison

In Table 9.1 you can compare what BP said in their advertisement to try and make amends in the aftermath of the Gulf oil spill and what United Airlines said after the pet tragedy. The statements were almost the same. The interesting thing about both these statements is that they each say it was a tragic accident that never should have happened. Of course they never should have happened. However, the point is that *they did happen!* Is that the message an organization wants to give after the fact? How is it that two companies end up saying almost the same thing in the aftermath of major foul-ups? One can only speculate why this might be and these personal opinions could stand as possible explanations:

- It's a coincidence.
- It's a cliché handed down through the industry.
- They hired the same PR firm.

Why does BP say one thing that highlights their own system failures – "… never should have happened"?

Had United used the 4-point formula in the aftermath of the dog tragedy, this is what it would have sounded like.

Point 1 – humanize

We at United would like to express our deepest sympathy to the family who suffered the tragic loss of their beloved pet, Kokito, and to all the passengers who also witnessed the sad event.

Explanation: If all reports on social media are correct based on observations by the passengers who put their first-hand accounts on Facebook and Twitter, not only was the flight attendant informed by Kokito's owners that there was a dog in the carrier, but the dog barked after takeoff when there was still time to save him. More than one passenger heard the dog.

Table 9.1 Compare what they said

What they said – BP	What they said – United Airlines
The Gulf oil spill was a tragedy that never should have happened.	This was a tragic accident that should never have occurred.[22]

There are a couple of questions that arise. Why did none of the other passengers say anything? Could it be because they are afraid of the perception of a persona possibly using "strong-armed" tactics? I am just offering opinions based on industry analysis. I am not saying I believe this, but a misperception left unchecked becomes a perception (see Chapter 2, technique #11), which is something United would want to change. It all goes to create the ripple effect that leaves an organization having to deal with the intangible issues that can destroy a lesser/smaller company, such as those relating to Congress, PETA, unions, customers, and ultimately market share.

Given all of the above, why would you want to say, "This was a tragic accident that should never have occurred, as pets should never be placed in the overhead bin"?

Of course it should never have occurred. But it did! By saying this statement an organization is implying that something went wrong – with their procedures, their training, their concern for the care of the pet, their concerns for their passengers, etc. This is the same thing – almost verbatim – that BP said, and one has to wonder why that is. It didn't work for BP and it was not as effective as it could be for United. However, it was more effective than other statements have been in the past.

Point 2 – make yourself part of the process

Many of us at United share in your grief as we are pet owners ourselves and realize that pets are like family to those who love them.

Note: "He was my best friend. I slept with him," Sophia said. "He was a big support for me."[23] This quote from the child indicates feelings towards the pet.

> For most kids, pets are more than just animals their families own – they're members of the family and the best of friends. […] And that can be very hard. After all, family pets often are the first to greet kids in the morning and after school. Your pet may be the one your child looks to for comfort and companionship when ill or feeling unpopular or upset.[24]

Explanation: I did not work with United on this event, but I am certain that many employees of United are pet owners and this had to be a horrific thing to see – even for non-pet owners. This is the time to make themselves part of the process. It is not offensive. It has to be a terrible thing for the other passengers as well.

Point 3 – defer to the experts

While we don't know exactly what happened to cause this tragic event, and while we, along with the family, wait for the results of the necropsy, United is going to take the following steps …

Explanation: This closes the door for United on the details of the event and allows them to open the door to focus on the actions they are taking.

Point 4 – give the facts

We have already taken steps to ensure that this will never happen again. The airline will begin issuing brightly coloured bag tags to customers traveling with in-cabin pets. The visual tags will further help our flight attendants identify pets in-cabin.

This issue does and does not go away for United. It does not in that a very controversial event happened one year prior that resurfaced in light of this situation. This issue brings out United's record for pet fatalities in comparison to competitors. They have an interest group in PETA. They have a union in defence of their employee. The issue went viral because passengers used social media.

It does go away more quickly because it was a pet and not a human who lost their life. It goes away more quickly because there was a rapid settlement. They did not bring out their CEO. You don't bring out your CEO for an event like this because you want it to go away quickly and bringing out a CEO elevates an issue to a higher level. It goes away faster because United used social media to get their message out quickly. The general public never heard any more about the WOOFF Act. They never heard any more about the criminal charges. One wonders if it had happened to one of the other mainline carriers if they would have received the same treatment as United.

Conclusion

Publishing on social media is instantaneous and has changed communication forever. Everything is on the spot and anyone can become a reporter. Reporters in mainstream media today often get their news feeds from local social media. Whether you or your organization engage in social media or not, those around you do, so it is a reality of today's world – and it can become your reality. As in the case of BP, they used social media, but adversaries used social media against them by establishing a fake social media profile that had more followers than they had. However, in the end social media cannot override a bad strategy all the way up the line.

Chapter summary

1. Forms of social media

- Facebook
- Instagram
- Twitter

- Hashtags
- YouTube
- Blogs

2. Case studies

- Case study 1 – BP
- Case study 2 – United Airlines
- Communication comparison

Notes

1 Doug Stanglin and Greg Toppo (2013) "Social Media Often First at Tragedy Scene," *USA TODAY,* July 7.
2 "Social Media," https://www.merriam-webster.com/dictionary/social%20media?src=search-dict-hed.
3 "Number of Social Media Users Worldwide from 2010 to 2021 (in billions)" (2019), https://www.statista.com/statistics/278414/number-of-worldwide-social-network-users/.
4 Dave Chaffey (2018) *Smart Insights,* March 28.
5 Internet WorldStats (2018), www.internetworldstats.com/facebook.htm.
6 Saskya Vandoorne (2010) "Continental Airlines and Mechanic Guilty in Deadly Concorde Crash," CNN, December 6, http://edition.cnn.com/2010/WORLD/europe/12/06/france.concorde.trial/index.html.
7 Anita Balakrishnan and Julia Boorstin (2017) "Instagram Says It Now Has 800 Million Users, Up 100 Million Since April," https://www.cnbc.com/2017/09/25/how-many-users-does-instagram-have-now-800-million.html.
8 Bruce Einhorn (2015) "AirAsia CEO Turns to Twitter for Crisis Management," *Bloomberg,* January 5.
9 Mark Matousek (2018), "Southwest Says It's 'Devastated' After Major Engine Failure Leads to a Fatality," *Business Insider,* April 17.
10 Gus Lubin (2010) "BP CEO Tony Hayward Apologizes for His Idiotic Statement: I'd Like My Life Back," *Business Insider,* June 2.
11 *Ibid.*
12 Kenneth Bazinet (2010) "BP Boss Svanberg says, 'We care about the small people' after oil spill faceoff with President Obama," *New York Daily News,* June 17.
13 MSNBC.com (2010) "BP Chairman Carl-Henric Svanberg's Apologized Wednesday for 'Clumsily' Referring to People Impacted by the Gulf Oil Spill as 'the Small People,'" http://www.nbcnews.com/id/37739658/ns/disaster_in_the_gulf/t/bp-boss-sorry-about-small-people-remark/#.XC7GLM1ME2x.
14 CBS/AP (2010) "BP CEO Tony Hayward 'Deeply Sorry' for Oil Spill," *CBS Interactive Inc.*
15 Michael Bush (2010) "BP Print Ads Promise to 'Make This Right.' Message, However, Is Undercut by Ongoing Spill," *AdAge,* June 2.
16 Ann Gerhart (2010) "BP Chairman Talks About the 'Small People,'" *Washington Post,* June 17.
17 Ki Mae Heussner (2010) "Fake BP Twitter Account Mocks Oil Spill PR Efforts," *ABC News,* May 25.
18 Quentin Fottrell (2018) "United Airlines Had Most Animal Deaths in 2017 – and They Doubled in Just One Year," *Market Watch,* March 14.
19 *Ibid.*
20 Yaron Steinbuch (2018) "Mom Pleaded With Flight Attendant Not to Stow Dog in Overhead Compartment," *NY Post,* March 14.

21 Brianna Nolan (2018) "PETA Statement: Dog Dies on United Airlines Flight After Being Put in Overhead Bin," PETA, https://www.peta.org/media/news-releases/peta-statement-dog-dies-on-united-airlines-flight-after-being-put-in-overhead-bin/.
22 Karma Allen (2018) "Family accuses United Airlines flight attendant of knowingly stuffing dog in bin, where it died," ABC News, March 14, https://abcnews.go.com/US/family-accuses-united-airlines-flight-attendant-knowingly-stuffing/story?id=53732538.
23 FOX5NY.COM Staff (2018) "Family Heartbroken by Death of Dog in Jet's Overhead Bin," http://www.foxdetroit.com/news/dog-dies-overhead-bin-flight.
24 Steven Dowshen (2018) "When a Pet Dies," Kids Health from Nemours, https://kidshealth.org/en/parents/pet-death.html.

10 Case study – Allegiant Air, the FAA, and *60 Minutes*

There are many recent examples where organizations are perceived to have done a good job or a bad job communicating. I have picked examples in which I had no hands-on working knowledge and talk about them in terms of the strategy and messages discussed in this book. I have no knowledge of how they developed their internal strategies or the technical issues that resulted in their need to publicly communicate. These case studies are studies in how they communicated, their messages, the delivery of them, and how they fit together, and not the regulatory, enforcement or safety issues that resulted from their need to communicate. Although communication may seem like just the frosting on the cake or the least important issue, if an organization does not get their communication right, it could have ripple effects – commercial, financial, political, and regulatory. This is not an analysis of their regulatory or safety operations. It is in respect of their strategy, messages, and communication only.

Allegiant Air

On April 15, 2018, *60 Minutes* aired a story on Allegiant Air that portrayed the airline in a negative way, particularly in respect of their safety. Every organization has their backstory but because I never worked with Allegiant and I do not know their backstory, I will stick to what appeared and the analysis. The analysis of this case study does not concern whether or not the airline is safe, does a good job, or anything else. It is only concerned with the parties to the segment and whether they communicated their messages to support a strategy.

Background

First, some background. Allegiant Air is a low-cost airline founded in 1997 and is currently based in Las Vegas, Nevada. They had been operating MD80s, which are older aircraft that were first certified in 1979, but this model was to be replaced by the end of 2018 by the A320. There have been exposés about safety concerns regarding Allegiant, but this is nothing unusual for a low-cost airline. There are many misperceptions about low-cost airlines being less safe than traditional operators; in fact, a low-cost operator should not be any less safe than any other operator. If a low-cost operator has a misperception problem about their safety in the minds of the public, it is important that they be aggressive in checking the misperception. If that is not done, then they will always be playing catch-up and be vulnerable if any incident takes place. As we said in Chapter 2, technique #11 (Defuse negative words or inaccurate statements), a misperception left unchecked becomes a perception.

If you go back several years, Allegiant had experienced a number of events. These events resulted in a regulatory review, which is one of the positive aspects of the aviation industry's built-in system of checks and balances. This would not be any different from findings or actions that could occur with any other airline. It is all part of a system to proactively enhance safety in the name of prevention. Findings, if there are any, may be attributed to a number of things, but it's how an organization communicates on these issues that can cause more significant problems.

The basic premise of the *60 Minutes* story was that Allegiant Air is one of the US's most profitable airlines but also one of the US's most dangerous based on a more than normal number of events. Their perception was that the regulator, in this case the FAA, had a less than aggressive regulatory approach. Interviews were conducted with a number of industry experts to support the story. An FAA executive was interviewed about the agency's enforcement policies, as were passengers from Allegiant about their personal experiences and some industry experts. No one from Allegiant Airlines appeared in the story.

The specific criticisms of Allegiant Air and the FAA

The *60 Minutes* piece said that there had been a higher than industry norm in-flight breakdowns for Allegiant. It suggested that the FAA had taken a less than aggressive approach to the concerns of industry professionals in that they did not diligently follow up on complaints from the pilots' union, did not aggressively enforce, and had a policy that was so focused on compliance that enforcement got lost. So, in this story both Allegiant and the FAA were criticized for these reasons. Some of the other concerns that were brought up were the age of the fleet, the large number of incidents that occurred with this airline, the airline's business model, and the apparent prioritizing of profit over safety. The concern was that budget airlines would cut costs on safety. It also appeared that there were almost as many criticisms against the regulator as there were against Allegiant.

In this segment, it was therefore important to have a strategy, with the aviation messages being that of a system of checks and balances were in place, they showed proactivity for prevention and safety, and for safety to be bolstered, and explained in a proactive rather than reactionary way. Both the airline and the regulator knew the theme of the story and therefore had ample time to prepare a strategy. In the case of the regulator, if the airline is under fire, it is imperative that they have a strategy that shows they are there to ensure the safety of the system.

An operator and the regulator need to correct the misunderstanding of the compliance and enforcement process in the eyes of the traveling public. The message would be that punishment in the form of fines does not add to the safety culture, as it intimidates people to not report issues, resulting in problems getting "swept under the carpet." Nothing is learned by the airline or, more importantly, the industry. The eventual message for a breakdown in compliance is the remedy of enforcement. It is not an either–or situation. But to understand this, the audit and enforcement process needs to be explained.

The enforcement process

The enforcement process is a multistep process. The first step would be the audit for compliance. These audits can take place for any one of a number of reasons, including regular surveillance, current or former employee complaint, e.g. whistle-blower or a problem with a customer. The certificate holder may get a letter of no action or administrative action.

If the regulator sees that an administrative action is all that is required, a warning notice is issued. The notice indicates the available facts and information about an incident or occurrence and says there may be a violation. A letter of correction confirms the FAA's decision in the matter and states the necessary corrective action the alleged violator has taken or agrees to take. If the agreed corrective action is not fully completed, legal enforcement action may be taken. This is all done with the objective of prevention. This prevention philosophy brings certificate holders into compliance rather than inflicting strong enforcement actions. This helps voluntary reporting without fear of retribution, which improves safety trends. This philosophy has been a contributing factor to the positive safety trends the industry has experienced.

An enforcement action becomes necessary where the FAA legal staff determine that a violation has occurred. Action may take the form of a civil penalty or a certificate action. One thing a regulator may not do is take arbitrary action. Although there may be complaints of one form or another, they can only take actions on their findings. Those actions have to be consistent with the findings. If a regulator does not like an operator or feels that perhaps an operator deserves one thing or another, they cannot "throw the book at them" based on that.

When an operator is getting criticized and under scrutiny by the public and in the media, the regulator is criticized as well. The main point of criticism of the regulator is that "this would not have happened if the regulator was doing their job" is almost as strong or stronger than the criticism against a certificate holder. Therefore, if the regulator does a poor job communicating, the operator will look bad as well. If the operator does a poor job but the regulator does a good job, the regulator can pull the operator up.

Overview and analysis of the FAA preliminary background letter to **60 Minutes**

Prior to the *60 Minutes* segment on April 11, 2018, the FAA sent a letter to CBS clarifying points previously provided regarding the upcoming *60 Minutes* segment on Allegiant Air. I asked the FAA official, whose signature was on the letter, who drafted the letter. He informed me that it was a group effort. I will first relate the letter and then provide an analysis of the letter based on the principles from earlier chapters.

The FAA letter to 60 Minutes

"This is to follow up and expand on the information we previously provided you about our safety oversight system and our oversight of Allegiant Air. (**paragraph 1**)

"The commercial aviation system in the United States operates at an unprecedented level of safety. The FAA has zero tolerance for intentional, reckless behavior, flagrant violations, or refusal to cooperate in corrective action by air carriers. When warranted, the agency routinely takes legal enforcement action against violators. (**paragraph 2**)

"In fiscal year 2016, the most recent year for which full data is available, 820 million commercial passengers flew in the Nation Airspace System. Since 2009, there has been no fatal domestic passenger air carrier accident in the U.S. and commercial aviation fatalities in the U.S. have decreased by some 95 percent over the past 20 years, as measured by fatalities per 100 million passengers on board. (**paragraph 3**)

"The FAA is vigilant in scrutinizing the operations of all airlines and is prepared to act on new information brought to its attention from data, from inspectors' observations and findings, and from any reliable source about any carrier at any time. (**paragraph 4**)

"The FAA's comprehensive oversight system provides a standardized, methodical approach to verify that all airlines comply with our mandate to provide the highest degree of safety. Our oversight system provides detailed insight into each airline's operation to identify potential risks before they become serious problems and take corrective action. The process is dynamic and requires that the FAA and the airlines we regulate constantly strive for safety improvements. The FAA adjusts our oversight of individual airlines based on analysis and risk identification. For example, the FAA typically puts airlines under heightened oversight when patterns of risk are identified as well as when carriers experience labour issues or financial distress, which may cause impacts to operations. In this regard, in 2015, the FAA heightened our oversight of Allegiant which was experiencing pilot labour issues. (**paragraph 5**)

"In 2016, we moved up Allegiant's 2018 scheduled review, known as a Certificate Holder Evaluation Process (CHEP). This review did not find any systemic safety or regulatory problems, but did identify a number of less serious issues, which Allegiant addressed. It is not uncommon to discover such issues during regular audits and inspections and to require air carriers to address them. Since the 2016 CHEP, the FAA has conducted ongoing evaluations of Allegiant's safety compliance, as it does with all carriers, and has not identified any significant or systemic problems with the carrier's current operations. Had we identified such problems, the FAA would have taken immediate action." (**paragraph 6**)

SAFETY CULTURE AND COMPLIANCE

"The key to continuous improvements in airline safety is to create a sustainable culture of safety through an open and transparent exchange of information and data between the FAA and industry. Beginning in the 1990s, the FAA established a framework for air carriers and others to share safety data in a non-punitive setting, through programs such as the Aviation Safety Action Program (ASAP) and the Voluntary Disclosure Reporting Program (VDRP). (**paragraph 7**)

"In 2015, during the tenure of then-Administrator Michael Huerta, the FAA further refined this approach by transitioning to the Compliance Philosophy, which incorporates safety-management principles to address emerging safety risks. Compliance Philosophy recognizes operators make inadvertent mistakes, and those mistakes can provide valuable data and information to help mitigate future problems. Compliance Philosophy is the most effective way to obtain actionable information to identify and address risks. Attached are the two FAA directives that can provide more insight in this area. (**paragraph 8**)

"So, in cases where a deviation results from factors such as flawed procedures, simple mistakes or a lack of understand, the FAA uses tools like training or documented improvements to procedures – before enforcement action – to ensure compliance. When the FAA encounters intentional reckless behavior, flagrant violations, or refusal to cooperate in correction action by carriers, it undertakes legal enforcement actions. If an air carrier is unwilling or unable to comply with laws and regulations, the agency can – and does – revoke the company's ability to operate. (**paragraph 9**)

"You can read more about this on our Compliance Philosophy page, located at https://www.faa.gov/about/initiatives/cp/."

FURTHER BACKGROUND ON ALLEGIANT

"I am also sharing some further points that will provide additional information for your viewers about the questions you have raised.

"The FAA's oversight of Allegiant has produced results. The rate of incidents reported by Allegiant to the FAA's Air Traffic Organization has trended downward in recent years. These incidents include diversions and emergency landings, as well as other events such as passenger disturbances and medical events. In Fiscal Year 2015, Allegiant reported 0.003225 events per 1,000 departures; in Fiscal Year 2016, 0.002075; in Fiscal Year 2017, 0.002875; and in the first two quarters of Fiscal Year 2018, Allegiant reported 0.0015 events per 1,000 departures. (**paragraph 10**)

"Also, the 2016 articles in the *Tampa Bay Tribune* about the FAA's oversight of Allegiant contained a number of inaccuracies, some of which have already been brought to your attention. For example, the reporters relied upon retired FAA personnel as subject matter experts who were not familiar with the current FAA practices, and the impact those practices have in improving aviation safety. The articles also suggested that FAA personnel somehow gave Allegiant a "clean bill of health." The FAA continually assesses airlines' operations and does not provide one-time signoffs such as this. (**paragraph 11**)

"I hope this information has clarifies issues you have raised. The FAA is the world's preeminent aviation safety organization and has been very successful in our mission of regulating air carriers to the highest level of safety. The primary mission of all 45,000-plus FAA employees – including the 7,400 assigned to the safety oversight division – is to provide the safest airspace system in the world. We are never content with the status quo and the FAA is continually working to enhance safety for the flying public." (**paragraph 12**)

Analysis of FAA's preliminary letter

The first four paragraphs were an opportunity to deliver the strongest message the FAA had considering the fact they were dealing with a highly sophisticated news magazine program that had spent months researching this segment and had a negative message that needed to be counteracted.

The FAA began with generic messages such as "The commercial aviation system […] operates at an unprecedented level" and uses the fact that there had been "no fatal domestic passenger air carrier accident in the U.S. since 2009." According to the FAA, an accident is an unplanned event or series of events resulting in death, injury, or damage to, or loss of equipment or property.[1] The danger with using incidents and accidents as a measurement of safety is that it comes back to haunt you. Sure enough, two days after the *60 Minutes* segment there was an aviation fatality (not Allegiant).

In the first four paragraphs, the letter is written as though the recipient is an inexperienced organization that requires an elementary explanation of what the FAA's mandate is, as opposed to a sophisticated organization with a 50-year track record which carries out in-depth research on frequent exposés. The letter did not appear to inform but rather dictate. Does *60 Minutes* really think that the FAA has "tolerance for intentional, reckless behavior, flagrant violations, or refusal to cooperate in corrective action by air carriers?" If an organization wants to make a strong point, it should be done immediately and clearly. You should not wait until the last paragraphs of a letter where you are a party to an exposé with an organization like *60 Minutes*.

In the second segment, "Safety culture and compliance," the letter starts with a mundane and elementary historical background taking two long-winded paragraphs to come up with their strongest sentence of "If an air carrier is unwilling or unable to comply with laws and regulations, the agency can – and does – revoke the company's ability to operate." This is far too basic for the sophisticated *60 Minutes* which has researchers who can google this information. Considering the fact that the segment is criticizing the FAA for their enforcement weakness, they should have begun with this. It would be similar to a person going for an interview and saying, "I was born in a small town, I went to elementary school, high school, college, blah, blah, blah, and I am now a doctor, lawyer, pilot, and engineer." That statement started from a position of weakness. You would have a stronger statement if you began by saying, "I'm a doctor, lawyer, pilot, and engineer. Let me tell you how I achieved all these things." At least if they fall asleep after the first sentence they will have had the main point.

Mistake #1 – Taking two or more paragraphs to build up to your strongest point.

Countermeasure to mistake #1 – Always start with your strongest point, especially if you are trying to correct a misperception.

Mistake #2 – When trying to make a point with a sophisticated news organization like *60 Minutes*, you refer them elsewhere so that they can understand what you want them to.

Countermeasure to mistake #2 – Have clear, simple, and obvious messages up front in the first paragraphs, backed up with support points.

In the next segment, "Further background on Allegiant," the letter gives data defending the safety record of Allegiant. However, when you provide data, you need some industry comparison for it to have any meaning. The letter goes on to discredit the *Tampa Bay Tribune*'s 2016 reporting on Allegiant Air and the former FAA sources they used. The letter also says that the retired FAA personnel used as subject matter experts were not familiar with the current FAA practices. The majority of retired aviation officials I have met stay up to date on practices and procedures after retirement. Enforcement procedures are public. It does not make sense to have a strategy that discredits others and does not strongly articulate your own message.

In paragraph 12, the letter states, "The FAA is the world's preeminent aviation safety organization." Acclaiming one's self as the world's preeminent anything on paper without the messages to back it up is never a good strategy. It is arrogant and could perhaps be offensive to all of the other world regulators, safety associations, and organizations that work every day to try and make the system safer. The letter ends with the message of "We are never content with the status quo and the FAA is continually working to enhance safety for the flying public." That is a good message but is better stated by saying, "The FAA will never consider ourselves to be at 100 percent because that would be the first sign of complacency. We are always looking to improve on our past performance because to us safety is a marathon with no finish line, but we are 100 percent safety-conscious." However, this is a message they should have used up front to set the tone and backed up with support points, rather than at the end. Why wait until the conclusion to promote your strongest message?

The *60 Minutes* interview and the FAA

I did not work with the FAA on this segment, so I have no working knowledge of how the FAA prepared for the *60 Minutes* segment. There were many opportunities to talk about the mandate and deliver the regulatory process during the on-screen interview process. While the FAA may well be fulfilling their mandate, their ability to communicate that was poor. When dealing with an on-camera *60 Minutes*–type interview you do not go just to answer questions. In my opinion, based on 30 years in this industry, it appears that this is what happened.

Because the aviation industry is based on a system of checks and balances, if an operator is under scrutiny, so is the regulator. If the operator does not appear in the segment and the regulator does, the pressure is on the regulator to defend their position in the process of checks and balances, thereby indirectly defending the operator. If the regulator is weak in their communication, it will not look good for the industry.

In the defense of the FAA and Allegiant, the data was old news and the aviation philosophy worldwide for safety is that efforts are done "in the name of prevention." It appeared that the FAA was there to answer questions and not take control of their message, whatever their message may have been. The FAA could have done numerous things to change this. Their strategy should have been to talk to the people who were listening and not the person asking the question. This did not appear to be the case. Below are some examples.

To paraphrase the *60 Minutes* interviewer: Are you alarmed that the head of the pilots' union that represents the Allegiants pilots was alleging that mechanics were telling pilots not to report issues?

Recommended: Once someone says, "This person told us this – what do you have to say about that?" they are getting you to start a dialogue supporting the point they want to make. The way you get out of it is to have a message of your own and not be there to just answer questions. You stop it with messages like this:

1. "I can't speak for what the head of the pilots' union told you." [close the door]
2. "I can only tell you what the FAA requires of all the industry." [the message]
3. "There are mechanisms in place for pilots who have concerns to be part of the process." [the message]

The message would be followed by support points such as:

1. Hotlines
2. Through their union
3. Through the inspector general

To paraphrase the FAA interviewee: I'd be concerned. [There is no message here or attempt to take control of the interview.]

Recommended: Certainly, discouraging pilots from reporting would be against the law. The pilots know it and the union knows it. Either one of them who participates in this activity becomes part of the problem – and jeopardizes people's lives. (This preempts the interviewer's next question.) Why is *60 Minutes* pointing out that what he described is against the law? This is not the media's fault. It was an opportunity not taken for the FAA to look proactive.

To paraphrase the *60 Minutes* interviewer: Was this against the law?

To paraphrase the FAA interviewee: Yes.

To paraphrase the *60 Minutes* interviewer: What is the requirement of pilots?

Recommended: There was another message here that the FAA failed to point out.

Message:

1. "Pilots who failed to report these violations are admittedly part of the problem and the union president is aware of that."
2. "Pilots are passengers on these planes themselves, as are their families."

To Paraphrase the FAA interviewee: Pilots are required to report and if they are discouraged from doing so it would be a worry to the FAA.

Recommended: What *60 Minutes* described goes beyond a failure to meet safety standards. It's against the law. That the FAA "would not appreciate it" is a very weak response to how they would feel about illegal behavior. This exchange would not have continued had they used the message when the behavior was first identified.

Recommended message: Let me explain how the FAA initiates an enforcement action.

This would have preempted many other questions. It is an opportunity to educate.

To paraphrase the *60 Minutes* interviewer: Is this the first you've heard of this?

To paraphrase the FAA interviewee: Yes.

To paraphrase the *60 Minutes* interviewer: Will you investigate this?

To paraphrase the FAA interviewee: We do investigate.

To paraphrase the *60 Minutes* interviewer: This particular situation?

To paraphrase the FAA interviewee: We will continue to be diligent.

For example, I know that the FAA articulated those points somewhat (paragraph 6) to CBS in writing to the investigation on April 11 prior to the April 15 interview, but failed to disclose them during the on-camera interview. The public did not read the FAA letter. They could have said, "As part of our proactive program for prevention we moved up Allegiant's surveillance program."

By using techniques, the FAA representative could have established credibility for viewers by gaining the attention of the viewers with simple phrases like, "Let me explain how the regulatory process works" or "What's important for the traveling public to understand is …" and using messages to make a point. This would have been an opportunity to educate.

Table 10.1 shows the messages the FAA could have delivered to the segment criticisms and the techniques they could have used to deliver them.

Table 10.1 Potential FAA messages to *60 Minutes*' criticism with techniques

Criticism	Technique to deliver message	Intended message
FAA should have been looking at safety culture	Let me correct the general misunderstanding about the global enforcement process (technique #4, 6)	Enforcement is not arbitrary
FAA saw a termination letter but nothing else	I don't know where you get your information but this is what happened (technique #13)	We looked at numerous things, for example …
FAA's passive approach to correcting Allegiant's difficulties	That is not correct (techniques #9, 10)	Preemption in the name of prevention accomplished through compliance has played a key role in the reduction of accidents internationally over the past 20 years. The traveling public, you included, are the beneficiaries of that.
Change of policy focuses less on enforcement	But what is more important to understand about safety is … (technique #10)	Compliance is not in lieu of enforcement. It is not an either/or.

204 *Case study*

The FAA's missed messages and opportunities during the interview

1. Government and industry working together proactively and internationally over the past 20 years has reduced the accident rate due to a compliant philosophy.

    The transition on how this would work:
    "The international industry has a number of programs that harmonize proactive safety throughout the industry."

2. The traveling public should appreciate that governments around the world work with industry proactively to prevent accidents. The decrease in accidents and the increase in safety is the proof of success.

    The transition on how this would work:
    "Let me explain how the compliance process has caused the accident trend to decrease by 95 percent over 20 years."

3. Enforcement is many times after the fact and it could be too late. Which is better for the traveling public?

    The transition on how this would work:
    "There is a misunderstanding about how enforcement works. Let me explain it …"

The 60 Minutes *segment points against Allegiant*

While Allegiant Air did not appear in the program, they had given a full statement to *60 Minutes*. The statement was delivered in part during the program but was also on the Allegiant website. The part of the statement they read said, "All of us at Allegiant are proud of our strong safety record, as noted in the most current, comprehensive FAA audit. Safety is at the forefront of our minds and the core of our operations."[2] Note:

1. The basis of this statement is accurate, focusing on where they are today in the aftermath of the audit and the findings; however, it is unclear what they mean by "their strong safety record." That is a message with no support points. The theme of the entire segment appeared to be that Allegiant did not have a strong safety record, that a string of incidents is one measurement of a safety record, and that the current enforcement philosophy is possibly permissive. However, in the full statement, which did not appear in the *60 Minutes* segment, Allegiant Air pointed out that they not only complied "with all mandatory safety regulations and guidelines, but also participate[d] in numerous voluntary safety programs."[3] These are two examples of support points, of what they do proactively.

2. Allegiant in their statement said, "Thanks in large part to the efforts of the FAA, the airline industry has never been safer."[4] In fact, the FAA does play

a role in making the airline industry safer but how they have done that needs further explanation, especially by the FAA. If the FAA does a poor job of explaining this, how can industry be expected to?

3. The part of the statement that says, "Safety is at the forefront of our minds and the core of our operations" is a PR cliché; there isn't an airline in the world that I have come into contact with that hasn't said that. It is a non-message. Do we ever hear a company say, "We are just in it for the money and not safety"? When you are up against a program like *60 Minutes*, the last things you want to use are PR clichés. They will never hold up, and as a matter of fact will reinforce the points the news program is trying to make.

Data was old

The examples used in the segment are old news. Allegiant Air was correct on that point. The data was based on past events and the FAA had recently concluded an audit of Allegiant Air. However, it was the issues that were of most concern, because the issues they brought out in the interview were ones reflective of systemic culture. Data can change from year to year, but it is ongoing safety culture that should be most concerning. The problem with safety culture is that it is difficult to measure – compared to, for example, numerical data.

Aging fleet

Allegiant has an aging fleet, but is an aging fleet a safety issue (see Chapter 5)? Generally speaking, the age of an aircraft should not be an issue if an operator has the manpower and resources to maintain proper airworthiness. Is the fact that experts or others would not fly on Allegiant an issue? No, because Allegiant's demographics are their demographics. Their client base will continue to fly them for the reasons they fly them now, whatever those reasons may be. Is the traveling public going to remember this long enough to have an impact on Allegiant? Probably not, because the traveling public have a short memory.

More maintenance incidents

Organizations go through times when they have more frequent incidents, and this may be blamed on the aging fleet. That is a message but not a technical explanation.

Pilot firing

This is a labour management issue. Every organization that is unionized has labour management issues. In addition, there is often a lawsuit involved, so it is a workplace situation.

Cuts corners on safety for profit

Because of the system of oversight between government and industry, the FAA could answer this. It is their issue to answer.

Table 10.2 shows the segment criticism of Allegiant, the potential messages that could have offset the criticism, and the techniques that would have been used to deliver that message.

The interviewer

In the old days, the *60 Minutes* type of interview included many aggressive ambush-type interviews where they catch the interviewees (if you want to call them that) off guard. This interview was not of that nature. I have also heard interviewees say in the past that they were "taken out of context." That did not appear to be the case in this context. In my professional opinion, Steve Kroft did an admirable job giving each interviewee time and space to offer a message and/or an opinion should they have one.

You can see in Chart 10.1 the parties that appeared in the *60 Minutes* story. *60 Minutes* was the media, of course. This is the same pie chart we saw in Chapter 1. The story may have been generated by the previously fired pilot, but *60 Minutes* would not have followed through on the story had they not believed there to be a story. What the media and traveling public may believe is a story may be something else to those intensely involved in the industry. On the other hand, something that is forgotten by the media or the traveling public in the near future may be remembered a lot longer by those who work with the issues on a daily basis.

The political style of communicating was represented by those who had been the passengers, or witnesses. They related their observations or experiences. It is the same type of situation where the media may come forward and say, "Witness have said …" or "Sources have told us …"

Table 10.2 *60 Minutes'* criticism of Allegiant Air with potential messages

Criticism	Technique	Message
Disturbing questions raised about performance	Admit mistakes (technique #20)	There were concerns but here is where we are today
Company not paying attention	Establish credibility – perhaps you are unaware what we are doing (technique #4)	If airline is doing something, and the audit program with government oversight
Business model too aggressive	Have a message (technique #1)	Many operators have an aggressive business model but that is not in lieu of safety
Older fleet	Correct a misunderstanding about the aging aircraft issue – an industry issue, not Allegiant (technique #4)	Economic not safety
Management seems to denigrate safety	Have a message (technique #1)	System of checks and balances

Case study 207

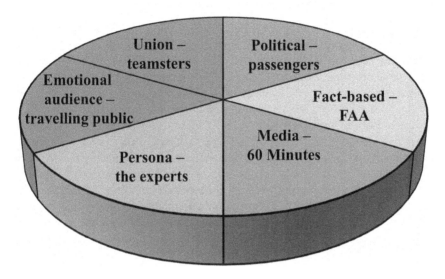

Chart 10.1 Parties to the *60 Minutes* story on Allegiant Air with FAA, April 2018

The teamsters' union represented the pilots of Allegiant and they were speaking on behalf of the fired pilot by giving the pilots' perspective in general.

The personas were the experts – in this case generally well known to those in the industry. One of them was a former FAA official with years of experience who knew the process whether or not they had been away from the FAA for a period of time. The other one was a former National Transportation Safety Board (NTSB) board member who had gone through the Senate confirmation process not once but twice, and no matter how long he had been away was qualified to speak on the process and the technical aspects of the subject. Sometimes experts may have been with an operator but not a regulator or an investigator. Having the expertise of a regulator gives insight into many operators and having the expertise of an investigator provides insight into a number of investigations. Because of the stature and background of this former NTSB individual, he was an expert on the subject regardless of the story. The fact that he had been the lead on a number of public investigations and the fact that he had been sought for his expertise in other events made him a persona in this case.

All those watching as lay-people who were part of the audience or travelling public could be categorized as the emotional audience.

The FAA deals in oversight and is part of a system of checks and balances, so that made them the fact-base party to the event. They had all the data, process, and actions. They had all the messages to potentially mitigate any criticism.

Potential impact on Allegiant Air

Financial

It was reported that shares of Allegiant dropped 8.5 percent in the immediate aftermath of the *60 Minutes* segment, followed by another 3 percent the day after the story aired. Meanwhile, the CEO's net worth dropped by $52 million.[5] "That company, which was valued at $1.9 billion ahead of its *60 Minutes* feature, is now valued at about $643 million – pointing to just how painful bad publicity, warranted or not, can leave lasting scars."[6] Whether or not these are lasting scars remains to be seen. Other companies have had much worse events with much more controversial issues and rallied. The initial statement issued by Eric Gust, the firm's vice president of operations, to the *60 Minutes* segment was, "It is unfortunate and disappointing that CBS *60 Minutes* has chosen to air a false narrative about Allegiant and the FAA. Allegiant's team members safely operate thousands of flights each week, which will transport more than 14 million passengers this year."[7]

Political

If a story evokes a response from an emotional audience, that emotional response can trigger the political audience. You can see from Chart 10.1 that the emotional audience in this story is the traveling public and the traveling public can be everyone – certainly a large number of a politician's constituents, and the politicians themselves.

In response to the *60 Minutes* investigation into the FAA's oversight of Allegiant Air, Senator Bill Nelson, D-Florida, penned a letter to the Department of Transportation (DOT) Inspector General Calvin Scovel calling for an investigation into the FAA's enforcement actions and its correspondence with the budget airlines: "The traveling public deserves to know whether the FAA is conducting thorough safety oversight of Allegiant. Anything less could lead to disastrous consequences."[8]

The FAA's response to that challenge was: "The FAA and our 44,000-plus employees are committed to pursuing the highest level of aviation safety. Commercial aviation in the U.S. is safer than it's ever been because airlines, manufacturers, pilots, mechanics and our own controllers share the same commitment. We are never satisfied with the status quo and always look for ways to make the world's safest aviation system even safer. To that end, we welcome any outside review of our safety oversight system, and we welcome the opportunity to present a complete and accurate picture of how that system works."[9]

Customers

Within ten days of the *60 Minutes* segment, the *Las Vegas Review-Journal* reported: "Allegiant Air on Wednesday said a *60 Minutes* segment that questioned its safety record caused fliers to steer clear, but added business is returning to normal. Since the segment aired April 15, the Las Vegas-based airline experienced cancellations and a reduction in bookings."[10]

Passengers are loyal to airlines for different reasons. Passenger who fly a low-cost carrier fit a certain demographic. They are going to continue to fit that demographic. The reality is that the traveling public has a short memory. Even those in the aviation industry who take my classes have to think really hard to recognize an event that I describe for them, if that event is not in the recent past. Organizations that have events that are more controversial and tragic than Allegiant's recover financially and commercially in a short period of time. In addition, if something more compelling happens that overshadows this in terms of publicity, Allegiant will be "out of sight and out of mind."

The public is much more likely to remember the one communication error, if it is a large one, than the event. Recall the comment by the CEO of BP in the aftermath of the Gulf oil spill: "I'd like my life back." It is a single comment that is still remembered to this day. If I ask a class, "Which event is it where a plane came apart over Long Island?" they have to think before they say, "TWA Flight 800." These are aviation people, not lay-people. However, if you ask, "What do you remember about the Gulf oil spill," they remember many things, but the first thing they recall is the quote of the CEO. You can do many things right, but you make a major communication mistake and it will long be remembered!

What did the FAA have to say?

When asking some FAA professionals – both currently employed and retired – for their thoughts on the *60 Minutes* segment, I was surprised to get the same bureaucratic responses I have received over the years. There is a standard response I hear when it comes to *60 Minutes*, and that is, "They always spend an hour with us and then they end up cutting and pasting what they want." That did not happen here. You can tell by watching the interview. You also know when *60 Minutes* calls and you did not generate the story, they most likely got their story from another source.

In my discussion, I mentioned to the FAA that I saw no messages delivered and no techniques to say, "What we'd like the traveling public to know is …" or "You may not be aware of how the enforcement process works. Let me explain." These might have helped deliver some proactive and positive aviation messages for the FAA. These techniques are for a strategy designed to educate the public. However, the comment by the FAA was, "It wouldn't pay to get adversarial with *60 Minutes*." Educating the public by using those messages would not be considered "adversarial," but the opportunity was missed.

However, in defense of the FAA, they do good work. There is a good story to tell but you have to prepare and you have to tell the story. The preliminary letter sent by the FAA that was analyzed above shows that they communicated their messages as though they were talking to novices. They had the opportunity to tell the story, but they failed.

Timing is everything

Two days after the *60 Minutes* segment aired, another airline suffered a tragedy. There was one fatality and seven others sustained injuries when an engine exploded in mid-air and a woman was partially sucked out of a window. It was the first time there had been a fatality in an aviation event in the United States since 2009, when a commuter plane crashed in New York. The NTSB said that they found evidence of metal fatigue in one of the engines. A similar episode happened in 2006 with the same operator, but it resulted in no fatalities or injuries. This immediately shifted attention away from Allegiant but not away from the FAA. And this is precisely why you do not use fatalities to measure the safety of the system (FAA letter, paragraph 3). You use the amount of effort an organization puts in proactively in the name of prevention.

Chapter summary

1. Allegiant Airlines
    - *60 Minutes* story and overview
    - FAA preliminary letter
2. The *60 Minutes* interview and the FAA
    - Messages, points, interviewer
3. Potential impact on Allegiant

Notes

1 US Department of Transportation, FAA (2017) Order 8000.72, Appendix A, p. A-1.
2 Caroline Linton (2018) "Allegiant Air Responds to Critical *60 Minutes* Report," CBS News, April 16, https://www.cbsnews.com/news/allegiant-air-60-minutes-defensive-2018-04-16 (accessed April 2018).
3 *Ibid.*
4 *Ibid.*
5 Lucinda Shen (2018) "Allegiant Air CEO's Net Worth Is $52 Million Lower After *60 Minutes* Segment Questions Safety," Fortune, http://fortune.com/2018/04/16/allegiant-airlines-nasdaq-stock-60-minutes/.
6 *Ibid.*
7 *Ibid.*
8 Blair Guild (2018) "Senator Calls for Investigation into FAA after *60 Minutes* Report on Allegiant Air," CBS News, April 16, https://www.cbsnews.com/news/allegiant-air-faa-investigation-lawmaker-calls-for-review-live-updates-2018-04–16/.
9 *Ibid.*
10 Eli Segall (2018) "*60 Minutes*' Segment Causes Dip in Allegiant Business," Las Vegas Review-Journal, April 24, https://www.reviewjournal.com/business/60-minutes-segment-causes-dip-in-allegiant-business/.

11 Summary of mistakes and countermeasures

Chapter 1: Introduction to aviation communication – it's more than you think!

Mistake #1 – Having a strategy that says, "How do we know what our message is until something happens?"

Countermeasure to mistake #1 – An understanding of aviation messages should be learned as a tool during initial aviation training for new employees. After all, aviation is your business. No tickets can be sold without an air operator's certificate.

Mistake #2 – Practicing for all situations with the same strategy by using briefing book with questions and answers is acceptable.

Countermeasure to mistake #2 – Do not practice for all situations with the same strategy. Determine if you are going to educate, clear up a misunderstanding, or fit into a situation whose theme has already been determined.

Mistake #3 – Preparing for all situations with the same strategy.

Countermeasure to mistake #3 – The lead for these strategies should be the safety/operations departments to ensure they do not conflict with their ability to effectively deal with their target audience.

Mistake #4 – "We don't have a union, so we don't need a strategy for dealing with a union."

Countermeasure to mistake #4 – Incorporate into your communication strategy the idea that your organization may need to deal with a union, whether or not your organization has one.

Mistake #5 – Organizations strategize to talk to the media.

Countermeasure to mistake #5 – Have a strategy that considers your audience beyond the media.

Mistake #6 – "It's the media's fault!"

Countermeasure to mistake #6 – Understand it is not the media's fault. It's the people who use the media.

Mistake #7 – Organizations compartmentalize communication. "We have people to do that!"

Countermeasure to mistake #7 – There needs to be an established and vetted policy statement and corporate/organizational definition for communication with accountability (making it every employee's responsibility) and the policy should be harmonized throughout the organization.

Mistake #8 – "We have executives who communicate for us, so we do not have to worry."

Countermeasure to mistake #8 – Make sure that all employees understand it is their responsibility to communicate and that clear and transparent communication is the foundation of a business, as opposed to meaningless public relations clichés. It does not belong solely to a "department" or a "person."

Mistake #9 – "We are protected because we have a 'policy.'"

Countermeasure to mistake #9 – Have a communication policy that meets reality with an empowerment statement that is non-punitive.

Mistake #10 – Spokespeople are those who speak to the media.

Countermeasure to mistake #10 – Define a spokesperson as any employee who has to speak to any audience on behalf of the company.

Mistake #11 – Not taking into consideration other countries' cultural styles of communication and working them into your strategies.

Countermeasure to mistake #11 – Have a plan to consider the cultural style of communication for every area in which you do business and ensure that your representatives in those countries are equipped and empowered to act on your behalf.

Chapter 3: The 4-point formula and extra – your absolute safety net

Mistake #1 – Organizations think they are in control of how they are notified. Not true! You find out how you find out.

Countermeasure to mistake #1 – Mandate that every employee be equipped with the 4-point formula which is the ultimate safety net in the event an employee is caught off guard. Also, understand how to communicate on the message when you are blindsided (see Chapter 2).

Mistake # 2 – Because the subject is communication, organizations think the lead communication strategists should be the offices of corporate communications.

Countermeasure to mistake #2 – These are not public relations events. An airline is not an airline unless it has an air operator's certificate. The people who are responsible for that are the ones who should be the lead communication strategists. They are the keepers of the message. The corporate communication departments are support to the organization.

Mistake #3 – Organizations believe they are in control of who can and cannot speak to the media. Not true! Everyone who represents the organization to any audience is a spokesperson.

Countermeasure to mistake #3 – Employees who may be confronted by the public should be empowered to communicate without the fear of punitive action, because they may very well end up on the news. They should know what the federal airworthiness regulations are. You do not want someone telling a family that a child who is over two years of age must be held in a parent's lap ending up on the evening news. All the regulators in the world will know that the staff is not familiar with federal airworthiness regulations.

Mistake #4 – Organizations believe that their policy determines who is the "spokesperson." Not true! The people who decide who the spokesperson is are the ones *asking* the questions.

Countermeasure to mistake #4 – Have all employees equipped with the basic aviation messages that are the reality of the entire industry no matter what country or what part of the industry you operate in. You do not have to wait for something to happen to know what they are. Aviation is the product – not seat pitch. These messages should be taught during initial aviation training (see Chapters 5 and 6).

Mistake #5 – "Our CEO/DG/director is our spokesperson." Not true! They may be one of your spokespeople but if you think they are your only one, you do not have a strategy that meets reality.

Countermeasure to mistake #5 – Everyone should know the 4-point formula. It is the ultimate safety net. It is better than saying "No comment" or "I'm not authorized" or "Call our office of corporate communications."

Mistake #6 – Many organizations think that point #4 is the centerpiece of this formula. That is incorrect.

Countermeasure to mistake #6 – Remember that point #3 is the centerpiece of this formula. You need to defer to the experts before you give the facts. That closes the door.

Mistake #7 – "We can't train everyone on the 4-point formula."

Countermeasure to mistake #7 – This is the one time when employees can get caught off guard with no time to refer to a manual or have time to make a phone call for guidance. Companies who deal with this proactively can equip all employees with the 4-point formula on a small card, which they can keep with their IDs or in their wallets so that it is readily available.

Mistake #8 – "If we do nothing and wait long enough, it will go away."

Countermeasure mistake #8 – Doing nothing is not an option in the tragedy scenario.

Chapter 4: The accident investigation process and associated scenarios: who is *really* in charge?

Mistake #1 – The operator or the manufacturer leads the investigation.

Countermeasure to mistake #1 – Aviation organizations should educate employees on the accident investigation process during their initial aviation training process.

Mistake #2 – The operator or the manufacturer can send their lawyers or other individuals who may best represent their interests.

Countermeasure to mistake #2 – Have those who could potentially represent an organization's technical interests in an investigation prepared to communicate on their behalf and understand the international process.

Mistake #3 – The operator should make the decision about what information is best for the families to hear.

Countermeasure to mistake #3 – Operators need to know "what lane they are in and stay in their own lane." Survivors want to hear what they want to hear. You will know what they are by the questions they ask. Be prepared to answer.

Chapter 7: Communication response worksheets – learning to plan it all *before* something happens

Mistake #1 – "If the media goes away quickly, I did a good job."

Countermeasure to mistake #1 – It is a mistake to think the media goes away in this case if you did a good job. That is not always the case. Sometimes it is because it is just not entertaining enough. The key is to close the door and not elevate it into a large-scale event with your strategy.

Chapter 9: Social media and aviation communication: when and when not?

Mistake #1 – Social media is a relatively new phenomenon.

Countermeasure to mistake #1 – Recognize that a successful strategy is one that needs messages and empowerment prior to an event to communicate on the spot.

Mistake #2 – If you have a social media plan in your communication strategy, you can assume you have a plan that meets the reality of today's world.

Countermeasure to mistake #2 – In order to have a sophisticated social media strategy, you need to take into account a strategy to counteract the "fake" social media campaign (as in the BP case).

Chapter 10: Case study – Allegiant Air, the FAA, and *60 Minutes*

Mistake #1 – Taking two or more paragraphs to build up to your strongest point.

Countermeasure to mistake #1 – Always start with your strongest point, especially if you are trying to correct a misperception.

Mistake #2 – When trying to make a point with a sophisticated news organization like *60 Minutes*, you refer them elsewhere so that they can understand what you want them to.

Countermeasure to mistake #2 – Have clear, simple, and obvious messages up front in the first paragraphs, backed up with support points.

Index

Note: Page numbers in **bold** type refer to **tables**
Page numbers in *italic* type refer to *figures*
Page numbers followed by 'c' refer to charts

accident 27
accident investigation process 71–92, 216; case study 90–92; communication levels 78–79; communication rationale 78; families 82–84; insurance companies 82; international participants 74; investigation board formats 75–78; investigators 79–81; lawyers 82; media 84–85; regulators 81; standards and recommended practices 74–75; state of manufacture 85; state of occurrence 85, 90; state of registry 85, 90, 97; variables for reality 85–86; victim nationality 86
accredited representative 28
Advisory Circular (AC) 24
aggressive communication 18, 19
aging aircraft 104, 124, 156–157, 195, 205
Air Accident Investigation Branch (AAIB, UK Ministry of Transport) 23–24, 76, 83
Air France Concorde crash (2000) 2, 49, 180
Air France Flight 447 crash (2009) 105
Air Line Pilots Association, International (ALPA) 10, 24
Air Operators Certificate (AOC) 24
air traffic control, causes and aviation event guidance 122
air traffic issues 103
Air Transportation Action Group (ATAG) 4
AirAsia Flight 8501 crash (2014) 2, 63–64, 181
aircraft: accident question guidance 123–124; age 104, 124, 156–157, 195, 205; maintenance 124, 156–157
aircraft component loss 166–167

Airworthiness Directive 24
alcohol 102, 129, 149
Allegiant Air *60 Minutes* case study 194–210, 218; aging aircraft fleet 205; Allegiant criticism and potential messages **206**; Allegiant statement 204–205; background 194–195, 198–199; enforcement process 196; FAA and *60 Minutes* interview 201–204; FAA letter analysis 199–201; FAA missed interview messages/opportunities 204; FAA preliminary background letter 197–201; FAA view 209; interviewer 206–207; maintenance incidents 205; old data 205; parties 207c; pilot firing 205, 206; potential customer impact 208–209; potential FAA interview techniques **203**; potential financial impact 208; potential political impact 208; safety culture and compliance 198, 200, 205; segment points against Allegiant 204–206; specific criticisms 195–196
American Airlines Flight 587 crash (2001) 104
anger 38–39, 40
animals, death guidance 127
Annex 13 (ICAO) 27, 68, 72, 77, 97
Annex 19 (ICAO) 27, 75
apology vs. humanization 120–121
Asia, cultural differences 19, 144–145
Asiana Airlines Flight 214 crash (2013) 19, 65–66, 176
audience: external 96–97; political 97, *see also* emotional audience

220   *Index*

audience analysis 12–17, 39; educating 13; and misunderstanding clear-up 13–14; pre-determined theme 14–17, 211
Australia, cultural differences 20–21
Australian Transportation Safety Board (ATSB) 24, 77–78
authority 53
Aviation Disaster Family Assistance Act (ADFAA) 24, 82, 84
Aviation Safety Action Program (ASAP) 198

baggage, lost 107
blogs 182–183
bombing, Pan Am Flight 103 (1988) 83
BP oil spill (2010) 113, 176, 178, 179, 209; social media case study 183–187, 186c, 189–191
Branson, Sir Richard 9
bridging technique 36, 118, 159, 162, 163, 165, 167
briefing book 211
brushfire 168
Bureau d'Enquêtes et d'Anaylses/ Investigation and Analysis Bureau for Civil Aviation Safety (BEA) 24, 77
business continuity guidance 131

cabin attendant issues 101–102
cargo issues 106–107
cargo security 106–107
Category 2 status (CAT 2) 26
CEO: the businessman 89–90; communication styles 89–90; the politician 89; the technocrat 89
Certificate Holder Evaluation Process (CHEP) 197, 198
Civil Aeronautics Board, Bureau of Aviation Safety 75
clichés 66–67
closing-the-door technique 32, 36, 125, 138, 139, 141, 142, 159, 162, 163, 165, 167, 174–175, 202
codeshare 25, 108; communication response worksheets 151–153; 4-point formula 57–58
commercial issues: communication response worksheets 150–153; 4-point formula 61–62; messages 107–108; pet death 61; property damage 61–62
communication: definition 4, 15; levels 78, **79**, 81, 82; media misperception 7; rationale 78; thought process 6–7; three points 5–8
communication failure 87–89

communication response worksheets 134–157, 217; accident with deaths/ injuries 135–139; basic template 134–135; codeshare partners 151–153; commercial 150–153; engineering issues 156–157; ethics 147–150; financial situation 153–154; maintenance error 139, 140; proactive strategy 136–137, 138–139, 140–143, 144–145, 146–147, 151, 154, 155; reactive strategy 138, 139, 142, 145, 147, 152–153, 154, 155; safety 145–147; technical issues 156–157; workplace scenarios 154–155
communication success 86–87, **88**, 89
communication techniques 30–42; and terminology 23–47
community event guidance 128–129
community groups 98
company information guidance 128
Compliance Philosophy 198
confidentiality 154; guidance 122–123
controlled flight into terrain (CFIT) 25
controversial questions guidance 125–131
Convention on International Civil Aviation (1944) 71–72, 77
corrective action 25
crash scenarios, 4-point formula 54–59
credibility 91; establishment 33, 164, 203; other party credibility establishment 33
criminality 25
cultural communication stereotypes 21
cultural differences: Asia 19, 144–145; Australia 20–21; communication 18–21, 144–145, 185, 212; Europe 19; France 21; Latin America 20; messages 114–115; Middle East 19; United States of America (USA) 19–20, 21
customer reputation, and financial situation 127–128, 153–154

dangerous goods 106
death: in-flight 102–103; press statements 158–161, *see also* pet death
defuse negative words technique 36, 173, 195
design issues 104–105
disagreement 37
discrimination 109
do nothing option 64–65, 216
don't know answer response 117–118
dos and don'ts 131–132

educating: communication audience analysis 13; and press statements 174–175
emotional audience 6, 9–10, 38, 41, 52, 60, 65, 69, 82, 83, 87, 88, 96, 98, 99, 102, 113, 116, 119, 125, 184, 185, 188, 208

Index

emotional-style communication 9–10
employee firings guidance 126, 144, 145
employee training 130
employees 96
empowerment statement 95, 212; authority 18; organizational communication 17–18; rationale 17–18
enforcement investigation reports (EIR) 25
enforcement process, FAA 196, 202
engineering issues: causes and aviation event guidance 121; communication response worksheets 156–157; messages 104
English as a second language 132–133
environmental events 127, 168–169
environmental issues 113–114
equal employment opportunity (EEO) 25, 59, 155
ethics: communication response worksheets 147–150; 4-point formula 62–63; guidance 120; messages 112–113; press statements 170–171
Eun, D. 176
Europe, cultural differences 19
European Aviation Safety Administration (EASA) 25
European Civil Aviation Conference (ECAC) 25
event/situation causes: air traffic control 122; aviation event guidance 121–122; engineering 121; maintenance 121–122, 124, 143; operations 121; security/ terrorism 122, 124; weather and environment 122
executive resignations guidance 126, 144–145
experts, defer to 32–33, 52–53, 54, 69, 135, 140, 141, 159, 161, 162, 167, 168, 169, 190–191, 215
extended-range twin-engine operational performance standards (ETOPS) 25
external audiences 96–97

Facebook 65, 66, 178, 179–180, 184, 186, 187, 189; contexts 179; downsides 180; emergency 179–180
fact-based communication 9
facts, use 33–34, 53, 54, 69, 135, 145, 146, 157, 160, 161, 162, 163, 164, 168, 170, 171, 175, 191
families: accident investigation process 82–84; accident question guidance 124–125; and money 83, 125–126, 137–139
family assistance representatives 81

fares, low 128
fault 169–170; guidance 126–127
Federal Aviation Administration (FAA) 25, 172; Allegiant Air *60 Minutes* case study 194–210, 218; enforcement process 196, 202
Federal Family Assistance Plan for Aviation Disasters 25, 84
Fernandes, T. 2, 63–64, 65, 181
financial reports, guidance 128
financial situation: communication response worksheets 153–154; and customer reputation 127–128, 153–154; messages 108; press statements 108, 127, 153, 154, 172; and reliability 127, 153–154
firing: employee 126, 144, 145; pilot 205, 206
Flight Data Management (FDM) 26
Flight Operations Quality Assurance (FOQA) 26
Flight Safety Foundation 25
4-point formula 91, 95, 135, 137, 138, 139, 151, 189, 214, 215–216; accomplishments 53; background 48–52; case studies 54–63; codeshare partner/affiliate 57–58; commercial scenarios 61–62; crash scenarios 54–59; and different audiences 67–68; ethics scenarios 62–63; expert deferment 52–53, 54, 69; fact use 53, 54, 69; humanization 52, 69; investigators 56; manufacturers 55; non-party status 56–57; on-site airport operators 58; operators 54–55; part-of-process technique 52, 69; party status 57; rationale 53–54; regulators 55–56; tour operator 58–59; travel agent 58–59; workplace scenarios 59–60; worst-case scenario 48–70
France: Bureau of Enquiry and Analysis for Civil Aviation Safety (BEA) 24, 77; cultural differences 21
Freedom of Information Act (FOIA) 26
fuel issues 113
funerals, attendance 139

Global Air Safety Plan (GASP) 26
government 98
ground handling agents 26

harmonization 26
hashtags, and Twitter 182
Hayward, T. 184–185, 186
high road technique 34, 89, 138, 165, 166, 170, 173
hijacking 112

222 Index

humanization 34–35, 38, 52, 69, 92, 135, 137, 159, 161, 166, 168, 169, 189–190; vs. apology 120–121; without responsibility acceptance 38

in-flight death 102–103
incident 27
initial aviation training 51, 211, 216
injuries 158–161
Instagram 178, 180–181
insurance companies, accident investigation process 82
insurance guidance 120
insurance professionals 68
internal notification channels 49
International Air Transport Association (IATA) 26, 107; Operational Safety Audit (IOSA) 26–27, 108, 152
International Association of Machinists and Aerospace Workers (IAM) 10, 26
International Aviation Safety Assessment Program (IASA) 26
International Civil Aviation Organization (ICAO) 27, 71, 72, 85, 106, 146; contracting states 72–74
International Society of Air Safety Investigators (ISASI) 28
intoxicated passenger issues 102
investigation board formats: Air Accidents Investigations Branch (AAIB) 76; Australian Transport Safety Bureau (ATSB) 77–78; Bureau of Enquiry and Analysis for Civil Aviation Safety (BEA) 24, 77; National Transportation Safety Board (NTSB) 75–76; Transportation Safety Board of Canada (TSB) 77
investigators: accident investigation process 79–81; audience advice 68; 4-point formula 56; messages 99

Joint Airworthiness Authority (JAA) 28
just culture 28–29

Las Vegas Review-Journal 208–209
Latin America, cultural differences 20
law enforcement 111; vs. aviation 119
lawyers, accident investigation process 82
letter of correction (LOC) 29
letter of investigation 29
line-oriented flight training (LOFT) 29
lip service 29
livestock 169
living environmental event 168

lost baggage 107
low fares guidance 128
low-cost carrier (LCC) 29

maintenance 103; aircraft 124, 156–157; causes and aviation event guidance 121–122, 124, 143; communication response worksheets 139, 140
maintenance repair and overhaul (MRO) 29
Malaysia Airlines Flight MH370 disappearance (2014) 4, 72–73, 81, 97; communication safety net 73
management: reputation 49, 51, 91; safety 30, 75
managers, safety 87, 88
manufacturers 55
marketing strategy guidance 128
media 212; accident investigation process 84–85; and animosity 98; audience advice 68; messages 97–98, *see also* social media
media misperception 7
media-style communication 11–12
messages: accident investigation objective 100; accident investigation process 99; affiliate 99; aging aircraft 104, 124, 156–157, 195, 205; air traffic issues 103; cabin attendant issues 101–102; cargo issues 106–107; cargo security 106–107; codeshare partners 108; commercial issues 107–108; community groups 98; contractor 99; cultural differences 114–115; dangerous goods 106; delivery practice 6, 31, 39; design issues 104–105; discrimination 109; employees 96; engineering issues 104; environmental issues 113–114; ethics 112–113; external audiences 96–97; financial concerns 108; fuel issues 113; government 98; hijacking 112; in-flight death 102–103; intoxicated passenger issues 102; investigators 99; law enforcement 111; maintenance error 103; media 97–98; occupational accidents 110; organizational 5, 30–31; outsourcer 99; part failure 103; personnel issues 109; pilot suicide 101; pilot training 100; political audiences 97; potential pilot error 100; privacy protection 110; public reputation 108–109; regulatory actions 105–106; and religious issues 114–115; remedial training 100; sabotage 107; safety 106; and saving face 114; sexual

harassment 110; and strategy 93–115; streamlining 39; terrorism 111–112; unions 98–99; unscheduled stop controversy 100–101; weather-related delays 107; whistle-blower 109–110; wildlife issues 113–114; workplace issues 109–110
Middle East, cultural differences 19
mistake admission 39–40, 130, 164, 170, 171
mistakes and countermeasures 211–218
misunderstanding clear-up, and communication audience analysis 13–14, 31
money question 83, 125–126, 137–139
monthly active users (MAU) 29

National Air Disaster Alliance/Foundation 82
National Transportation Safety Board (NTSB) 24, 29, 65, 66, 75–76, 82, 84, 210, 2017
negative-into-positive technique 35, 170, 171, 173
negativity, and rising above 34
no comment technique 41, 51, 53, 95, 96
no-winning acknowledgement 118–119
non-living environmental event, press statements 168–169
non-party status, 4-point formula for 56–57
Notice of Proposed Certificate Action (NPCA) 29
Notice of Proposed Civil Penalty (NPCP) 29

Obama, Barack 184, 185
occupational accidents 110
oil spill 168; BP (2010) 183–187, 189–191
on-site airport operator 58
operations, causes and aviation event guidance 121
operators 54–55
outside party speculative statements 167–168

Pan Am Flight 103 bombing (1988) 83
part failure 103
part-of-process technique 14, 42, 52, 69, 89, 91, 113, 114, 135, 151, 156, 159, 161, 164, 165, 166, 168, 169, 170, 171, 172, 185, 190, 202
party status, 4-point formula for 57
party system 28

passengers, intoxicated 102
pencil-whipping 29
People for the Ethical Treatment of Animals (PETA) 188, 189, 190, 191
persona communication 9
personal opinions, avoidance 40–41
personnel events guidance 119
personnel issues 109
perspective 34, 140, 141
pet death 61, 68, 127, 168–169, 176; social media case study 187–191
pilot: accident question guidance 123; experience 129–130, 160; firing 205, 206; potential error messages 100; pre-flight drinking guidance 129, 149–150; suicide messages 101; training messages 100
polite persistence technique 40
political audiences 97
political-style communication 9, 206
politician 126
positive communication 18, 19
potential parties: emotional-style communication 9–10; event 8c, 9–12; fact-based communication 9; media-style communication 11–12; persona communication 9; political-style communication 9, 206; union-style communication 10
pre-determined theme, audience analysis 14–17, 211
press briefings 66
press conference 65
press statements: aircraft component loss 166–167; deaths/injuries event 158–161; and educating 174–175; ethics 170–171; fault 169–170; financial troubles 108, 127, 153, 154, 172; no death/injuries event 161–162; outside party speculative statements 167–168; regulator defence 172–173; regulatory event 162–163; regulatory fine 163–164; safety 165–166; security scrutiny 162; security/terrorism concern 164–165; templates 158–175; third world industry misperception 173–174; whistle-blower 171; workplace event 166
privacy protection 110
proactive strategy, communication response worksheets 136–137, 138–139, 140–143, 144–145, 146–147, 151, 154, 155
proactivity 43
property damage 61–62

public reputation 108–109
punitive measures, employees 130–131

reactive strategy, communication response worksheets 138, 139, 142, 145, 147, 152–153, 154, 155
regulator defence 172–173
regulators 6–7; accident investigation process 81; audience advice 67–68; 4-point formula 55–56
regulatory action 105–106
regulatory event 162–163
regulatory fine 163–164
regulatory surveillance 43
reliability, and financial situation 127, 153–154
religious issues, and messages 114–115
remedial training, messages 100
repair station certificate 29
reputation management 49, 51, 91
resignation, executive 126, 144–145
Royal Flying Corps (RFC) 76

sabotage, messages 107
safety 106, 156, 165–166, 195; and 100% safe notion 146–147; communication response worksheets 145–147
Safety Management System (SMS) 30, 75
safety managers 87, 88
saving face, and messages 114
security 43, 44; causes and aviation event guidance 122, 124
security concern 164–165
security procedures, guidance 129
security scrutiny 162
Service Difficulty Report (SDR) 30
sexual harassment 59–60, 154–155, 110
situation causes *see* event/situation causes
situational awareness 116–121; don't-know-answer 117; don't-know-but-want-to-respond 117; ethics 120; getting out of trouble 118; humanizing vs. apologizing 120–121; insurance 120; know-answer-but-don't-want-to-respond 117–118; law enforcement vs. aviation 119; and leaving situations 116; personnel event 119
60 Minutes, and Allegiant Airways case study 23, 194–210, 207c
social media 7, 8, 16, 49, 63, 64, 65, 66, 95, 176–193, 217–218; BP oil spill case study 183–188, 189–191; forms 176–183, *see also* Facebook; Twitter; YouTube

Southwest Airlines 66
Special Assistance Team (SAT) 30
spokesperson: appropriate criteria 93–94, 95; CEO communication styles 89–90; lowest possible level 94–95, 96; role 16–17, 50–51, 213, 214, 215
standard operating procedures (SOPs) 30
Standard and Recommended Practices (SARPs) 29, 72, 74–75
State Safety Programme (SSP) 74–75
statistics, use 33–34
streamlining 39
suicide 60, 101
support points 135, 145, 148, 151, 155, 156, 158, 160, 163, 166, 171, 172, 173, 174, 202; development 32, 42–45; technical data sheet development 42–45
Svanberg, Carl-Henric 184
Swissair Flight 111 crash (1998) 7–8, 69, 177

Tampa Bay Tribune 200
technical data sheet 158; support point development 42–45, 55; template 43–45
technical issues, communication response worksheets 156–157
template notification, basic anatomy 141
terminology, and communication techniques 23–47
terrorism 164–165, 111–112
third world industry misperception 173–174
thought process, communication 6–7
tone-setting technique 38, 161, 164, 170, 171, 172
tour operators 58–59
Traffic Collision Avoidance System (TCAS) 14, 30
training: employee 130; initial aviation 51, 211, 216; line-oriented flight training (LOFT) 29; pilot 100; remedial 100
Transportation Safety Board of Canada (TSB) 30
travel agent 58–59
trends, use 34
Twitter 66, 178, 180–182, 185–186, 187, 189; and hashtags 182; and inaccuracies 181–182

union-style communication 10
unions 6, 212, 98–99
United Airlines 176, 178; pet dog death social media case study 187–191, 188c

United Express Flight 3411 incident (2017) 10
United Kingdom (UK) Ministry of Transport, Air Accident Investigation Branch (AAIB) 23–24, 76, 83
United States of America (USA), cultural differences 19–20, 21
unnamed sources, and arguments 37
unscheduled stop controversy 100–101

ValuJet Flight 592 crash (1996) 8
Victim Support Tasks (VSTs) 84
Victim Support Team (VST) 30
Virgin Atlantic 9
Voluntary Disclosure Reporting Programme (VDRP) 198

weather, causes and aviation event guidance 122
weather-related delays 107
Welfare of Our Furry Friends Act (WOOFF) 188, 189, 191
whistle-blower 30, 60, 109–110, 128, 155, 171, 171, 109–110
wildlife issues 113–114
witch hunt 118
workplace events 166, 109–110; communication response worksheets 154–155; 4-point formula 59–60; sexual harassment 59–60, 154–155; suicide 60

YouTube 65, 177, 178, 180, 182; positive uses 182